REMEMBER
Smith's Weekly?

REMEMBER
Smith's Weekly?

A Biography of
An Uninhibited National Australian Newspaper
Born: 1 March 1919
Died: 28 October 1950

GEORGE BLAIKIE

RIGBY LIMITED

Rigby Limited, James Place, Adelaide
Sydney, Melbourne, Brisbane, Perth

First published 1966
Reprinted May 1967
Copyright 1966 by George Blaikie
Library of Congress Catalog Card Number 66-21203

Printed in Australia by The Specialty Press Limited, Melbourne
for Rigby Limited, Adelaide, and registered in Australia
for transmission by post as a book

For Claude Eric Fergusson McKay

CONTENTS

CONTENTS

ACKNOWLEDGEMENTS

The author wishes to thank John Fairfax & Sons Ltd, Sydney, for their generous permission to use literary and art work from the bound volumes of *Smith's Weekly,* over which they hold copyright; also Stan Cross, who provided most of the material on the early *Smith's* artists, and the many artists and journalists who contributed their memories of the paper; Angus and Robertson Ltd, Sydney, for permission to use material from "My Life Story — The Autobiography of Sir James Joynton Smith"; The Public Library of New South Wales staff for never-faltering patience under two years of fire.

"I have to confess a plebian liking for *Smith's Weekly* — the liveliest and most audacious thing printed in English." Tom Clarke, Editor, *News-Chronicle*, London, 1934.

"A man at Mt Gravatt, Brisbane, hatches 100 eggs with one hen. He puts the eggs in a barrel and sits the hen on the bunghole." — *Smith's Weekly*, 14 January, 1922.

CHAPTER ONE

Vol 1 No 1

"For gorsake, stop laughing — this is serious!"
or
"Mon Dieu, pas plus de rire — voila ce qui est sérieux!"
or
"Um Gotteswillen, nich mehr lachen — 's ist ernsthaft!"
— *Smith's Weekly*, July 1933.

There was no need to slap *Smith's Weekly's* broadsheet bottom to make it draw its first breath on 1 March 1919.

The paper came jazzing from the inky womb of the press, roaring full toot, doing back flips to make people laugh, and offering to fight any man in the House, State, World, or Universe. *Smith's* was born with a complete set of teeth, an ulcer-proof digestion, and an inbuilt complex of loves and hates. It first appeared with a Digger hat on the back of its head and an Australian flag indelibly stamped on its sun-tanned forehead. Throughout its lifetime it never removed that hat, even in the House, or obscured that flag.

Smith's was a pure Australian mechanism that ever pursued the loftiest ends in the national interest with what its critics considered to be the zest and tactics of a larrikin. "It's *Truth* in trousers!" one observer cried.

The paper was irreverent towards established ways of life that savoured even faintly of pomposity. It was critical, raspberry firing, fast punching, and capable of smelling a sacred cow from afar off against the wind. (It kicked almost all sacred cows fair in the udder as a matter of simple principle. And if the cow dared squirt back in anger or self-defence, out would come the pole-axe.)

Smith's was also cheerful, chuckling, hopeful, vital, and incapable of apologizing if it made a mess in the corner, which its uncontrollable enthusiasm caused it to do regularly.

It was born a twopenny conglomerate of gags, dreams, criticism, comment, drawings, bulldust, satire, and demands for justice.

1

And it died unchanged in spirit. Only the price had altered. That had gone up to sixpence.

In the thirty-two years of its life it punched more noses and raised more belly laughs than the rest of the papers in Australia combined.

At any one time it was seeking to be a number of things — the Public Conscience, a crutch for the fallen, the champion of the underdog, an *amica re in tempora incerta,* a vehicle of entertainment, both dramatic and comic, a belter of hell out of the mean, the wicked, and the pompous, the voice of the Digger, and anything else the editors happened to think of from day to day.

There was no limit to what *Smith's* could and did do. It smuggled opium into the country and peddled cocaine to prove there was a big drug-racket going on. It sold white girls by auction to Chinese merchants to spotlight a lively white slave-market in Australia. It fought for the right of a dog to attend golf matches at the exclusive Kooyonga Golf Club, Adelaide. It forced a Federal Government to give the inventor of the Owen Gun a reasonable reward.

Smith's regarded only two things as untouchable—the Salvation Army, because it was good beyond criticism; and venereal disease, because it was too dirty.

Pompous bottoms and inflated egos attracted the paper like a wasp to whatever wasps can't resist. And the sting always sank deep. And good causes set it playing on Angels' harps.

There didn't seem to be a middle course. But that was the very attractive thing about *Smith's.* It said what it thought one way or another with all the zest it could muster, and more often than not, it spoke with the voice of the majority of Australians.

Smith's loved:

Australia	Bertie Oldfield
White collar workers	Nurses (Angels of Mercy)
The Salvation Army	C.S.I.R.O. Scientists
The steel and sugar industries	Good Jews
The genuine unemployed	Billy Hughes
Sweated seamstresses	Old Age Pensioners
The White Australia Policy	Wholemeal bread
Diggers	Jokes
Underdogs	Claimants of fortunes in
Australian success stories	chancery
Bold enterprise	

2

Smith's hated:

Spivs	Bureaucrats
Tipsters	Perversion
Profiteers	Pomposity
Military Police	"Dagoes"
Jehovah's Witnesses	Bad Jews
White bread	Communists
Japs. In the north	Go-getters
Black men with white women	Bodyline
Red tape	

In addition the paper was ready to love any Australian who could invent perpetual motion, devise a cure for cancer, or produce a genuine bunyip.

Because of its gay nature and its free swinging style of journalism, *Smith's* attracted the free souls of the Australian literary and art worlds to its staff. These writers and artists proved to be the best at their crafts in Australia. They were given pretty much a free go to demonstrate their talents, and at times the results were spectacularly brilliant.

No regular reader could ever guess what the next copy of *Smith's* would look like but he did know he could bet on some shocks, some laughs, and an up-to-the-minute picture of what the hell was wrong with Australia — in *Smith's* enthusiastic opinion at any rate.

For many, the best thing about *Smith's* was the comic art work — the masses of gags that fairly flooded each issue. In the mid-1920s, some London press leaders considered *Smith's* team of black-and-white artists was the best in the world. It probably was, too. And the writers down the years were a star-studded team of poets, satirists, humorists — Kenneth Slessor, Lennie Lower, Adam McKay, Edgar Holt, Hugh Dash . . .

In 1934, Mr Tom Clarke, Editor of *The News Chronicle*, London, and Lord Northcliffe's right-hand man, wrote a book following a long visit to Australia, and in it made this comment: "I have to confess a plebian liking for *Smith's Weekly* — the liveliest and most audacious thing printed in English. And I would not miss this weekly joy of brilliant writing and brilliant drawing. There is nothing quite like it. I forgive it all its acid for its cleverness."

This full-blooded compliment is a crown for the brow of Claude Eric Fergusson McKay, who dreamed up the concept of *Smith's,* assisted at its birth, guided and moulded it through most

3

"You plurry fool! You spent your tixpence, an' where you bin, eh?"

of its thirty-two years of life and, sadly, saw it die of financial pneumonia as he came rushing through the door just too late with a cure.

Claude, a journalist and publicity expert, had been loaned by J. C. Williamson's to direct the publicity of the Eighth War Loan in 1918. He did a spectacular job and won the admiration of Sir James Joynton Smith, Lord Mayor of Sydney and Chairman of the War Loan Committee.

Indeed, Sir Joynton was so impressed that he sought to reward Claude with a cheque for £500 which the latter calmly refused. Sir Joynton, who had left England as a one-eyed cabin-boy and had become a millionaire, was bewildered and declared: "You're the first man I ever knew to refuse money!" Later, over a cup of tea he said: "You once said you would like to start a weekly newspaper. I'll back you for £20,000!"

You bet Claude wanted to start a weekly! He had lots of ideas he wanted to test. Also he wanted to make a packet of money.

4

One of his theories went this way:

There are other things besides fires, murders, and accidents in which the average man is vitally interested. After all he doesn't expect to be murdered. If there's a fire his premises are insured. And accidents are always what you read of as happening to someone else. But every man is interested in his own daily life — where he lives, what he does. He's interested in his affairs and so are we. We don't want stories of murders or violence, but cases of economic cannibalism. We want the facts about injustices, unfair sackings . . .

And Claude, with his Presbyterian background, felt there were a lot of people not getting a fair go who needed someone to speak out for them — bank clerks and other white collar workers, and pensioners. And then there were the Diggers coming home. He was worried about them. Once their uniforms were off . . .

Fair Question.

Claude felt too, that there was need for brighter entertainment in the press. His experience as house poet with J. C. Williamson's had polished up in him an innate flair for devising both dramatic and amusing situations. Why not comic drawings featuring jokes of a native Australian flavour?

Sir Joynton had the money, Claude had the editorial ideas. All they wanted was a manager. Claude turned to a newspaper friend, Robert Clyde Packer, then a sub-editor of *The Sun* (Sydney), and invited him in to form a triumvirate. Packer had worked with Claude on the promotion of the Eighth War Loan and had an impressive record as an administrator and editor. Two small rooms were taken on the top floor of Somerset House in Martin Place, Sydney, and there, late in 1918, McKay and

Packer began to work on the format of a new Australian weekly.
A name was needed — something striking and different.

Through his war-loan raising, Sir James Joynton Smith, Lord
Mayor of Sydney, had become a national figure, a symbol of
patriotism . . . "We can't waste all that free advertising," McKay
and Packer cheekily decided and went to work on Sir Joynton
whose frail defences were quickly beaten down. And so the
curious title, "Smith's Weekly" was devised.

News got round Sydney that a new type of paper was in the
making. When journalists from the dailies began climbing up
to the top of Somerset House to have a sniff, Claude and Clyde
briefed the bright ones on what was expected from contributors
— the types of stories and paragraphs required.

Up the stairs one day came the celebrated former Editor of
The Bulletin, J. F. Archibald, then aged over seventy, his eye
twinkling. Was there a table and chair for him? He wanted to
discover if "the old mill could grist again." Archibald had a
genius for subbing paragraphs — soling and heeling, he called
the work. He was given table, chair, pen, and a stack of paragraphs.

And so Claude McKay, Clyde Packer, and J. F. Archibald
produced Volume I, Number 1, which was printed by William
Brooks in the Sydney suburb of Zetland. The first edition, dated
1 March 1919, sold 35,000 copies at twopence throughout Australia. Fair. Just fair.

McKay who had dropped a salary of £30 a week to take £10
a week from *Smith's* kitty until the new paper turned the corner,
and Packer who had also dropped a good income for £10 a
week, didn't know it then, but they were on their way to wealth.

The very first issue set the pattern which, with only the
slightest adjustments, was to make *Smith's* a favourite with the
public and a gold mine for its owners. This pattern was very
much Claude McKay's interpretation of what Australians liked,
wanted, and needed. It was designed with the sense of showmanship that was natural to Claude. There were drama, comedy,
surprise. There were impertinence, tears, and roars of defiance.
Past history, prediction, and imaginative analysis of the current
scene. Funny drawings with jokes underneath and solemn ones
pointing heavy morals.

Above all, *Smith's* showed it could get news and cook up
exciting angles quite beyond the imaginations of other papers.

The big topic in Australia when *Smith's* was born was the
Spanish 'flu. *Smith's* was bound to recognize this fact in Volume

1, Number 1 (1 March 1919), but what was there left to say? The dailies had already played up sickness and death, so Claude and Packer decided to concentrate on the economics of the epidemic — what it was costing the community — and marked the idea down for their page one lead.

But nobody knew what the cost was, because no one was keeping tab. This meant that *Smith's* simply had to have a go at estimating: "While it is practically impossible to obtain reliable figures regarding weekly loss to the Australian community due to the 'flu epidemic, *Smith's* has calculated these losses — Retailers, £50,000, Hotels, £20,000. . . . "

It became practice after that for *Smith's* to be the unofficial authority on all matters of public interest on which there was no official information. The paper took this function so seriously that its surveys were often deep and accurate. And if it was ever proved wrong . . . ah well, the error had been made in good faith and in seeking to serve the public.

Rudyard Kipling was the No. 1 patriotic poet of the Empire at the end of World War I, and the battle of Villers-Bretonneux the pride of the First A.I.F.; Billy Hughes, Australia's wartime Prime Minister, was the darling of everybody in Australia. Like a playwright, Claude McKay set about weaving the whole three — Kipling, Villers-Bret, and Billy — into a plot which would have special appeal to Australia, and so make a second story for his first front page.

The legendary Kipling had been paid as high as 1/- per word for his writing.

Claude cabled to Billy Hughes, then in London for the Peace Conference, requesting him to offer Kipling a commission to write "The glorious story of Villers-Bretonneux whereby the Australians saved Amiens" at the fantastic fee of 5/- a word.

The Prime Minister, a close pal of Claude McKay's, came to the party. He wired back to Australia: "Will approach Kipling if you wish, but as he declined our invitation to visit Australian battlefields he can hardly write effectively. Conan Doyle knows all about it. Shall I approach him?"

Claude replied: "Exhaust Kipling. Doyle unwanted."

Billy Hughes answered: "Kipling declines."

Nevertheless *Smith's* was left with an unusual story involving important people and events, and above all, the paper was able humbly and profitably to make the point that it had been prepared to go to world-record expense to serve the Australian public.

This angle of the big and dramatic offer to a prominent public figure remained a favourite gimmick with *Smith's*. It reached its peak in 1921 when Billy Hughes, still Prime Minister, but wrestling desperately with his followers, was offered, in a front page splash, the editorship of *Smith's*. Terms were £10,000 a year for five years.

The story shocked Billy's supporters so much they packed in behind him and the fiery little Welshman never did go on to *Smith's* payroll. But the offer had been a very serious one. Claude McKay knew that when Billy had written a weekly feature, "The Case for Labour," for *The Daily Telegraph* in Sydney before the first World War, the paper's sales had jumped 11,000.

On page two of the first issue *Smith's* had a go at satisfying the Godly by printing, "The Lost Miracle — a real-life story demonstrating that God is always good."

The story, written by J. F. Archibald, the famed ex-editor of *The Bulletin,* would have left many a reader more spiritually thoughtful had not the paper printed immediately under it a philosophical piece on the art of committing suicide. *Smith's* tartly claimed that anyone who had a shot at taking his life and failed wasn't fair dinkum. Using as its text and inspiration the fact that a melancholy but determined man had hung himself from a railway shed in Sydney with a pocket handkerchief, *Smith's* claimed that it was "fatally easy to suicide if your mind is made up. . . . " The half-decided man takes his pick of the pharmacopoeia poisons and is stomach-pumped back to life; or he buys an expensive revolver and misses himself." (*Smith's* was wise before its time. Later it was to become general knowledge that the majority of attempted suicides were performed to win sympathy and not eternal oblivion.)

The *Weekly,* which committed itself utterly to anything it ever attempted, had a deep-down hate for anyone who wasn't fair dinkum in the pursuit of an avowed objective — even suicide.

Of course there had to be a Financial Section in the first edition. Page three was led with a serious sermon on how best to invest £500 in bank stocks. But before the bottom of the page was reached, *Smith's* could no longer keep a straight face and strange paragraphs like this began to appear: "Australia owes £648,000,000 or roughly £129 per head. In DEBT we are not divided!" And there was a curious assessment of business risks attributed to Cecil Rhodes: "Thirty-two per cent more people lose money in farming than in mining. Forty per cent lose more in manufacturing than in mining. . . . "

This jolly note in Australian financial journalism, sounded in the first issue, continued to ring through *Smith's* until death quelled it.

In the sad days of the great Depression, the only smile that many a melancholy businessman got was from reading *Smith's* which cheerfully defied the financial heavens to fall. Right in the middle of its financial page *Smith's* would plonk a big joke block featuring something like:

Jacky, sitting thoughtfully on pub veranda: I wouldn't be surprised if these plurry bad times weren't the cause of the plurry Depression!

While Claude McKay may have had plenty of bright material for most sections of the first edition of his paper, he was obviously desperately short of copy for a sports page. His main

"What's up, Jacky—won't they serve you a drink?"
"No—I bin plurry well declared black."

problem was that he couldn't dig up an experienced turf writer. Show business had taught him that one must not dry up on stage. Do anything, say anything, but don't just stand there petrified. So he went to a leading Sydney surgeon who took an interest in the turf and invited him to write the first *Smith's* racing page under the banner, "Punters and Plungers by a Leading Surgeon."

The surgeon had a go and produced probably the oddest hotchpotch of literary horse manure ever printed. For material he even worked his way back into the eighteenth century. Still, there was no blank space and a time was soon to come when *Smith's* turf page, written by Cliff Graves ("Iroquois") was the best in Australia.

As for the remainder of sports copy in the first edition — well, let us simply say that its cornerstone piece was an article entitled: "Fan Tan — How It Is Played."

Throughout its lifetime, *Smith's* made continuous use of what Claude called the Siedlitz Powder technique for creating an exciting story. And this technique was perfectly demonstrated in Volume I, Number 1, under the headline "Hun Method — our Madness."

The idea was to mix two subjects which on their own were stale and uninteresting, but, mated with each other, produced an explosive effect. Element "A" in this case was, "Hun Method — an account of how Germans treated their prisoners of war," and Element "B" was, "Our Madness — an account of how German prisoners are gently treated in Australia."

Smith's supplied a swizzle stick:

> He who can read the first column (Hunatrocities) without seething with rage too deep for words, must have water and iron instead of good red blood in his veins. He who can read the next column (our kindness) without shamefaced disgust ought to be in the Federal Government.

There followed a recital at lurid length of German atrocities to P.O.W.s overseas. And then came Element "B" — a story about pleasant conditions at Holdsworthy, the main German internment camp outside Sydney. According to *Smith's,* internees didn't have to work unless they wished to. And if they did lift a hand, they were paid. There was even a café running in the camp, and the inmates were permitted to stage lavish entertainments. Cried *Smith's* in apparent rage:

> Blame the powers that be which allow such misplaced, such maudlin, such all but treacherous privileges to the blood brethren of the brutes and bullies enumerated in the parallel column.

With the war only a few months finished, this story was tailored to an emotional nicety. The soldier was still a sacred symbol. Having read his Ruskin, Claude McKay knew that when peace was firmly restored there was no one less wanted than the soldier who had made it possible. He was determined that the Australian Digger would not be forgotten, and to that end, announced in his first edition the dedication of a full broadsheet page in perpetuity, to present the case of the returned serviceman: "*Smith's* intends to make it impossible for any expeditionary to be able to say truthfully that he has not had a square deal. To that end it will devote this page every week. . . ."

A bright young lawyer, fresh back from the front, was employed to conduct the page. This was William Bede Dalley, son of the famed politician. He attacked his assignment with a near-religious zeal, and, for a start anyway, adopted the maxim, "The Digger is always right, bless him."

He set a busy pace on his first page, by demanding that no non-returned military policeman should be permitted to lay a hand on a Digger: "Control of the A.I.F. must be undertaken by fighting men only!" This tirade was sparked by a complaint to *Smith's* by an old Dig that a non-returned M.P. had struck him with a baton. "Any person or persons who witnessed the alleged assault will assist the ends of justice by communicating with *Smith's Weekly*," the paper trumpeted.

MO: *"What is remorse?"*
JO: *"The period between one night out and another."*

To its eternal credit, as many as two pages per week in every edition from first to last were devoted to the cause of the returned serviceman. *Smith's* became rightly known as "The Diggers' Paper" and established, perhaps for ever, the image of the Dig as a magnificent fighting man, with a heart of gold and an innate objection to bumptious authority.

For its first political column, the *Weekly* elected to attack "Bolshies" and profiteers. The paper never ceased to fear these two forces, always insisting that "the profiteer is the mother and father of revolution." With the Russian Revolution still red raw in 1919, *Smith's* could see the forces that had inspired it causing trouble in Australia decades ahead — a perfect piece of crystal-gazing. The paper died in 1950, still shouting, "Beware the Communists and the Profiteers."

11

One of the most interesting aspects of the first edition was the mass of minor features, each of which was designed to display a specific type of paragraph — "Gossip from Here, There, and Everywhere," "Strange But True — or Things That Happen Occasionally," "Anthology of Anecdote" (Stories of Wits and Wags), "By The Way" (Casual Paragraphs), "Leaderless Legion" (Complaints). . . .

Here the skilled hand of J. F. Archibald, the former Editor of *The Bulletin* could be seen. All the paragraph features he established in the first edition remained as fixtures for the next thirty years. One of their secrets was that they inspired the public to "send it to *Smith's*" — anything from a bellyache (Leaderless Legion) to why Hangman Jones of Victoria suicided (Strange But True). (Here's why Hangman Jones of Victoria allegedly did himself in : "He suicided rather than execute Mrs Knorr — née Minnie Thwaites — who had killed twenty-five infants. Mrs Knorr feared that her skirts would blow up and show her legs when she went through the trap.")

Claude McKay early saw that public contribution of paragraphs was a good publicity and sales promotion medium. He insisted that every par printed carry the name and town — "P. Phillpot, Moe, Vic." — of the person who sent it in. Thus shearers could boast in shed and pub that they were writers for the papers. "Wanna bet?" And out would come the tattered clipping that represented the proof. Normally the material had been soled and heeled into a new shape from that sent in, but the contributor would swear that never a word had been altered from his original copy. Such is the vanity of writers fortunate enough to get their work printed.

Thousands of pars poured into *Smith's* every week. And every week thousands of people eagerly bought the paper to see if their contributions had got into print. Many, on scoring a hit, would buy half a dozen copies to hand to relatives and admirers. After all, one did not graduate as a journalist every day.

One of the most shadow-casting items in the first edition was an allegedly comic drawing by artist, Cec Hartt of a joke put forward of J. F. Archibald: In a foine Irish household, mother was beaming on her son Patrick and saying with all the soul in the world, "We'll make little Patsy a praste, plaze God." Father was belting the table and roaring, "We will make little Patsy a praste, plaze God or not."

The Irish Self-Determination League in Australia called for a boycott of *Smith's Weekly* for that gag. And thousands of Irish immediately bought the paper to see what was going on. Claude McKay reports that Clyde Packer commented profoundly : "Now if we could get a few more boycotts, we would be home on the bit."

That joke block was the foundation stone of a new school of black-and-white art in Australia.

> "For all its boasted courage *Smith's Weekly* does not always print the truth even though it is aware of it. The present editor, for instance, knows full well that my parrot at home, every time he hears the gate click, shouts: 'How's yer bum, Luv?' But will *Smith's* print that simple truth? It will not!"
>
> — Snowy Howell, V.C., of *Smith's*
> Advertising Staff, circa 1931.

MRS RYAN (*to her husband*): "*We'll make little Patsy a praste, plaze God.*"

RYAN (*decisively*): "*We will make little Patsy a praste plaze God or not.*"

CHAPTER TWO

Vol 1 No 2 to Vol XXXII No 35

After a few months in 1919, during which they produced the paper in Martin Place, Claude McKay and Clyde Packer talked Sir Joynton Smith into letting them move their operation into the Imperial Arcade which the knight owned in Pitt Street. The arcade had a nice basement that was promptly filled with printing machinery, as McKay and Packer had decided the time had come to do their own printing.

The first night the presses roared they produced more than a newspaper. They produced a mass exodus of guests from the Arcadia Hotel which was part of the arcade. The pub was built like a violin, Joynton complained, and every vibration in the basement was faithfuly passed on through floors, walls, window sashes, and pipes to the very top ceiling. From then on, it was necessary for the hotel to accept only guests who were prepared to sacrifice one night of sleep per week while the building was in labour producing a new edition of *Smith's*.

Circulation which started at 35,000 in March 1919, moved upwards steadily and reached 75,769 in January 1921, nudged just under 100,000 by August 1921, and hit a magnificent 150,000 in December of that year. These figures denoted success. The cost of achieving them had been just on £100,000, represented by a bank overdraft backed by Sir Joynton.

About this time Sir Joynton Smith decided to reward Claude McKay and Clyde Packer for their parts in establishing his paper while they worked on the token salary of £10 a week each.

Calling the two men to conference, he handed them each a document to read saying that if the contents were satisfactory to the readers would they please sign at the bottom. The contents were satisfactory. Sir Joynton had given McKay and Packer one-third of the paper each and kept one-third for himself.

In two years of inspired toil, the two journalists had become very wealthy men. It was an Australian success story of the type *Smith's* delighted to publish as a symbol of the rewards available in this country for those with the wit, energy, and ambition to have a go.

Beloved of the Diggers and the white collar workers, *Smith's Weekly* went bustling ahead, providing in many homes what radio and T.V. offer today — humour, satire, drama, surveys, news behind the news. . . .

By January 1923, the circulation was 165,648. The print figure went over 200,000 in 1927.

Meantime, the McKay-Packer-Smith triumvirate had added another Phar Lap to their newspaper stable. In 1922 they moved *Smith's Weekly* from the Imperial Arcade to new premises, specially built in Phillips Street, Sydney, almost opposite Police Headquarters.

Then, in July 1923, they caused a sensation by launching a new style morning paper — *The Daily Guardian* — which, after eighteen months, climbed to nearly 100,000 circulation and topped 300,000 in 1926. The team had the Midas touch in newspapers.

In 1927, with *Smith's Weekly* and *The Daily Guardian* at peak popularity, the triumvirate suddenly split up.

Old journalists still argue about the fundamental causes of the split. But crisis point arrived with an argument over whether wrestling matches, then booming in Australia, were faked or genuine.

Jim Donald, Smith's boxing writer, wrote a number of stories claiming that wrestling was a racket, a phoney, a take. Big pressure was put on Sir Joynton Smith to leave wrestling alone and he urged Claude McKay to call Jim Donald off. But Claude was an old style Editor-in-Chief who would not take pressure from anyone. He had extreme ideas about honesty in a newspaper. He would not accept drapers' advertisements in *Smith's* because he believed they would not produce results that were value for money. And if an advertiser sought to influence the editorial, using his patronage as a lever, Claude's rage would be explosive. He said that if any people objected to what Jim Donald was writing about wrestling being a racket, they were welcome to take out a writ.

Sir Joynton Smith offered to resolve the deadlock by selling out his one-third interest to McKay and Packer. Quixotically, Claude McKay said he would sell to the other two. His offer was accepted. And so the man who had dreamed up *Smith's* walked away from it in 1927. He was then aged only forty-nine. Wealthy and weary from the task of producing newspapers, he decided to spend the rest of his life living in England and playing endless golf.

Clyde Packer and Joynton Smith added a Sunday paper — *The Sunday Guardian* — to their newspaper empire.

In 1928 the brilliant journalist, Frank Marien, was brought over from *Truth*, at a record salary, to be Editor-in-Chief.

Associated Newspapers, then the biggest newspaper group in Sydney, grew more and more concerned as *The Daily Guardian* ran rings round its morning paper, *The Telegraph*, and *The Sunday Guardian* severely punished its Sunday sheet, *The Sunday Sun*. When, in 1929, Packer and Joynton Smith cheekily announced their intention of entering the Sydney evening field, Associated Newspapers decided to buy off the enemy and offered £575,000 (£175,000 cash and £400,000 in Associated Newspapers preference shares) for *The Daily Guardian*, *The Sunday Guardian*, and a guarantee that a new evening paper would not be started.

The bid was accepted. Packer and Joynton Smith were left with only *Smith's Weekly*. To keep their machinery warm, they purchased two ancient sporting papers, *The Referee* (extremely respectable) and *The Arrow* (originally *The Dead Bird* and dreadfully unrespectable). Meanwhile Claude McKay went on playing golf and was right out of the business.

The new owners of *The Daily Guardian* merged it with *The Telegraph* and joined *The Sunday Guardian* with *The Sunday Sun*. The mixtures went bad and £1 ordinary Associated shares dropped to 1/6, while £1 ordinaries fell to about 6/-.

Clyde Packer had received most of his shares from the sale of the two *Guardians* in Associated preference shares. When he was invited to join Associated Newspapers as Managing Editor to see if he could pull the show together and, of course, protect his own equity, he sold out his interest in *Smith's Weekly* to Joynton Smith and went to Associated in 1930. So now only Joynton Smith of the three founding fathers remained on *Smith's*. And he didn't have any idea of how a newspaper should be run. The Depression was thumping the economy.

At this point Claude McKay reappeared from England utterly bored with the retired life and eager to tilt at any likely windmills. Joynton Smith invited him to lend a hand with *Smith's*, and McKay wasn't the father to turn away from his own infant, particularly when the poor creature was ailing. But he wasn't as welcome in the office as the flowers are in May. Frank Marien, the new Editor-in-Chief, an Italo-Irish romantic with a tight contract, wasn't going to take editorial advice from anyone.

Smith's advertising boss and a director of the paper was Frank Packer, Clyde's only son. He said he wasn't going to agree to Claude McKay returning. Joynton Smith answered that one with hard cash. He bought out Frank's shares in *Smith's* for £27,000 and the young man went off with bulging pockets to join his father at Associated Newspapers.

(By 1932, Clyde Packer had built Associated Newspapers ords up from 1/6 to 18/- and prefs from 6/- to 18/. An impressive performance in two years. Being ill, he then retired but died at sea early in 1934, aged fifty-five, when returning from a visit to England where he had sought treatment. His son, Frank, founded *The Australian Women's Weekly* in 1933 and developed the vast newspaper complex that is now Australian Consolidated Press. He was knighted in 1959.)

Meantime, Claude McKay retired to a panelled room on the top floor of the *Smith's* building and confined himself to financial problems, while a stepfather (Marien) attended to the vital editorial development of his child. They were sad days for Claude McKay. And it was no joy to Marien, down on the second floor to know that the former partner was up there on the top floor glowering. In fact Claude only stayed long enough to stabilize the finances, then retired from the paper again.

Then in July 1936, Frank Marien died suddenly. This sad event and the ever increasing virulence of the Depression caused great concern to Sir Joynton Smith. The paper's very survival was in doubt. Kenneth Slessor, the poet, and the paper's main-stay on the writing side, took over complete editorial leadership as well.

An outstanding journalist and editor, Harry Cox of Sydney, was invited to take the paper over as Editor-in-Chief in 1938. He brought with him as skilled a team of craftsmen as Australia could provide. But the kiss of death seemed to be on the paper's brow, and in spite of tremendous efforts by the staff, the circulation went down to a hopeless 80,000 in 1939.

It was a time to think of undertakers and gravediggers.

On the eve of World War II, Claude McKay appeared yet again. Like a king in exile, he had been waiting a chance to return. He believed he could make the paper successful again if he was in unconditional control of it. With a little army of investors, including ex-senator Sir Victor Wilson and W. J. ("Knockout") Smith, the glass king of Australia, Claude McKay was able to get control of what remained of *Smith's*. A capital of only £60,000 was more than enough to do the job.

SERGEANT: *" 'Ere's a message from H.Q. wishing all you blokes a Merry Xmas."*

In the week he took over an event happened that restored the paper to the public — World War II.

If the Depression had left *Smith's Weekly* with one valuable asset, it was the reputation of being "The Diggers' Paper."

Skilfully, Claude, who had invented the title two decades before, saw that full use was made of it in rehabilitating the anaemic paper. With him from exile he had brought an editor, George Goddard, a genuine "Old Dig" who knew the serviceman's taste perfectly.

At the same time Claude restored to *Smith's* the foundation image he had given it, when he defined it as:

The champion of the rights and liberties of the people of Australia.

Their defender against the depredations of public and private batterers on the body politic.

The forum for the expression of individual opinions.

The journal that will ever find a *causa belli* in the abuse of privilege on the part of those occupying positions of public trust, the dipping of unauthorized fingers into the public purse, and ill treatment of the underdog by those clothed with a little brief authority.

Though now aged sixty-one, Claude McKay went to work like a four-round prelim boy determined to become another Les Darcy. And his staff went roaring with him. Not that he had much staff, because all the young ones went to war. Still, those he had were good, and between September 1939, and September 1944, the circulation rose from 80,000 to 250,000. It went on to over 300,000. Once again *Smith's* was "the paper that cared," "the Public Guardian."

It was moving at a hand gallop when the war ended. But rising costs and other problems steadied it down until, in 1950, powerful shareholders decided they wanted to get out. They sold to interests which wanted a building rather than a newspaper, just as Sir Keith Murdoch of *The Herald* (Melbourne) came into the bidding with his purse open.

The last issue of *Smith's Weekly* Volume XXXII Number 35 — was dated 28 October 1950.

CHAPTER THREE

The Eye of the Author

Wise man: It says here that a single fly can lay 400 million eggs in a season!
Innocent youth: Cripes! What about the married ones?
—*Smith's Weekly*, 1922

Of the hundreds of people who worked for *Smith's Weekly*, a large number solemnly swore in and out of their cups, in public and secretly, that one day by God they would write a book about *Smith's*. For the paper had a story of its own that appealed strongly to the instincts of newspaper folk.

Had all the vows been kept — and none were — there would now be scores of different versions of the *Smith's Weekly* story.

Smith's meant different things to different people. There'll be plenty to quarrel with the way I saw it — through the startled eye of a rather inhibited Presbyterian type who grew to love the paper well in twenty years of service, but never became sophisticated enough to forgive it all its sins or understand all its eccentricities.

To hold a spot on *Smith's*, one had to be a character. I rated mainly because in my first few years with the paper, starting 1931, I provided an endless source of entertainment to the artists and journalists as the most innocent creature ever to join the hard-bitten staff. I have been assured by expert observers that I would have caused surprise and even alarm on the Salvation Army's paper, *War Cry.* On utterly uninhibited *Smith's,* I was little short of a riot.

My father, a conscientious Sydney bank manager, became convinced, when I was fifteen, that I had been born to the newspaper writing craft. He was inspired by the fact that a highly principled Sydney weekly paper, *The Sydney Mail,* printed on the purest white glossy paper, published a poem of mine. The poem had been lifted from a school magazine and republished in a Special School's Issue run by *The Sydney Mail,* to attract a packet of school and drapers' advertisements. According to this paper my poem "typified schoolboy spirit." First verse ran:

> Study and learn, boy, while you may,
> The loafer is nought but a fool.
> Tata, tata, tata, tata (I forget that line)
> You've done your best for the school!

My father bought many copies of the issue and insisted on showing it to all of his clients, among whom was Sir James Joynton Smith, the money behind *Smith's Weekly*. Sir Joynton read the poem with his one good eye and then for a long time puffed his cigar through a gold-mounted lobster claw holder. When my father managed to get him speaking again he did not comment on the work but he did say he would give me a job. And that was a terribly big victory, for the great Depression was raging at the time, and openings were scarce even for young poets of promise and/or purity.

Looking at the poem with now mature eyes, I am convinced that Sir Joynton could well have had a nasty overdraft at the time and had to choose between bankruptcy or me. Still, he could well have been comforted by the thought that he would only have to pay me 25/- a week for a start and maybe I would die young because you know how it is with the good.

When I use the word "good" I have my youthful self in mind. Morally I was something extra special — a highly-trained Presbyterian lad, Sunday school teacher, Bible class leader, and an ex-Chancellor of the Rockdale Order of the Burning Bush (a church club for youths, the motto of which was "Christ and Character" and the object of which was "to be pure in mind and speech and useful to Jesus Christ and our fellows.")

I joined *Smith's* as a copy boy on 24 December 1931, and on that date took home the first copy of *Smith's Weekly* my family had ever seen.

My mother cried throughout Christmas Day and Boxing Day, believing that her second son, the poet one, had been delivered up to Mammon for a miserable 25/- a week.

Work pretty near stopped on the paper for a couple of days while the staff quizzed me and obviously marvelled at my ready answers. I explained the significance of the St Andrew's Cross in my lapel (all active members of The Order of The Burning Bush wore one) and created a considerable impression by stating that I was prepared to take responsibility for filling four pages of the paper a week.

What did I have in mind to fill the pages? One page about

"What are you doing this week-end?"
"Oh, nothing to speak of."
"I thought you'd given up that sort of thing."

youth activities, one page on school sport, one page on schools generally, and one perhaps with a universally appealing religious flavour — that's what. Everyone, breathing heavily, agreed that I had just the right ideas to give *Smith's* a new slant. But first my writing powers had to be tested, and, what's more, tested with a front page assignment.

Reg Harris, later Press Secretary to numerous Federal ministers, was kind enough to give me my briefing: "Write a thorough essay on 'A Thinking Man's Interpretation of the First Four Books in the New Testament'."

By day I ran messages swiftly and eagerly. By night I wrote with great power and earnestness. In a week, I delivered my first 5,000 words representing Part One of what promised to be a ten-part serial. Alas, I did not make the front page as anticipated. Reg explained that if I had written my story just one thousand nine hundred and thirty one years earlier it would have been NEWS. There was no denying this sad logic. I had missed the bus by ages.

John O'Donnell, Chief of *Smith's* Investigation Staff (a sort of newspaper private eye, I was to discover) suggested I try my novice quill on "The Evils of Alcohol in Both High and Low Places." This was an easy assignment as I was well versed in temperance matters. I could and did prove that Napoleon took wine before the disastrous Battle of Waterloo, and the Duke of Wellington drank only pure water. Why did the artist, Vincent Van Gogh cut his ear off? Because he was under the influence of alcohol! I also had a most impressive case of a famous French Chef who cooked for kings in palaces, until he took to sucking at

BARMAN: *"'Ere, yer don't wanter sit there; the beer's drippin' on yer."*

BOOZE ARTIST: *"Whasser matter (hic) with that, s'long as I can 'old me (hic) mouth shtraight."*

the wine he should have stirred into the custard and so inevitably ended in the gutter.

A dreadful warning rang clear through every one of the 10,000 impassioned words I wrote. My final line needed four exclamation marks to hold it back: "Let no man foolishly imagine that he can trifle with alcohol with impunity!!!!"

No *Smith's* reader ever saw the story because it was never printed, but every artist and journalist in the building read it and the majority came to the little dog box in which I sat waiting the call to do messages to take a good look at me. Most of them asked me questions on various points and I was able to explain anything they couldn't understand.

(Later, when I secretly investigated the curious fact that the

C

average artist and journalist on *Smith's* found need to leave the office about ten times a day, excluding lunch hour, I discovered that fate, my father, and Sir Joynton had plunked me down in the middle of the hardest drinking newspaper team in Australian, if not in Empire history.)

It was explained that my alcohol story failed on three major counts: (a) It was not hot news that alcohol befuddled the brain, caused mothers to forget to feed their babies at times laid down by baby clinics, encouraged immorality among both old and young of both sexes, and caused husbands and fathers to get home late for tea with their pay envelopes seriously invaded, and (b) the story would give offence to many good people who took alcohol for medicinal purposes on doctors' prescriptions and would be taken as a personal affront by King George V and the Royal Family who sometimes took wine with their meals. (c) I had unfairly omitted to state that the Bible recommended a little wine for the stomach's sake, a fact of which I, as a Bible student, must surely have been quite aware.

"You must develop a nose for news, boy, otherwise you will never become a great journalist!" And what was news? News was what was happening right there and then.

The main thing happening there and then in Sydney was a police chase after a mysterious murderer. I inquired of senior reporters like Ken Slessor, Gus Walker, Reg Harris, and Clem Cleveson, if a story about the murder would be satisfactory as news. They agreed that it certainly would be and urged me to keep my eyes and ears open.

How I wanted to corner that killer, get an exclusive story out of him, and then, of course, hand him over to the authorities, as any decent citizen would have done.

Within two days, I got one of those breaks a copy boy dreams of. I was told to answer a phone in the newsroom. "Newsroom," I cried with shrill authority into the mouthpiece.

A sinister voice hissed: "Say nothing to anyone. This is the man the police are after for the killing. I want to make a statement to a reporter. Above all, don't call the police."

Young and inexperienced as I was, I knew a hot story when I hit one. I shouted that I wouldn't tell the police, and the sinister voice told me to pipe down or the police would hear me in any case.

The killer didn't want to be switched to a proper reporter. He liked my voice and felt he could trust me. He would make his exclusive statement to me and no one else. But if I breathed a word to anyone the exclusive was off, see? I agreed to these terms.

"Would you please come up to the office and ask for me?" I requested.

The killer laughed hollowly. Did I think he was such a fool as to walk into such a simple trap? I'd have a dozen policemen waiting for him. He said he knew how shrewd newspapermen were.

I assured him I was to be trusted. I was prepared to take oath. But he was touchy and he explained that he meant no offence to me personally but he could not afford to trust anyone. After all, his life was at stake. He'd get the rope without doubt if caught, wouldn't he? I eagerly assured him he would, and he suggested I break down my enthusiasm a bit if I wished to maintain the level of mutual trust we had established.

We had reached an impasse which the killer broke by suggesting we could meet out in the open. Would I be prepared to meet him on the corner almost opposite *Smith's* in ten minutes' time? (Police Headquarters were on that corner.) I agreed to that arrangement. The killer wanted to know how he would recognize me. I explained I would be wearing a fawn suit with a St Andrew's Cross in the button hole. His only further request was that I hold my hands slightly out in front of me so that he would be able to see I was not holding a gun. I assured him I would never dream of carrying a gun, and didn't actually know how to use one even. The man said he still wanted to see those empty hands. Fair enough!

It took me less than a minute to get to the Police Headquarters corner where I took up position with my hands held slightly in front of me. Nine minutes to go. My eyes took in everything that moved. Could be that the killer was watching me right then!

The appointed time came and went. No killer. I checked the badge in my lapel. It was still there. Impatiently I waited. Several people from *Smith's* found me on the corner and asked what on earth I was doing. I told them quickly and urged them to move away from the secret rendezvous.

Gus Walker, a senior reporter, seemed particularly worried about what I was getting myself mixed up in. Had I ever handled a killer before? What if the man was after another victim? Had I planned my counter moves in case of an attack?

To that moment, I had not given any attention to these lines of thinking. Gus said it just proved how untrained I was. While he did not possess the cold courage to stand with me, he said he was prepared to go into the Assembly Hotel opposite where I stood (the Assembly was beside *Smith's*) and observe from the saloon bar window. He would shout a warning if he thought I was in any danger. Thereupon he retired to the bar and kept giving me encouraging waves through the window. He got other people to wave too. There was comfort in all this.

At the end of one and a half hours I began to feel the game was lost. Then I happened to look at the *Smith's Weekly* building opposite. There were scores of windows in that building and every one was filled with beaming faces looking down on me.

It was from that moment I began to change into the man who in later years, as head of the reporting staff of *Smith's Weekly*, was to write without flinching such front page sensations as "Nude Dancing in the Slums," "Black Men and White Women," "Half-caste Harvest," and "King's Cross — City of Sin."

The hard grind of journalism steadily changed me from a gentle youth who was "pure in mind and speech and useful to Jesus Christ and his fellows" to a somewhat cynical, bald-headed journo. who is not absolutely convinced that the world is round or that the provisions of the Oaths Act (1908) are warranty that people signing statutory declarations are necessarily endorsing the truth.

I came to love much that *Smith's* stood for, although I don't think my mother ever did. There was a stage quite early in the piece when I seemed to be successfully talking her into understanding that behind all its brashness the paper was really a seeker after truth and the public good.

Unfortunately, at that critical moment I happened to take home *Smith's* baby brother, a wild little racing sheet printed on yellow paper called *The Arrow*. At birth, *The Arrow* had been christened *The Dead Bird*, and while in the passing of time it changed its name, it never changed its nature. It aimed at entertaining turf and dog enthusiasts between bets with spicy, true life stories.

The issue I took home contained on the centre double spread an exposé of the main brothels of Sydney with pictures of the premises and some of the merchandise, the story of a man who got stabbed in the face with a spoon by an angry mistress, a choice bit about an actress who had become a drug addict and had extra puffy thighs from all the needles she poked into herself, and lots of other rollicking tit-bits. It didn't mean much to me, aged sixteen, but it did startle my mother who long argued that any paper coming out of the same stable as *The Arrow* was not likely to be a Christian messenger.

My "office" as a copy boy consisted of a tiny room no more

FIRST SCENE SHIFTER: *"Nothing ever happens in this place, Joe."*
SECOND SCENE SHIFTER: *"No; same old scenery every night."*

than four feet by four feet. It was full of card index files, old papers, a tiny desk, and me. If a second person squeezed in, bodily contact could not be avoided unless I stood on my chair or desk.

Now it appeared that most of the artists and journalists were greatly concerned about my over-purified attitude towards women. I sternly refused to listen to off-colour stories and counselled all who would heed me that a woman must be regarded as a sacred temple which must not be violated. A good man respected all women as he respected his mother. Kissing and cuddling and other rude things should be left until after a couple were married.

I now know that I was taking the whole business a little too seriously. Everybody on *Smith's* knew it right then, and it was secretly agreed that my eyes should be opened just a little bit in the matter of sex.

To that end, a pretty young woman from the Tivoli Ballet was briefed to call at *Smith's* and ask for me personally. An inquiry desk clerk brought her to the door of my tiny den. From the start I did not trust her. She smelt too good for one thing and her dress was so short that even as she stood at my door I could see above her knees — never a good sign. Her eyelids were painted (beware of painted women!) and her lips becarmined. She was really very pretty, but I well knew that beauty was only skin deep.

The girl explained that she had heard I was the most understanding reporter on the staff and she wished to get me to write an exposure story about the terrible things that happened to chorus girls as a warning to innocent young creatures who might think the theatre was decent and romantic. I suppose I should have told the young woman that I was only a copy boy and ill-equipped to handle a big exposure. Indeed, the words were forming on my tongue when the girl stepped forward. To avoid intimate contact, I had to take one pace backward which resulted in my sitting down hard in my chair. In a flash the dancer was inside my dog box. She shut and latched the door then seated herself on a tiny stool beside my desk. Her silken knees rested hard against mine because there was nowhere else in the room she could fit them and that's the honest truth.

I could not bear to look at her painted eyes. My alternatives were to look at her silken knees and the considerable portion of thigh which had come into view as soon as she sat down, or to look at the roof. I compromised by doing half and half so that my head kept going up and down in a desperate nodding motion.

The girl began telling me terrible things about dandies who waited at the stage door with bunches of flowers and jewels and things. They didn't just want the honour of esquiring nice young ladies to supper. They wanted more than company and conversation. They were after IT! They were devils disguised as men.

As the young dancer told her sorry tale, she kept patting me on the knees with a dainty hand to achieve emphasis. She achieved that all right. My terror was that someone might come and find my door locked, insist on entering, and find me . . . How would I ever be able to explain the dreadfully compromising situation?

A foreign sound broke through my dazed condition. It was just like a snigger. Now, the walls of my little room were about seven feet high — wood for the first four feet from the floor and then frosted glass. I became conscious that there was not a square inch of frosted glass against which the impression of a face was not showing. (Reg Harris will vouch for the veracity of this little tale. After all, he organized it.)

As one might imagine, the things that happened to me during my first few weeks on *Smith's* caused me considerable confusion of mind. It was dear old Adam McCay, leader writer on *Smith's* and doyen of Sydney journalists at the time, who explained to me what the hell was going on.

Adam was a first-class honours graduate in classics and was much given to reading Latin in the raw as well as writing very rude verse with the most delicate touch.

One day I carried a hot meat-pie to his room for his lunch. Adam peered at me through his pince-nez which were perched at the very end of his thin nose and ordered me to sit down. He took a bite of his pie then whipped out his upper plate and popped it in a drawer. "You have been witness, boy, to an act of supreme honesty of mind. When I've got my plate in, my palate is blotted out and I can't even taste meat-pie. *Ergo,* except when dining at Government House I make a practice of removing my teeth when dining." This I have since worked out was Adam's way of getting me to relax.

He said he had been watching me and imagined I was not happy with my new vocation. He was darned tootin' right in his imagining. While his gums busily chomped pie, he chatted merrily on, popping out words and flakes of crust at me. I was to understand that *Smith's Weekly* was like no other paper that had ever been born. It was an assembly of free and happy souls. "We make a game of producing the paper," wise old Adam orated. "We play pranks on one another and get lots of laughter out of living. And that gets reflected in the paper we produce. Kill all that and you kill *Smith's.* The fact that they have been playing pranks on you proves they like you. You are now initiated into the brotherhood of the happiest souls in Australian journalism."

Adam finished his pie, put back his top plate, and began writing slowly and laboriously with a plain steel nib. I was too entranced to leave his presence, for here indeed was great wisdom. As he wrote, he told me that his father had been a Presbyterian Minister who had been so fiery in the pulpit — a mood inspired by Scotch Whisky before breakfast, Adam claimed — that he ended up with a congregation of only five — his five sons. "We all put 2/- each in the plate and took the money back after the service." This seemed to end the lecture and I turned to leave the wise man's presence.

"One last warning, boy. If you should read Holy Willie's Prayer by Burns you will note a line which says, 'Oh Lord, forgive this fleshly thorn.' See that you never have need to voice such a prayer through consorting with chorus girls." I blushed mightily, and Adam's roars of delighted laughter followed me as I fled to the refuge of my dog box.

All this is not intended to be an attempt to foist a lump of my autobiography on an unsuspecting public, but to demonstrate why my interpretation of *Smith's* and its people may well differ from that of many others who saw and experienced the same events as I did.

I was to serve *Smith's* in sickness and in health etc. from December 1931, until its death in October 1950. Thus I knew it intimately for two-thirds of its life.

My only regret is that I missed the first third which was the richest bit.

CHAPTER FOUR

The Founding Fathers

Sir James John Joynton Smith	(1858-1943)	(Financial)
Claude Eric Fergusson McKay	(1878-)	(Editorial)
Robert Clyde Packer	(1879-1934)	(Managerial)

"Once upon a time there was an Englishman, a Scotsman, and an Irishman. . . . "

When an Englishman, a Scot, and an Irishman are mentioned in combination, the thing most likely to follow is a dirty story.

In the case of the combining of Sir James Joynton Smith (English), Claude Eric Fergusson McKay (Scottish), and Robert Clyde Packer (Irish), the result was *Smith's Weekly*. Each man brought to the venture a special element. Joynton provided the cash, Claude, the editorial planning and direction, and Clyde, the administrative skill. The result was something of a newspaper miracle. Also in the miracle class was the fact that three such dominant bulls should have been able to graze along happily in the same paddock for as long as they did with only one cow between them.

At the time the triumvirate came together in 1918, each had established himself in the rugged individualist class and was beginning to gather the anecdotes which turn men into legends. Joynton Smith was then aged sixty, Claude McKay, forty, and Clyde Packer, thirty-nine. Joynton was a knight and a millionaire, Claude and Clyde were working journalists who wanted to be millionaires.

The key to Joynton Smith's success was that he could "smell a quid" from a great distance. Expert opinion insisted he was a nut when he announced, in 1918, that he was going to do a solo performance of backing a new weekly newspaper. Nut or not, for an initial hard cash investment of £20,000 he collected £300,000 out of *Smith's*.

Thanks mainly to a delightful autobiography of Joynton Smith, ghosted by Claude McKay in the mid-1920s, a sugar-coated history of the curious financier is available to posterity. His enemies who called him, among other things, "a one-eyed cockney crook" were never game to put their sentiments on paper. If there was a dark side to his life, little trace of it now remains.

He was born in London in 1858 as plain James John Smith, son of a gas fitter of cockney background. By the age of five, impressed though he was at his father's amazing capacity to create light where there was darkness, he determined that the gas business was not big enough for him. Thus when, at the age of twelve, his Dad considered he had been educated enough and sought to make a gas fitter out of him, the youth rebelled.

After a frustrating year, Smith (snr) surrendered to his son's demands to be launched in a business career and apprenticed him to a London pawnbroker. The wages were poor (2/6 a week) and the hours long (8 a.m. to 8 p.m.) and, in addition, the boy had to sleep each night on top of the shop counter where he acted as a human burglar alarm.

Nevertheless, this was a happy period of his childhood and early business career. While London slept, he would gather together a selection of pawned musical instruments and con- stitute himself a one-man band. With banjo, mouth-organ, and concertina he would make music, supplying dramatic percussion effects with a cymbal strapped to his right foot and a drum stick tied to his left.

His star piece was "Just Before The Battle, Mother":

Dearest Mother I may never
Press you to my heart again.
But if I fall in Abyssinia
I trust in Heaven we'll meet again!

This constituted probably the one cultural period of Smith's life and it ended when he fell four floors down a light well, breaking an ankle and ruining himself as a pawnbroker's apprentice.

The wounded child bettered himself by getting a job with a stationer. He still received only 2/6 a week but he got a half day off on Saturday. His Pa still took half his wages. And one day young Smith, with a flash of psychological insight, sensed that his dear old Dad would be happy to receive that 1/3 ad infinitum, providing that he had no reason to believe that his boy was earning more than 2/6 a week.

Cunningly, young James Smith built his income up to 15/- a week with a variety of jobs. He gave 1/3 to his Dad and spent the rest attending London theatres, at one of which he was entranced with the lesson to be learnt from the pantomime, *Dick Whittington.*

His bright mind saw a blueprint for his future success: clear out of London with or without cat, make a million, return, and become Lord Mayor.

It seemed to him that going to sea was the No. 1 logical step, and he wandered the wharves seeking a berth. None was offered. But hard cash solved the problem. For 1/-, young Smith — he was fourteen at the time — bought a discharge from a sick cabin boy and so joined the crew of a tiny grubby coaster. His functions included cooking, to wit, frying in fat a mix of flour and water — the sole dish at all meals. After three weeks, with 3/- in his pocket and bruises on his brow, James Smith returned home convinced that the quick way to wealth was not via the galley of a small coaster. The big overseas ships were the ticket!

The boy, with his discharge certificate to aid him, graduated to big ships. On his sixteenth birthday, in October 1874, he concluded that big ships weren't much chop either. He was then receiving 1/- a month clear. So when his ship berthed at a New Zealand port he went ashore and stayed ashore. For a time he worked as an assistant barman in a Port Chalmers pub for 15/- a week plus keep. Here he learnt much about the subtle art of bluffing. American sailors came swaggering in to the bar with huge knives swinging from their hips and fierce curses on their bearded lips. They took umbrage at the least provocation and out flashed the knives threatening bloody death.

But for real drama, you had to watch two of these American dreadnoughts, heated with neat spirits, squaring off to each other. "With cat-like tread" they circled the bar room floor working their keen blades in the air and stating in bloodcurdling detail the various parts of the adversary's anatomy that were to be sliced away from the main trunk at any instant.

Young Smith came to know that when these dreadful clashes were over, though the heavens had thundered and hell's gates had opened wide, there was never any blood on the floor because no one had been cut. And yet, all who had witnessed such a duel went away swearing they had seen bloody murder done. Smith concluded that it's the impression you make that counts and not the things you actually do.

At this stage the youth elected to take another crack at the nautical road to glory and went to work as a steward on a New Zealand coastal line. By the age of twenty-three, he was a chief steward, the youngest in the shipping company's history, and had £300 in savings.

He now turned back to the land. With his £300 savings and

£800 credit, he got control of the Prince of Wales Hotel in Wellington. He quickly developed a big clientele by staying open all hours of the night. The fines were big, but the sly grog profits were bigger.

Impatient for progress, Smith sold out the Prince of Wales and bought control of the bigger, posher Post Office Hotel in Wellington. Here he employed a new gimmick. He made his pub the sporting heart of the North Island of New Zealand. Inside its walls he conducted a Tatt's Club. As a sideline, he formed the Seaman's and Fireman's Union of New Zealand and took the job of president. When ships were in port, his public bar was always busy.

By the time Smith was twenty-eight, he was a wealthy man. His business was worth the enormous sum of £10,000. But he was tired. For the five years he had run the Post Office Hotel he had not slept more than four or five hours a night.

Why not return to London and show 'em what young Jimmy had made of his life?

So he sold out and sailed for home. On the voyage, relaxing in his first-class comfort, contemplating ways of investing his fortune, he had what he felt was a perfect idea. The bookmakers of England were wide open to a punter with a bank big enough to keep on attacking them. If you backed favourites only, and increased your stakes to cover past losses and allow for a profit, you would have to win.

It took Smith some months and the loss of £9,500 to discover that his thinking was faulty somewhere. But when he did, he confessed himself beaten and resigned as a punter forever. There's a big difference between gambling and taking a legitimate business risk.

Back to New Zealand went the humbled Smith. With no capital, he was on the labour market again. In Wellington, the best job he could find was as secretary of the Maritime Cooks and Stewards Union. He plugged along at that until 1890 when, with £54 in his pocket, he walked out and went to Sydney with no ideas and no prospects. But he was still full of fight and ambition.

While hunting for an idea, he read in a newspaper of a man in Germany who attended funerals, took shorthand notes of orations at the graveside, and produced a framed report which he sold as a memento to grieving relatives of the deceased.

The young cockney had taught himself shorthand in New Zealand. All he needed to go into the funeral memento business was a silk hat and a black frock coat. He purchased these and began attending three funerals per day — the three most promising he could find listed in the newspapers.

Mourners took him to be a high-class newspaper reporter, probably from *The Sydney Morning Herald,* and eagerly supplied him with their names and addresses. Graveside orations took a flowery turn when speakers noted the solemn man in the silk hat taking down every precious word.

Smith designed a big card heavily decorated with blue forget-me-nots and crying out in letters of gold "So Loved. . . . So Mourned." On these he had printed his version of the funeral orations, plus the names of all present. It only remained for him to call on the mourners whose addresses he had and offer them framed copies of the card. Average price was 30/-, but when the market was ripe, as much as £3 could be asked and received.

Within a short time, the business was returning between £20 and £30 a week. But its proprietor found it boring. After he had saved some money he sold out the goodwill and his stock of "So Loved. . . . So Mourned" cards for £100 cash, and turned to the field he knew best — pubs. The best job offering was the managership of the Grand Central Coffee Palace which was sadly run down and apparently beyond revival, for Sydney folks shied clear of it. Smith took the hotel over and soon had it filled. As a result of his work as secretary of the Cooks and Stewards Union in New Zealand, he knew almost all the stewards on the New Zealand-Australia run. He got these men to act as his agents and steer New Zealand visitors to his Coffee Palace. Of course when the place was filled to overflowing with overseas visitors, Sydney people wanted to stay there too.

In 1896, after some five years at the Coffee Palace, the shrewd cockney had a small bankroll behind him and decided it was time he became his own boss once more. He looked round for a run-down hotel and found a perfect specimen in the Imperial Arcade Hotel in Pitt Street. The only people who drank there were bar flies of the lowest order and the boarders were poor types who spent their nights gambling and buying grog from a night porter who was making more than the proprietor. So poor was the proposition that the owner was happy to lease it to Smith for £12 a week for ten years. Even then, the wise men of the hotel trade agreed that the cockney was being robbed.

And yet this broken down pub was to be the starting point in Joynton Smith's march to millions. The first thing he did was to kick almost everyone out of the pub and redecorate the place so that decent people found it respectable.

The hotel was part of an old arcade that ran between Castlereagh and Pitt Streets. In time, Smith got the whole premises for a total of £147,500. Before he died in 1943, the property was worth over £1,000,000. This was the arcade in whose basement *Smith's Weekly* had its first real home.

Smith was one of the first, at the turn of the century, to sense the potential of the Blue Mountains outside Sydney as a tourist resort, and bought hotels and picture theatres there. He formed and controlled the Victoria Park Racecourse in Sydney. He played the role of Midas merrily.

In 1915, he was elected to the Sydney Municipal Council, and in his third year as an alderman, became Lord Mayor of Sydney, a function which won him a knighthood and led to his being made Chairman of the Eighth War Loan Committee, in which capacity he met Claude McKay and Clyde Packer.

In appearance, Claude McKay was the perfect picture of a cultured English gentleman. He was tall and slim and handsome, if you like rather narrowed eyes. His clothes were always in perfect taste and he even smoked cigarettes — which he bought wholesale and puffed endlessly without inhaling — with a highly polished elegance.

This façade was deceptive. Behind the reserved visage and the poise was one of the most impish minds Australia has produced. McKay had all the basic instincts of a Barnum, the pen of a playwright, and the logic of a lawyer, all mixed together and smothered in Scottish Presbyterian sauce. In addition, he was dangerously good at golf, both as a player and a sire. (His elder son, Tom was an Australian amateur champion.)

Claude was probably the only man who could have thought up such a strange phenomenon as *Smith's Weekly*. He certainly was the only person who had the knack of making it work profitably. Whenever he walked away, the till stopped tinkling. When he returned, financial health was restored.

Smith's sought to be sensational and spectacular and entertaining because Claude McKay was a showman. At the same time, it sought to be desperately righteous because of Claude's Presbyterian conscience. And McKay knew instinctively just how much of each to mix in. Even the brilliant Frank Marien, when Editor-in-Chief, couldn't match Claude's sure touch.

The best way to get something of the measure of McKay was to watch him smoking cigarettes in an elegant drawing room. He would select a cigarette with care, tap its ends on his thumbnail until they were just so, light the very tip, and puff generously without inhaling. The cigarette would then be used like a theatrical prop, as he waved it hither and yon like a firefly's bottom. And the ash? All the ash went steadily on to the Indian carpet and the butt got thrown over Claude's shoulder out of the window. And if by any chance the window wasn't opened, the hostess would never believe that her carpet had been burnt by that charming gentleman's butt.

It was useless pointing out Claude McKay in a crowd and saying to a stranger: "That man arranged to have a couple married on the back of an elephant to publicize a Sydney pleasure park long before World War I!"

The stranger would sneer at you and say: "Not that gentleman who looks like a High Court Judge!"

And yet Claude did pull that elephant stunt and many more way-out lurks like it in the unhallowed name of publicity.

Claude McKay had been born of high-class Scottish parents in the country town of Kilmore, Victoria, in 1878. He was unlucky enough as a teenager to obtain employment on *The Kilmore Advertiser* through the generosity of the owner-editor, Mr G. Goode, at a salary of nothing for the first year and 10/- a week for the second year. The "10/-" was mainly a figure of speech for it rarely materialized. Mr Goode used to go to the Bank to gather the money, but would call at the Royal Oak Hotel when returning with it.

But Claude gained valuable experience in the newspaper business. He wrote most of the paper, set up much of the type, helped print the thing and then delivered half of the result on horseback. (Total circ. 250). He was also required to do the office bookkeeping. In view of all this, it is hardly strange perhaps that he should have created such a multi-sided marvel as *Smith's Weekly*.

By the time Claude was sixteen, his salary on *The Kilmore Advertiser* had soared to £1 per week but, of course, he still didn't receive it. The salary's main value lay in its theoretical measure of the young man's worth.

In due course Claude, still a teenager, moved to *The Seymour Telegraph* in Victoria as an editor on 35/- a week. Being Editor, he could write what he liked. And what he liked caught the eye of the mighty *Age* (Melbourne) which did him the great honour of making him a junior reporter on its staff for £2.10.0 a week.

On *The Age*, he found that working time was "all the hours

you can stay awake." He didn't mind the hours but the standard required even of a boy from the bush was a bit beyond him and he got the bullet.

After that he worked for a Melbourne legal firm and then for all types of organs including *The Australian Mining Standard, The Warrnambool Standard, The Bendigo Advertiser, The Argus* (Melbourne), *The Courier Mail* (Brisbane) and *The Town and Country Journal*.

And there was something to be learnt from each new editor. Mr Tom Pritchard of *The Australian Mining Standard* told him that one did not improve the expression from the psalm "beside the still waters" by changing it to "contiguous to the unrippled liquidities." (Mr Pritchard was the father of Katharine Susannah Pritchard).

As a young chap of twenty-nine, Claude became interested full time in the theatrical business via a broken-down outfit called Wonderland Circus. He left *The Daily Telegraph* (Sydney) to play press agent to a sorry collection of animals and acts. Wonderland Circus represented the bits and pieces left over from "Wonderland City," a Sydney Coney Island that had failed.

Claude McKay, working on the side in 1907, had given Wonderland City its best publicity by creating a tremendous controversy over whether it was or was not nice to marry a man and woman on top of an elephant. This had never been done before in world history.

A happy couple were organized (at a fee of £15 each) and a clergyman agreed to do the job. Alas, on the big day, with 80,000 paying customers at a bob each eager to see the nuptial knot knitted, the clergyman had had second thoughts and would only perform the ceremony on terra firma and in privacy. Even this did not defeat Claude. After the ceremony, he had the bride decked as a houri and the husband as Ali Baba. An actor dressed as a minister, hopped on to the elephant with the couple and 80,000 Sydney souls cheered like fury as love triumphant and pure paraded through Wonderland City.

As press agent for Wonderland Circus, Claude went ahead to Brisbane, fully aware that the "star attraction" was a lion so ancient that it was toothless, hairless, and indifferent to whether it lived or died. Here was a true test of Claude's capacities. He got a controversy going in the Brisbane press over how long a lion could hope to live, and stirred up much bitter argument. At the right moment, he advertised that Wonderland Circus was presenting "Leo, the Oldest Lion in Captivity." To beat that lion as a major attraction, Wirth's Circus, the main opposition, had to produce "A Blood-Sweating Hippopotamus."

However, in spite of all Claude's bright ideas, the circus went broke, and he was obliged to return to newspapers. He did this for a time, and, about 1908, went to J. C. Williamson, the theatrical entrepreneur, as his secretary, house poet, and publicity expert. He launched new artists with wonderful and often dreadful tricks. His idea was to create news.

A famous swimmer at Manly surf beach was known as "Shark Bait" because of his courage. On the day he took cramp in the chill waters and was likely to drown, who should swim out and rescue him? No less a person than Ivy Schilling, J. C. W.'s newest importation. It just happened that plenty of pics of Miss Schilling in bathing costume were available for the press.

In the early hours of a Sydney day, a monster sought to climb a ladder and enter a Potts Point flat for who knows what evil purpose. Who fired the three pistol shots that roused the entire neighbourhood and drove the alleged intruder away? The lovely Miss Hilda Spong, J. C. W.'s newest importation.

Nellie Melba liked Claude's style so much that she signed him up as her secretary while she was in Australia. J. C. Williamson refused to let Claude go and insisted on Melba tearing up the contract. Melba then hired a man named Beverley Nichols as her secretary. He was a pretty good writer too.

Claude was still with J. C. Williamson when he was loaned to handle the publicity of the Eighth War Loan and so met Sir James Joynton Smith. He devised a sort of martial circus to capture public attention and sell bonds with Joynton Smith as the "ringmaster."

The Lord Mayor of Sydney issued a challenge to the Lord Mayor of Melbourne; each was to march towards Albury and meet on the Murray River to see who had collected the most money on the way. Joynton Smith, with Claude McKay at his side, advanced in an imitation army tank which fairly leaked patriotic flags. The pair set each new country town visited at the throat of the one before by urging it to beat the other's figures. Clyde Packer also helped on this loan-raising deal which proved tremendously successful.

When the loan campaign was over, the Lord Mayor of Sydney offered to back Claude in the production of a national weekly paper. Thus *Smith's Weekly* was born.

Once Claude had the money to realize his dream of starting a distinctive type of paper, he turned to Clyde Packer, a journalist of strong personality and outstanding organizing ability, and invited him in on the deal. Joynton Smith was happy to have Packer in the foundation team; he had got to know and admire him while he had been helping with the Eighth War Loan.

Robert Clyde Packer, born in Hobart in 1879, was of Irish background. He worked his way along a very hard road to success. Newspapers attracted him early and he took a job on a Hobart paper at 7/6 a week. His future seemed uninspiring until one Saturday afternoon, while attending a race meeting, he picked up a sovereign. He placed his find on a horse which won at 15/1.

Alert to the fact that the little people were working for him, Packer immediately took ship for the mainland and a wider stage on which to prance. Maybe he lost the little people on the water. In any case he could not get a newspaper job in Melbourne or Sydney. The best he could do to defeat starvation was to sell himself as an expert powder monkey at a Sydney quarry. He had never touched or even seen blasting powder in his life. Two old hands at the quarry identified the young man as a hungry trier and not only showed him how to use powder but kept him in tucker for a week until he could collect his first wages. In later years, Packer was noted for his affection for anyone who was a trier or showed signs of undernourishment.

When the quarry employment finished, the Tasmanian wheeled big bags of flour round a warehouse in Sussex Street, Sydney. This sort of work bored him. He walked out of the job and once more went in search of a newspaper that could find a spot for him. It was a long search and did not end until he reached Cairns, north Queensland.

Then, like Claude McKay, Clyde Packer worked for a multitude of country papers — Bellingen, Macksville, Tamworth included. He married, and leaving his wife and son (now Sir Frank Packer) in Sydney, took over the editorship of *The Dubbo Liberal,* owned by a widow. (Sir Frank comments cheerfully: "My father seemed to thoroughly enjoy that job at Dubbo. My mother thought he enjoyed it a little too much and, on hearing that the widowed owner was quite young and attractive, made a special visit to Dubbo to see for herself. I was too young to know what my mother saw, but I do know that father immediately left Dubbo and returned to Sydney.")

Clyde Packer marked his reappearance in Sydney by joining the staff of *The Sunday Times.* This was in 1908, and he was then aged twenty-nine, big, strong, and lively. The Editor of

The Sunday Times, T. R. Roydhouse, had been appointed Baden-Powell's representative in Australia, and was organizing scouting here. He grabbed Packer and appointed him "Chief Scoutmaster." The evidence is that Packer liked scouting and saw in it a means of promoting interest in *The Sunday Times;* he made sure that the paper carried large lumps of scouting news. He also saw that most able-bodied men on the staff spent their spare time in short pants and peaked hats. When, in 1912, Baden-Powell visited Australia, it was Clyde Packer who led the great demonstration of welcome at the showground. (Four hundred of the welcoming scouts were on horseback!)

In 1913, Packer became Editor of *The Sunday Times,* and was building a fine reputation for himself when the spectacular Hugh D. McIntosh won control of the paper from other shareholders. This was the McIntosh who had promoted the world heavyweight title fight between Tommy Burns and Jack Johnson in Sydney in 1908 and had the reputation of being the only man who had ever scared the giant negro, Johnson (allegedly with a pistol).

McIntosh didn't want Packer to continue as Editor, but couldn't sack him outright because a contract of service blocked that move. Pressure tactics were used as an alternative. On Saturday nights, when *The Sunday Times* was being prepared for the press, McIntosh would stamp arrogantly into the room of Editor Packer and hurl abuse. His hope was that the Editor would resign.

Once Packer appreciated the situation, he got a big, heavy ruler and next time McIntosh appeared at the door for his Saturday night pressure session the Editor shouted: "If you enter this room, I'll brain you with this!"

McIntosh tried operating his hate sessions from the doorway for a time, but soon realized he was making no impression. He bought out the remainder of Packer's contract in 1915 for the then considerable sum of £500.

Clyde Packer was made welcome on *The Sun* (Sydney) as a sub-editor and served on that paper until 1918, when Claude McKay invited him to join the *Smith's Weekly* venture. On *Smith's,* Packer specialized in administration and technical aspects of production, such as lay-out, for which he had an unusual flair. He studied many overseas papers and had a file of hundreds of strikingly arranged pages taken from them. He used lay-out ideas from these files for *Smith's* and later *The Daily Guardian* and *The Sunday Guardian.*

While Claude McKay was the man who saw that *Smith's* was

lively with ideas, Clyde made sure it was lively and attractive in appearance.

It was from examining American newspapers that Packer produced *The Daily Guardian's* biggest selling idea. He had noted that "Miss America" Contests had become more and more popular in America and concluded that surf and beach-minded Australians would like the idea or some variation of it.

From this thinking stemmed the first Miss Australia contest in 1926, run by *The Daily Guardian* in Sydney. The search for the typical Australian girl kicked *Guardian* sales from 160,000 to 300,000 and produced as winner, Miss Beryl Mills, a highly intelligent girl who had the exact measurements of Venus de Milo — arms into the bargain.

It was tragic, though understandable, that McKay and Packer should have fallen out. They were both strong, clever, and ambitious men. While they worked in harness as a team — Claude as Editor-in-Chief and Clyde as Managing Director — they were an unbeatable combination. But by 1927, when Claude McKay sold out his third share, they felt precious little sympathy for one another. And in fact after the break, a very strong antipathy grew. It was only after Packer, too, had left *Smith's* in 1930 that McKay was able to walk through the door again, and then only after Clyde's son, Frank, had been bought out.

It is interesting to speculate how big a figure Clyde Packer would have become on the Australian newspaper scene had he not died in 1934, aged only fifty-five.

Claude McKay was seventy-two years old when *Smith's Weekly* closed for ever in October 1950. He bought a patch of prime land at Exeter, about a hundred miles from Sydney, and to this day, is energetically breeding fine dairy cattle and writing occasional bright pieces for the Sydney press.

CHAPTER FIVE

Editors and Editors-in-Chief

"Let'em call me an Italian bastard if they care. The laugh will be on them, because I'm half Irish on my mother's side."
—Frank Marien, Editor-in-Chief 1928-1936

Only the most unusual and talented type of people were capable of steering *Smith's* from the editorial chair.

Not only did the paper require its helmsmen to be fearless fellows; it demanded that they be showmen with a strong sense of buffoonery, as well as poets, and chargers of windmills. They had to be psychic in handling their temperamental staffs of creative artists and writers, knowing just how hard to apply the knout to get good work done without precipitating a revolt. Above all, they had to be able to laugh at writs and rumours of writs without getting ulcers.

Had anyone ever thought of nailing up an editorial honour board in *Smith's* it would have declared in letters of gold:

Editors-in-Chief:

Claude McKay	1919-1927
Frank Marien	1928-1936
Harry Cox	1938-1939
Kenneth Slessor (June-Sept.)	1939
Claude McKay	1939-1950

Editors:

Reg Moses	1930-1935
Kenneth Slessor	1935-1939
George Goddard	1939-1947
Edgar Holt	1947-1950

Sometimes *Smith's* had an Editor-in-Chief. Sometimes it didn't. Sometimes it operated with an Editor only. Sometimes with an Editor-in-Chief *and* an Editor. Life is not long enough to explain the intricacies involved. Suffice it to say that the paper always came out bubbling with fun, fire, and fury whoever was stirring the pot.

Frank Marien was called in when Claude McKay pulled out of the Joynton Smith-McKay-Packer triumvirate and went off to England, wealthy and determined to spend the rest of his life playing golf. Like Claude, Marien had come up from the very bottom of the newspaper game by sheer merit and had demonstrated his necessary flair for showmanship by serving a stint as publicity manager and house poet with J. C. Williamson's, a job of enormous prestige.

Admirers of Frank Marien used to claim that he was an Australian Michelangelo, capable of brilliant professional performances as a writer, a painter, a musician, and an engineer. He was also an athlete of near-international quality.

He was born in Sydney in 1890 of Irish-Italian parents. His father's name was Marieni, but the final "i" was knocked off as the result of a pre-marital requirement stipulated by the strong-minded Irish lass from Tipperary he married.

At St Joseph's College, Sydney, the famous sporting school, Frank became captain of football, cricket, and athletics. As a change of pace, he edited the school magazine, did all the illustrations in it, and was a key figure in the designing of the college badge which is used to this day.

There were a number of varying opinions as to what career he should follow when he left school. Datillo Rubbo, one of the leading art teachers in Australia, insisted he should make art his life work. Other experts considered he was born to be an engineer. Sporting officials insisted that whatever work he took up he must not let it interfere with his sport.

Although Marien had drawings hung in the Art Gallery of Sydney, and played full-back for New South Wales at Rugby union, it was to journalism that he turned for a living. To begin with he took the craft rather casually. He found reporting for the *Freeman's Journal* (now *The Catholic Weekly*) just too easy. Assigned to write a colourful report on Cardinal Moran's birthday concert at the Sydney Town Hall, he did so with the aid of the programme. He didn't go to the concert, and nor did Cardinal Moran who became sick at the last moment. The show was cancelled and young Marien sacked.

After working on country papers for a time, he joined *The Daily Telegraph* (Sydney) in 1919, and then moved to the evening *Sun* in 1922 as a special writer. Fame came to him as a result of one story. Every morning as he went to work in the train, he looked down into the small garden of a tenement house at Erskinville. Suddenly he realized he had been able to interpret the lives and emotions of the young couple in the house by the condition of their backyard — weeds for sorrow, flowers for happiness, the coming of babies, the departure of guests, bottles for parties. . . . The story as Marien wrote it for *The Sun* (Sydney) attracted a fan mail of 4,000 letters. This is probably still an Australian record response to a single story.

In 1926, Frank Marien went from *The Sun* to *Truth* as Managing Director, and by his masterly approach to the human interest type of story, increased *Truth's* circulation by 200,000 a week inside two years.

When Claude McKay sold out his interest in *Smith's* in 1927 and resigned as Editor-in-Chief, Joynton Smith and Clyde Packer looked round for the best possible replacement. They decided in 1928 that Marien was the obvious choice.

Marien, then thirty-eight, was interested. His terms, gossip insisted, were the highest ever demanded and received by a journalist in Australia — a ten-year contract on a salary rising to £110 a week. The basic wage in 1928 was £4.5.0.

Frank Marien's personal ability as an artist enabled him to handle with great skill and understanding the brilliant team of black-and-white artists Claude McKay had built up. Any artist coming forward with a bright idea could have all the space he liked to display it to the world — one-third or half of a broadsheet page even. What artist could resist such treatment!

The feuding and fussing that went on between Marien and his artists, related elsewhere, was mainly fun and a technique for ensuring that no one got into a dull rut. Stan Cross nominates Frank Marien as "the best Art Editor Australia ever had," and many artists who worked for Marien would agree.

On the editorial side, Marien was also successful, though, in the opinion of most, he did not have the same touch for handling the *Smith's Weekly* formula as did Claude McKay. But this is no criticism of Marien, for the paper had been Claude's baby and no one ever understood it as well as he did.

It is one of the mysteries of Australian journalism that it was in Marien's régime, in 1932, that *Smith's* printed the "wicked beyond expression" Wilkinson story which almost destroyed the paper at the time and damaged its reputation permanently. How could such a skilled and devoted Editor-in-Chief have been hoodwinked into printing such material? One theory is that he was victim of a plot to kill his paper.

While Marien worked in his editorial sanctum on the second floor, his ear was ever attuned to the clacking of the linotypes on

"Oh why! Oh why can't I have a nice house and pretty clothes like other men."

the first floor and the roar of the big presses in the basement. His engineering instincts would never leave him alone. In 1935, when told that the highly specialized mechanical superintendent of *Smith's*, Geoff Coburn, had resigned, Marien appointed himself mechanical superintendent.

He quickly proved to doubters that he could strip down a Linotype or a Hoe press more quickly than anyone else in the office. And when he had put the lino together, he could sit at the keyboard and set a story into type as he composed it in his head. His secret was that at his home in the outer Sydney suburb of Miranda, he had one of the finest private engineering workshops in Australia. In the shop were lathes of all sizes, electric drills, automatic steel saws, and thirty feet of belt-driven shafting, driving a multitude of gadgets on a forty foot work bench.

His whole home was a mass of electrical wonders, all of which he installed himself. (He even did the wiring himself.) In the kitchen, he had a table that, when buttons were pressed or wheels turned, would briskly raise and lower itself, shoot out stools and work boards, and do everything short of sing.

He also maintained a full-scale movie projection room and screen in his back yard. Provision was made for fifty guests in the stalls and thirty in the dress circle directly above. From his projection box, the host could work batteries of switches to fade coloured lights in and out around the screen, and turn fans or radiators on his guests according to the needs dictated by the weather.

In the two years ending July 1936, he practically ran *Smith's* from St Vincent's Private Hospital where he received constant treatment for a severe illness. His sole complaint was that he could not get a decent feed of his favourite dish — cold baked rabbit. His strict diet denied him this simple delight. Ever a fiery man and one not easily thwarted, he briefed his younger son, Brian, a teenager, to sneak a forbidden rabbit to his room.

Brian was lurking on the stairs, a rabbit under his shirt, when he was waylaid and searched by the Mother Superior, the very famed, but severe Mother Patrick.

"You are trying to kill your father," she told the boy.

His father said this was rot and changed his tactics. There was a little balcony attached to his room. From time to time, under cover of darkness, Brian would toss a stone into this balcony from the ground. A weighted string would come from the gloomy heights and be quickly withdrawn when a cold baked rabbit had been attached.

One day in July 1936, Frank Marien's private secretary, Miss Louie Still, entered his office at *Smith's* and found him dead at his desk, a sheet of copy paper and a pencil before him. He had died a true journalist's death at the age of forty-five.

Before Marien died, Claude McKay had come back from overseas and, at Joynton Smith's invitation, had set himself up in the office as an unpaid manager, in an attempt to make the paper a more profitable concern.

Unfortunately the Scot, Claude McKay, and the Irish-Italian, Frank Marien, though each brilliant, were not compatible. For one thing, Marien would accept nothing from Claude in the way of editorial guidance. For Claude, the foundation Editor-in-Chief and father of the paper, this was galling.

When the paper became profitable again, Claude walked out and did not reappear until 1939, when he assumed complete control of his curious infant once more. He then carried on as Editor-in-Chief until the end in 1950.

There never was a list of rules as to the functions of a *Smith's* Editor-in-Chief or a *Smith's* Editor. For instance Reg "Mo" Moses, who held the title of Editor from 1930 to 1935 and the rank of "Literary Editor" for years before that, spent most of his time in writing rather than administration. This was very proper because no one in Australia could match him in his day for popular satire. His by-line, "Mo" invariably started readers giggling. A university man and classical scholar, he served his apprenticeship on Sydney daily papers before becoming J. C. Williamson's publicity expert. He joined *Smith's* in 1921, two years after it started, and quickly won himself a reputation as a rare wit.

The New South Wales Police Association tried him out as an after-dinner speaker at its annual dinner. Mo began, "I have often wondered what becomes of the illegitimate children of barmaids. As I stand here tonight and look about me, I see the answer to my wonder. They become policemen, of course." For the remainder of his life, Mo was the main speaker at New South Wales Police dinners and *Smith's* was a great favourite with the Force.

A short, round man, Mo had a very large and distinctive head. Claude McKay had George Finey draw a caricature of Mo's cranium making it larger than ever and printed it with the comment, "A magnificent head for a brain. Offers c/- this office. Please hurry." A happy little bit of trivia that delighted regular readers.

His resignation to go over to *The Australian Women's Weekly* in 1935 would have been a disastrous blow to *Smith's* had not Kenneth Slessor been on hand to take over the weekly satirical chore. Which of the two men was the better at this rare art was a popular point of argument in the 1930s.

Mo died in his first year with *The Women's Weekly,* aged only forty-six.

Kenneth Slessor succeeded Mo as *Smith's* Editor in 1935 and remained in the chair until 1939, when George Goddard took over. In 1938, Sir Joynton Smith sought to ease some of the enormous strain from Slessor who was performing the functions of editor, literary editor, leader writer, satirist, and main feature writer, all at the same time.

He brought in Harry Cox as Editor-in-Chief. Harry was a

Sydney journalist of tremendous energy and fast-flowing ideas, who provided a very sharp change of pace in *Smith's*.

He had had the reputation in his reporting days, of being able to outmatch anybody, even teams of men, on difficult assignments. With him to *Smith's*, he brought a string of name writers — Stewart Howard, the author, Ross Campbell, the Victorian Rhodes Scholar and later author, as well as Bill Rodie, Bill Band, and others.

Harry had arrived at a bad time. With the Depression wracking the economy, weekly papers had become a luxury. The new Editor-in-Chief used all his energy and ingenuity, experimenting with colour and a big variety of features designed to cater for all possible tastes. He even took a shot at attracting children with special comic strips — an extreme step indeed for *Smith's*.

Nothing would check the sliding circulation. Harry Cox left the paper in 1939 and the ever-faithful Kenneth Slessor once more took complete charge in an attempt to hold the paper together. Slessor, who is one of Australia's all-time great poets, is also one of her all-time great journalists, and his almost single-handed fight to save the dying *Smith's* just before World War II is one of the epics of newspaper history. He not only edited the paper but wrote the front pages, the leaders, the satire, the verses to go with the weekly caricature, the film reviews, and answered the phone to all who wished to register a grouch against the paper.

In a desperate search for readers, *Smith's* had introduced a feature completely foreign to its basic forthright nature — a weekly astrology column. For economy purposes this was retrenched. Immediately a tirade of protests came in from alleged devoted readers of the column. Slessor concluded that a small group of people were ringing up over and over again to create a multiple effect. Each time they rang to protest they wanted to know why, why, why "the best feature in the paper" had been dropped. Slessor's wit provided an answer which killed all argument: "We have had the paper's horoscope cast and our stars say we must drop the feature instantly or go out of business!"

The unbearable weight of office was taken off Ken's back when Claude McKay suddenly appeared late in 1939 with a powerful syndicate to take over the dying *Smith's*, sales of which were down to 80,000 a week.

Then came World War II. The Commonwealth Government grabbed Kenneth Slessor and appointed him Australia's Official War Correspondent. After serving his country well in Syria,

FIRST DIG: *(on leave): "Can I touch yer for a pound, dig?"*
SECOND DIG: *"For a pound yer can punch me ruddy face!"*

Crete, the Middle East, and New Guinea, like a true *Smith's* man Ken objected to being messed around needlessly by unimaginative higher authority. He resigned as a "W.C." in February 1944.

Ken has now long been the doyen of Sydney journalists, leader writer of *The Daily Telegraph,* and President of the Journalists Club, Sydney. In spite of all these activities the magic of his poetry has never dimmed. Even the bits he wrote as jingle for *Smith's* decades ago are rich with their original laughter.

Here are two verses Slessor wrote for *Smith's* in 1934 to go under a Syd Miller caricature of Billy Hughes who had retained his North Sydney seat with a record majority:

The old man of North Sydney
No destiny can dim.
As steak adheres to kidney,
North Sydney sticks to him.
Like perfume to the lily,
Or bridle to the bit,

North Sydney cleaves to Billy,
And Billy sticks to it.

He wrote verses like that every week. Bright catchy stuff.

But he also wrote for *Smith's* verses which would have given the paper the right to call itself a literary journal had it cared to do so. In the late 1920s, Ken's poems with Virgil Reilly's illustrations were attracting to *Smith's* as readers, poetry lovers who normally would have found little to their taste in the paper.

Slessor, who wrote Jim Donald's boxing column when the Sultan of Swot was on holidays, was always fascinated by the girls who went to the fights. Hence the sentiment behind "The Tiger in The Rose," published in *Smith's*, 2 June 1928:

Rosie at the stadium
Flaunts around her neck
Rubies rare as radium
Diamonds by the peck.
Furs of real Peschaniki
Staggering the press.
Rosie's not the simple little
Angel you suppose,
Down behind the dimple there's a Tiger
                              in
                                    the
                                          Rose.

Jungle creatures loitering
Down in Rosie's heart
Leap out reconnoitering
When the fighters start;
Fairies love ferocity —
Rosie starts to shout
Filled with animosity
'Bust him on the snout!'
Never mind the posy, disregard the pose,
Have a look at Rosie! There's a Tiger
                              in
                                    the
                                          Rose.

When Claude McKay returned in 1939 to reclaim his now mature, though ailing infant, he brought with him George Goddard, a highly trained journalist of admirable imperturbability whom he appointed to serve as Editor under his Editor-in-Chiefship. George, who had edited a number of daily newspapers and

"Yair, I got a job as cook because me principles are against carryin' arms—I don't believe in murder."
"Don't believe in murder? Then what ———— hell do you call the meals yer givin' us?"

had then tried his hand at business with Carrier Air Conditioning, had been glad to come back to his first love.

He proved an excellent choice. He was a World War I Dig, and when World War II broke out within a week or so of his joining *Smith's,* he and Claude knew exactly the patriotic diet to feed the excited nation. *Smith's,* which had been The Diggers' Paper since 1919, restaked its claim to the title with zest in 1939. Claude McKay, aided by George Goddard and the war, built *Smith's* back to a circulation of over 300,000 and enormous profits.

Round, plump, and balding, with a habit of parking his specs on his extra high forehead, Goddard gave the impression of being a rather gentle soul. But he was full of crusading courage and made a fine running mate for Claude who, if he wasn't looking for a fight, was forever hoping one would turn up.

Probably the ultimate test of an editor is how he acts if threatened with prison — a rare and terrible ordeal. During the war Claude and George were threatened with pokey by the Federal

Government for being in possession of allegedly "stolen documents" they had used to expose the massive secret profits being made by the services canteen organizations. Their response was to use *Smith's* front page to announce their danger. Never a hint of apology or regret. The two men were ready to take imprisonment for a principle. The Government backed down.

Goddard hated plagiarists and had a special letter he used to send them when returning their phoney mss:

> Dear Mr Brown
> There's a story told about Dame Constance D'Arcy, eminent medico of Macquarie Street. Do you know her? She's very big and very fat.
> One day she rushed down from her rooms to Macquarie Street, hailed a taxi and said: "Quick! drive me to the Women's Hospital, Maternity Section, Crown Street. . .!"
> The taxi driver replied: "No, you don't Missus! Not in this cab."
> Same applies to the enclosed ms. "No, you don't, Mr Brown! Not in *Smith's*!"
> > Yours truly,
> > G. Goddard,
> > Editor.

The years of World War II with their shortage of staff and attendant problems took much out of George Goddard. In August 1947, just when the going was smooth once more, he collapsed and died.

His successor was Edgar Holt, former leader writer of *The Herald* (Melbourne) and *The Daily Telegraph* (Sydney) who had been *Smith's* political writer for a couple of years. Edgar, like Ken Slessor, was a poet and a good one. His Political Form Guide in *Smith's* was noted for its waspish wit, and he had the art of making the dullest subjects sound bright, even important.

However, it was as a cooking writer that he found his most enthusiastic audience. He had a fine talent for cooking and an even better one for writing about his adventures with pot and pan. Under the podgy pen name, "Toby Belch," he produced a weekly column which rarely failed to set the taste buds glowing. Here's Edgar in full cry from the kitchen:

> Recently I wrote lovingly about duck and orange sauce. Today I write even more lovingly, and, fresh from preparing it, submit it for your approval.
> The duck had come fresh and exciting from a friend's poultry farm. Something special had to be done with it.
> I took my largest shallow pot with lid that fitted tightly.

Then with a quick reckless abandon, I melted nearly a quarter-pound of butter and set the bird to brown. I had the flame going vigorously and turned the duck frequently, frequently.

When I was happy about the colour, I poured over the duck in its butter a cup full of the very light stock in which I had simmered the duck's neck. Round the bird, I set the quarters of a large orange together with a little of the orange skin which had been trimmed to the length and thickness of match sticks. Seasoning in the ordinary way with salt and pepper, I then clamped down the lid and left the bird to cook gently in the steam for one hour.

When the lid was lifted, the duck was tenderly succulent. I set the bird on a dish decorated with orange slices and put it in the oven to keep hot while I made the sauce.

Here you must lavish all your skill and affection. Into the liquid in the pot, I poured two cups of white wine — a still hock — and allowed the whole to come to the boil. I then strained the sauce and skimmed from the top as much as I could of the grease, returned the sauce to the flame, and reduced it a little. As a final touch I took the sauce from the fire, and poured in as much Cointreau as would fill a small liqueur glass.

The bird fell gloriously apart and was served only with the sauce. I should add we drank a bottle of ten-year-old Hunter River claret — a delicate and noble wine.

Only a poet could have written such a recipe.

Edgar battled bravely right to the last edition of *Smith's*. It was no fault of his the paper expired when it did, the Liberal Party of Australia grabbed him and made him their Federal Public Relations Officer. From a poetic political writer who "knew his onions," he became probably the No. 1 P.R. man in Australia.

CHAPTER SIX

Smith's Artists—The Old Guard

"For a teetotaller I seem to suffer more from hard liquor than anyone else in Australia!" — shouted down the *Smith's Weekly* lift well by Sir James Joynton Smith at his Art Staff which was departing for the pub.
—*Circa* 1925

Many of the people who read *Smith's* regularly considered that its greatest merit lay in its black-and-white comic art work, Each week, the paper was packed out with masses of gags and comic strips and caricatures aimed bang at the Australian funny-bone. With no T.V. to entertain at night, *Smith's* had a very special place with folks who liked their fun to come in pictorial form.

From the start, the paper sought out the best comic artists in Australia. The bait at first was crude, but very effective money. If you were good enough to get on *Smith's* art staff, your salary would be triple what you could win elsewhere with your pen and brush. In time, first-class men tried to get on *Smith's* for the glamour and the gay-spirited company as much as for the cash.

By the mid-'twenties, it was the opinion of Fleet Street that *Smith's Weekly* out in Australia had the best team of black-and-white newspaper artists in the world. This probably wasn't far wrong. Magic names appeared at the bottom of drawings throughout the paper — Stan Cross, Joe Jonsson, Cec Hartt, Virgil, Driffield, Donaldson, Hallett, George Finey, Syd Miller, and Frank Dunne. Later came Jim Russell, Norman Mitchell, Les Dixon, John Endean, Emile Mercier, Eric Jolliffe, Joan Morrison, Mollie Horseman, Jim Phillips. . . .

Few who have been important in newspaper art in Australia since 1919 didn't serve on *Smith's* for some time at least.

The first artist to join *Smith's* was Cec Hartt, fresh home from World War I. He is more remembered now for his remarkable personality than for his artistic skill. He was a good draughtsman, with a ready sense of humour which had the genuine common touch. Cec was everybody's pal. An indication of his natural charm is that Henry Lawson, the poet, loved him like a favourite brother, even though he usually abhorred artists, suspecting that they were mountebanks and far inferior to literary people.

The pair were friends before 1914 and kept up a busy correspondence when the artist was overseas on active service. In the early part of the war, it was the vogue for Diggers to write home using the heavily coloured cliché "it is like taking the lid off hell!" to describe the German onslaught. The newspapers reproduced the expression with never-ending enthusiasm.

Cecil varied the theme when he wrote to Lawson: "Henry, the noise is hardly supportable. It's like working at home!"

Lawson carried a packet of Cecil Hartt's letters in his pocket, delightedly reading such excerpts to all who would listen, until the paper they were written on had been reduced to tatters.

Joan Morrison, Petrov, Virgil Reilly, Stan Cross, Joe Jonsson, Syd Miller, George Donaldson, Frank Dunne, Alex King, Jim Russell, Mollie Horseman.

While in Horseferry Road Barracks, London, after being wounded in France, Hartt amused himself by getting out a book of Digger drawings which proved to be a shock best-seller in England where Australian soldiers were very popular. Cecil, to his amazement, ended up being presented to His Majesty, King George V.

It was this successful bit of art work that particularly inspired the founding fathers of *Smith's* to grab Cecil. They planned to make their paper "The Diggers' Paper" among other things, and Cec was a natural drawcard for the old soldier audience from the very first issue.

There were times when Claude McKay had good reason for thinking that Cec had known every single soldier in the First A.I.F. Homecoming soldiers, on being discharged, rushed straight to *Smith's* to search out good old Cec and have a drink with him. Cec, as good a performer with a glass as with a pen, was ever eager to rewarm old wartime friendships. One secret of his attraction was the curious real life stories he loved to tell. His appearance in a Sydney bar would result in an audience gathering quickly to listen to his delightful chatter. One of his star stories concerned the first meal he had on returning home from the war.

Very conscious that Cec loved kidneys (cooked whole) beyond all known meats, his wife tramped to a myriad of butcher shops begging a kidney here and a kidney there until she had a splendid potful. Happily Cecil sat down to his first post-war meal at home with his dear wife and his little son, Laurie.

RICH OLD HUNKS TO CHARITY COLLECTOR: *"It's true I don't give much, but if you only knew how it hurts me to give at all you wouldn't wonder."*

He attacked the luscious favourite food from which he had long been parted. His wife ate heartily. But young Laurie would not lift his knife and fork to touch the kidneys. Between eager bites Cec urged the lad to tuck in. Young Laurie coldly refused to eat. At last, patience exhausted, father demanded, "Why in heaven's name won't you eat any?"

"Cos I've seen 'em hanging on dawgs!" cried young Laurie desperately.

Laurie was the central figure of many of his father's favourite crowd ticklers. Cec's home was in the Sydney seaside suburb of Dee Why, near to the local Salvation Army hall, where every Sabbath evening a brave brass band accompanied the hymns, and emphasized with musical phrases the vocal testimony of the faithful. Little Laurie seemed most intrigued and one Sunday evening announced that he would like to attend a Salvation Army meeting.

Mother and father were delighted that their offspring was interested in obtaining a basis of grace, and arming him with a hurricane lamp, sent him off on his misson, secretly watching his infant steps from afar. Later, going to collect the child, Cecil met the Salvation Army Captain who gave him this report: "Your little boy crept in and sat by himself in the last row. I felt I should specially welcome one so young and so alone. So I walked up through the rows of seats and sat beside him. I put a paternal arm round his shoulders and essayed an encouraging few words — 'And so, my little laddie, you've come to be saved?' But your Laurie dumbfounded me by his announcement — 'No, I've come to see the bloody wowsers!' "

Cec had spoken just a little too loudly and uninhibitedly at home. To show his repentance, he encouraged his son to attend Sunday School and tried to show the child that he was interested in what was being taught. As a result the following conversation took place between father and son:

"What did you learn today, Laurie?"

"Aw, nothing much. Just a story."

"Well, tell me the story. I'd like to hear it."

"Well, I'll tell you. They were having a shivoo and Jesus was there and someone came and told him the wine had run out. So he said fill up all the pots with water and I'll turn it into wine. And they did, and he did. And everybody was so drunk they didn't know the difference."

It was Cecil Hartt, with his love of a tale and a beer with merry pals, who initiated the tradition that all *Smith's* artists had to be jolly good company. Long after his death, when few who had known him remained on the staff, the tradition of gaiety still lived with the artists.

Hartt's comic drawings in the first few issues of *Smith's* attracted so much favourable comment that Claude McKay and Clyde Packer realized the comic art element was a winner and had to be exploited fast. But there weren't any other comic artists available in Sydney.

Ernie Brewer, first advertising manager of *Smith's*, offered a suggestion. He said that over in Perth was a young chap with a lot of promise working as a draughtsman in the Western Australian Railways Department, he thought, and doing a bit of freelance art work on the side for *The Sunday Times, The Western Mail,* and the *United Licensed Victuallers Association Journal.* Some samples of the young man's work were obtained. Claude McKay was most impressed and wrote to Perth, offering the unknown artist a job on trial at £5 per week.

Thus the now celebrated Stan Cross came from Perth to Sydney to win recognition as probably the finest black-and-white artist Australia has produced. Today, in his seventies, as creator of the famous daily comic strip, "Wally and The Major," he is the highest paid newspaperman in Australia. And, as his employer, Sir John Williams of The Herald and Weekly Times Ltd, Melbourne, is fond of saying, "worth every penny of it!"

It is impossible to believe that anyone could look less like the

REPORTER: *"Press"* (*passes in*).
JACKY: *"Press."*
TICKET COLLECTOR: *"What press you belong to, Jacky?"*
JACKY: *"Alonga McEvoy's plurry woolpress, o' course."*

popular conception of a free-and-easy comic artist than Stan Cross. Tall, athletic in build, eagle-eyed, and lofty browed, he had an absolutely magnificent patrician nose, a deep measured voice, and was immaculately dressed with an ever so slightly relaxed drape.

All this complex is deceptive enough, but what finally defeats the searcher after the Bohemian factor in Stan's mode of conversation is the subject matter he favours in barside discussion. In a gathering of artists he may initially be party to quips, gossip, and discussion of techniques, but inevitably his quick mind moves away into the fields of economic philosophy where he is a No. 1 bull. Because he is unchallenged king among Australian black-and-white artists, the court moves with him, not to argue but to listen, as Stan, utilizing spilt beer on the bar and a deft drawing finger, demonstrates the economic ills affecting the world and describes the appropriate remedies. His grasp of the subject appears to be profound and his expositions are dramatic.

Many of Stan Cross's admirers believe that he would have made perhaps a national name for himself had he become an academic instead of an artist. (He has written books on accoun-tancy, economics, and English grammar). But *Smith's Weekly* caught him in 1918, when he was in his early twenties, and began exploiting his magnificent talent for comic art.

On arriving from Perth, he joined Cec Hartt in a small room in *Smith's* attic in Somerset House, the paper's birthplace. The only other occupant of the room was a lay-figure Stan had brought with him. A fanatic for anatomical accuracy, Stan had had the life-sized figure of a man made for use as a model. The effigy was a work of art. It had movable joints at every appropri-ate point of the limbs, the neck, and the centre of the spine. The frame was covered with one of Stan's old suits, the papiermâché head crowned with a hat, and the feet shod with shoes. Stan could pose it in any complicated position he desired.

On one occasion "Dummy" was posed in a belligerent fighting pose when a somewhat tipsy Digger mate of Cec Hartt's dropped in to renew auld acquaintance. The visitor, his battle instincts still strong within him, could not resist the implied challenge and sparred brilliantly around the figure landing cleverly placed blows to head and body. In time he worked round behind "Dummy" and, as a *coup de grâce,* swung a vicious right-hander to the back, crying in the vanity of victory, "How's that for a kidney punch?"

He then cried out for another reason. His hard swung knuckles had landed on the great, round, iron spine-joint socket that nestled flatly under "Dummy's" coat.

From then on, the model was placed in the "Come and fight, yer mug" pose when not in use. Digger pals calling to see Cec invariably insisted on demonstrating their boxing skill — with a minimum of encouragement anyhow — and if they did not think of including an attack on the kidneys in their assault plan, a quick hint from Cec and Stan took care of that.

The first time Henry Lawson met "Dummy" he was filled with amazement. During 1919 he made innumerable visits to the art loft, in search of a conversation with his mate, Cec Hartt, and, equally important, a sixpence for refreshment. On entering one day with his hand out, he suddenly sighted the lay-figure and contemplated it suspiciously for a long time. He observed the quite good shoes that "Dummy" wore and then ostentatiously examined his own cracked footwear. He felt the quality of the suit with thumb and forefinger at lapel and compared it with his own battered raiment. He took off his greasy hat and matched it against the model's headgear.

Standing well back, he subjected "Dummy" to a further scrutiny, then walking forward towards it with his hand out he cried reproachfully, "Hey! You jolly well give me sixpence."

Stan's "Dummy" later became a well-known figure in Sydney. Teams of artists would carry him through the streets and pubs of Sydney on a stretcher to publicize forthcoming Artists' Balls. He would be solemnly sat at bars and drinks lined up in front of him until it was his turn to shout when he would show his sportsmanship by permitting his untouched whiskies to be shared around.

At first Henry Lawson took little interest in Stan Cross, believing him to be "only another artist," which made him, in the poet's opinion, somewhat less than the dust. This was the situation until one afternoon in a pub when Lawson was giving all his attention to Hartt and completely ignoring Stan. Hartt opened the latest copy of *Smith's* on the bar and displayed it page by page for Lawson's consideration and criticism, until a three-column joke block somewhere in the centre convulsed the poet with laughter.

"Stan Cross here drew that," Cec yelled.

Lawson straightened up, wheeled round on Stan, and saluted him over and over again in the elaborate military-like gesture he reserved for those who really captured his admiration. Stan, now seventy-seven, can remember few more magic moments in his career.

Stan Cross pioneered the comic strip in Australia in 1920. On the advice of Errol Knox (later Sir Errol of *The Argus* (Melbourne)) who had joined the editorial staff, Claude McKay had imported some strips from America where they were all the rage. The American stuff was no good to *Smith's;* anyhow the policy was to print one hundred per cent Australian material. But Stan took the technique and devised "a political quip" in strip form as a running weekly commentary on the Patterson butter arrangement, whereby Australia subsidized her local dairy industry to sell butter on the English market at prices lower than were being received at home. As the leading characters of his strip, which he called "You and Me," he created "Mr Pott" —

LIZA: *"I don't know why you don't like my boy friend."*
DAD: *"He seems such a vulgar cow."*

a plump little man — and "Whalesteeth" — a long, lanky, toothy chap. The cheerful couple opened the series full of glee in the belief they were going to get lots of cheap butter. The final picture showed them standing sadly on the wharf as the butter sailed away to be sold cheaply in England. Australia delighted in this new approach to political problems, but in time the strip ran away from the creator and became domestic in nature until the title "Mr and Mrs Potts" was substituted for "You and Me."

This same strip, or a vestigial form of it, is still one of the most popular in Australia. It was inherited by Jim Russell in 1940 and now appears in all States under the title of "The Potts." The addition of "Uncle Dick" and the grandchildren has increased its attraction.

Stan started a number of other strips on *Smith's*. His personal favourite was "The Vaudevillians" — Norman and Rhubarb. Norman was a top-hatted dandy and Rhubarb an ever-tipsy sailor who cracked topical gags together as they tripped the light fantastic. Another Stan Cross all-star winner was the original

DAD: *"Hey! Don't go too far, you'll be wanted down in the milkin' yard directly."*

Dad and Dave Strip which was Australian to the whiskers in the most cheerful and cheeky sense.

This strip reached its peak in popularity when Stan sent Dad and Dave abroad. Australia rocked for a full week over this sequence:

Dad and Dave looking very much tourist types (cameras, guide books, etc.) are in London doing the sights. Dad buttonholes an extra proper-looking Englishman and says, "Hey mate, what's that building over there?"

Very proper Englishman: Well, actually, it's the Bloody Tower!

Dad: Is the bloody thing worth seeing?

Country people were even more delighted with the strip depicting Dad and Dave inside the Bloody Tower.

Dave reads his guide book and then pointing to a beefeater guard, who has very, very skinny shanks, says authoritatively, "That bloke is a beefeater, Dad."

"Well," opines Dad, "it must be that chilled stuff that comes from the Argentine."

That strip was cut out and pasted up by almost every Australian cattleman, for the matter of cheap Argentine beef pinching Australia's English market was a very live question at the time.

Stan had the keenest eye, as did Claude McKay, for any matter of political interest which could be treated with laughter. His sense of satire was brilliant and his capacity to judge public taste from moment to moment limitless. All this coupled with the rarest talent for black-and-white work made him probably the greatest of Australia's newspaper artists ever.

Stan himself insists that George Finey, the caricaturist, deserves the honour. Claude McKay nominates Charlie Hallett. Some English judges plumped for George Donaldson. Sir John Longstaff, doyen of Australian portrait painters, used to barrack for Joe Jonsson. All these were *Smith's* artists.

But the mass judgement of editors and readers is overwhelmingly in favour of Stan Cross, whose current strip, "Wally and The Major," which he began drawing for *The Herald* (Melbourne) in 1940, has long been the most popular daily and Sunday strip in Australia.

In his *Smith's* days, Stan's sense of variety and his output of material were bewildering. In addition to the several strips and stacks of joke blocks which he did as routine, he was constantly devising new short-run features. "Things That Make Stan Cross" (political and economic criticism), "Places We have Never Visited" (Law courts, Parliament, players' room at a test cricket match), and "Firsts in Australian History" (the first barmaid, the first strike, the first football match.)

As *Smith's* did not stand for any political creed, nor, as a matter of fact, for anything bar "Hooray for Australia," Stan was free to throw his ink around just as his fancy dictated. The fun that resulted was delightfully uninhibited. It was often enough sharply pointed, but never cruel and mean, and the sternest critic could never say he found a blue note in any of Stan Cross's work.

Stan's idea of a bit of fun on the side was to gather a group of *Smith's* comic characters on the front page of an edition and send them adventuring in advertisements throughout the whole paper. By the time they emerged on the back page, the advertisers had been given a fine free run for their money. Stan didn't regard this sort of thing as work, but a pleasant exercise in ingenuity.

In July 1933 he crowned his labours with what has been popularly rated "the funniest joke ever produced in Australia." There are plenty of experts willing to back the joke for the all-time world title.

This was the celebrated "For gor'sake stop laughing, this is serious!" gag which convulsed Australia. Calls for reprints were so great that *Smith's* ran them off on glossy paper by the tens of thousands. A group of clerks was employed full-time mailing them away to all parts of the earth. Requests for copies came from such curious places as the Khyber Pass (from British Troops stationed there), Tristan da Cunha, and Mombasa.

There are a dozen versions of how this joke was born. Here in Stan's own words is the exact story of its creation. The detail in the story is important for it demonstrates perfectly how coolly the professional comic artist craftsman goes about his business. There is no mad creative laughter, or sudden unexpected inspiration, but a dour, logical progression to a comic result.

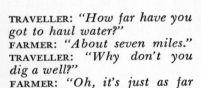

TRAVELLER: *"How far have you got to haul water?"*
FARMER: *"About seven miles."*
TRAVELLER: *"Why don't you dig a well?"*
FARMER: *"Oh, it's just as far one way as the other!"*

Says Stan Cross:

A young art student called to see Frank Marien, *Smith's* Editor-in-Chief, to see if he could get some of his work into the pages of *Smith's*. Frank inspected the work and saw the boy had made good progress with his studies. But none of the drawings submitted was suitable for publication, nor did the lad have any idea what would suit the paper.

So Frank Marien looked through the "pool" of joke suggestions that had been sent in by outside contributors — some people made small fortunes selling gag ideas to *Smith's* — and picked one which looked promising. The proposition was that a builder having slipped was hanging by his hands from the water guttering of a house. His mate, involved with the accident, was hanging on to his legs. The one hanging on to the guttering was laughing. The second was complaining: "What are you laughing for?" The gutter-hanger was replying: "Well, you're pulling my leg!"

The student made a drawing containing these elements and submitted it to Marien. It was impossible as a joke block — not a bit of fun in it.

Frank Marien called me in and handed me the original contributed joke. He said: "I want you to show this lad how to see the sort of thing we want — how an idea must be thought over, the essence of its humour extracted, and its presentation stage-managed into a funny scene." I decided that the contributed suggestion had its humour, if any, in the phrase "you are pulling my leg." But in this form, the joke was thin, obvious, and uninspiring.

I pushed the idea around and around until I had one man hanging perilously from a girder, far above the street. The second man had slid down his mate's body and, in clutching to save himself, had pulled his mate's pants down. I made them both roar with laughter, notwithstanding their great peril. Now I needed a line with a lot more punch than "you're pulling my leg." I settled for "For gorsake stop laughing—this is serious."

When the Stan Cross version of the gag was presented to Frank Marien, he was so amused that he was fearful he had overjudged the quality. To make sure that it wasn't funny to him alone, he left the original lying on his desk for several days. Every visitor to his office couldn't help but inspect it. (Marien didn't ask a single person to look). Some visitors laughed so hard they had to sit down. Others mopped their eyes. Marien, never afraid to shout his wares when he knew them to be good, presented Stan's drawing as "The Funniest Drawing In The World."

No one ever challenged this bold claim. Everyone was too busy laughing.

The Australian *Who's Who* states that Stan Cross was born in Los Angeles in 1888 and this causes much distress to Australians, who fear they cannot claim Stan as one of their own.

Stan was in truth born in America, but when his background is all sorted out, Australia has more right to him than any other country. His parents, both English born, met in Queensland and married in Sydney. Believing he could hear a fortune beckoning to him from America, father Cross took his bride to the land of hope where he imagined he would make big money as an architect. He had, however, to accept the more practical end of building — the saw and hammer section. As a carpenter he got interested in union affairs and he became secretary of the American Carpenters' Union.

At a convention of trade unions, Cross (snr) became friendly with the famous Samuel Gompers, father of the American trade union movement. Stan retains to this day a cigar Gompers, a cigar maker by trade, rolled by his own hands and presented to his father at that convention.

The family came to Australia and settled in Perth. Stan was four at the time. He entered the Railways Department to become a draughtsman, but while his employers fondly imagined him at Technical College learning draughtsmanship, he was actually at Tech. studying fine art, a simple lurk to carry him away from worrying about where to place seats in railway carriages and transport him to fame and wealth as a creative artist.

"Dinkum! You're the first girl I ever asked to come out with me while I set the rabbit traps!"

Number three man to join *Smith's* infant art staff was Alek Sass, a Melbourne artist with a delicate touch, and, more important to *Smith's* in its first year, highly skilled in the American technique of drawing for papers printed on fast rotary machines. More experienced than Stan Cross and Cec Hartt, he was named as first Art Editor of the paper.

Sass, whose real name was Williams, was somewhat serious in his outlook as a result of an attempt he once made to cure his old dad of the demon drink.

His father had two main loves — his garden and alcohol. His son determined to exploit one love to cure the other. One evening, when Pa Sass came home soused, young Alek waited until he had lapsed into a rum-bound swound and then removed the sleeper's great big boots. Donning these boots, the son stamped heavily all over the lovingly developed garden beds all round the house. His theory was that in the morning dad would identify the footsteps as his own, attribute the havoc to his own blind inebriation, and swear off liquor for ever.

Most of the plot worked out perfectly up to the point where Pa should have sworn off grog. Alas, his heart was so broken at what he believed he had done that he abandoned gardening and concentrated on his other hobby more or less full-time.

12.45a.m., MOTHER *(to daughter):* *"Are you engaged, dear?"* DAUGHTER: *"Very nearly, Mother."*

Sass's seriousness of mind, resulting from shame at what he had done left him wide open to the two playful pups on his staff who had not had time or experience enough to develop serious inhibitions.

Stan Cross and Cec Hartt were quick to note that the Art Editor took meticulous care with his work, ensuring that his drawings were very clean and very thorough. Their minds were on this one day when, returning from lunch to the Imperial Arcade, they found a large splotch of thin solder on the footpath beneath a leadlight window a workman had been fixing. The splotch was collected and taken to the art room, where a Sass drawing of a pretty girl, representing hours of earnest work, lay on a drawing board.

The splotch was covered in Indian ink and, when dry, placed on the face of the pretty girl. An empty ink bottle and dry cork were placed beside the splotch. When Art Editor Sass was heard approaching, Stan and Cec engaged in a fierce bumping wrestle which appeared to be at violence peak when the top man entered.

The lovely drawing! Ruined!

The two young men raced round apologizing to their raging Art Editor and hurriedly brought him blotting paper with which he attacked the bottom of the stain. The ink blot began to move up the tilted drawing board. . . .

This style of nonsense remained an essential part of the way of life in the art room as long as *Smith's* lived. In the Imperial Arcade days, the fun was so fast and furious, and the noise so constantly intense, that the many other tenants in the building often found it hard to concentrate on their prosaic businesses.

Landlord Sir Joynton Smith, pleased as he was with the progress of his new paper, was concerned for the comfort of his tenants for whom the "happy, laughing louts in the art room" seemed to have little consideration.

Joynton was unfamiliar with the ways of artists, but he learnt fast, and came to expect the worst from them. This led him into a most embarrassing situation. One of his most distinguished tenants in the arcade had some back trouble which caused him to walk almost doubled over. Joynton, bustling along the corridor, ran into a figure who appeared to be barging headfirst and blindly forward. Instinctively identifying an artist at play, Joynton jostled the bent figure aside, roaring in his most authoritative voice, "You damn fool, why don't you stop your nonsense?"

Then he discovered he was bawling out his highly respectable tenant. After humbly apologizing, he called thoughtfully into the art room and spoke some well-selected cockney words that made quite an impression for many minutes.

It took Joynton a long time to get used to the pace of the artists. A non-drinking man himself — in spite of the fact that his fortunes were based on pub ownership — he was much bewildered by the amount of time spent in bars by the artists he paid so generously.

When the paper moved to its Phillip Street building in 1922, Joynton often called to warm his one remaining proprietorial eye on his asset. He always looked into the art room, but he rarely found anyone at a desk. After one such visit when he

CLOVER: *"Strawberry is putting on airs lately."*
CHERRY: *"Yes, ever since she heard that her son's hide has been made into cricket balls for the Tests."*

found no artist at his toil, Joynton went to the end of the corridor, and, throwing back his head, roared as loudly as he could down the lift well, "For a teetotaller, I seem to suffer more from hard liquor than anybody in Australia!"

When the artists finally arrived back from their libations and heard what the big boss had said, they were delighted. Joynton went up very high in their estimation. They had little admiration for his wealth or fear of his power of hire and fire, but they loved him for that flash of wit. Indeed, they responded with a burst of work of unusual merit.

There was another good burst just like this when, sometime later, after receiving an encouraging report on the paper's income, Joynton poked his head round the art room door and announced, "If you gentlemen continue with your good work, I'll have beer laid on to the art department." The cheering was loud and long. And there were even some hopeful hearts who believed Joynton might have been fair dinkum.

The early work of Cross, Hartt, and Sass was studied with interest and delight by every art student and would-be artist in

70

Australia. Art contributions poured in, but few had quality enough to merit publication. One however, lampooning ship-owners in a fight they were having with workers on the water-front, pleased Claude McKay and he published it in October 1919. The very day it appeared, the unknown artist who had drawn it arrived at the office looking woebegone.

He was a small, thin chap, an ex-Digger with a bright eye, who anounced that until a few moments previously he had been a shipping clerk on £4 per week. Alas, his employers had associ-

Eamon De Valera,
Head of the Irish Free State.

ated him with the cartoon and hurled him out into the snow. This was the sort of situation Claude was adept at handling. "Do you think you could draw a cartoon a week?"

"I've no doubt about it."

"Then you've got £1 a week rise."

Thus it was that Charlie Hallett, one of the brightest pens of them all, came to join *Smith's* happy band of artists.

Charlie proved to be of the blood when it came to fun in the art room, and when Stan Cross and the boys introduced a back-wards jumping competition, Charlie entered into the contest with

F

such spirit that he not only won, but broke his ankle on the shiny floor in the triumphant effort.

Many of *Smith's* most famous artists turned up in the first couple of years. One of the most important early arrivals was George Finey, whom Stan Cross still nominates "best of 'em all." That he really has claim to this honour is debatable, though there is little doubt that Finey has not been matched in his specialty as a caricaturist. He had the rare talent of being able subtly to distort features so that a person's characteristics and temperament were writ plain. The truth of some of Finey's work was terrifying and even painful. George, a man of fearless spirit, would not be swayed by hope of heaven or fear of hell from portraying people as he personally interpreted them.

From Hughes to Bruce, or making the best of a bad job.

He initiated a popular feature, "The Man of The Week," and caricatured whoever was the most important figure in each week's national news. The very first job he did in the series in 1922, made it clear that he would make concessions to no one. His subject was Archbishop Mannix of Melbourne, at that time a most controversial figure for his alleged anti-British attitude. George's critical insight led him to emphasize the Archbishop's severe, and as he saw them, intolerant and unhappy characteristics.

There was no doubt that the caricature was a magnificent piece of art work. But was it wise to invite trouble from a large section of the community by publishing the study? Claude McKay and Clyde Packer normally game to have a shot at anyone or anything, wrestled for a long time with their consciences. Both had an innate distaste for hurting sincere church people. Finally, the conclusion was reached that publication would be "fair journalism."

At least two other people appeared to have concluded differently almost immediately after the edition hit the streets. When

Claude arrived at the Imperial Arcade office, he saw two priests of abnormal size, one with a thatch of ominous red hair, waiting grimly on the doormat. Clyde Packer, grinning, insisted it was the Editor's function to discuss editorial matters with interested readers, and Claude was the Editor.

Claude faced the issue bravely. The worst that could happen was that he could be cast forty feet from his balcony room to the concrete floor of the arcade. He permitted the visitors to advance upon him, and, as innocently as he could, inquired their business.

Was he the Editor? Yes!

The red-headed priest said they had called about the caricature of Archbishop Mannix.

Yes?

Archbishop Mannix.

"Well, I want to know if you'll sell me the original. I collect caricatures of His Reverence, and the one you have today is the best that's been done of him."

George Finey was a model of what the uninitiated would expect a Bohemian artist to be. He dressed *avant-garde*, usually scorning such fancy Dan items as a tie, tended to wear sandals, let his fine crop of hair fly wherever the breeze cared to blow it, and seemed to live for the day. His generosity was notorious. You didn't have to know George personally to borrow a quid off him. A short, sharp recitation of hardship, and, particularly on pay-day, George's purse was at the pleader's service. It was a divine weakness and one trusts the gods take it into account, for on earth George has not received the laurels to which his artistic brilliance entitles him. (Not that George particularly cares).

George, in his heyday on *Smith's*, pretended to have a monumental dignity and this enabled him to enjoy a world of fun. His battles with Frank Marien, the Editor-in-Chief, between 1928-36, were epic, for Marien knew how to play the nonsense game just as well as his art staff.

After one noisy argument, George Finey claimed that Marien had injured his dignity beyond all bearing. The following day, *Smith's* folk reporting for work, found George seated at an easel in the gutter outside *Smith's*, busily doing his normal work. They asked what he was up to and he declared he was not going back inside the building until he received a proper apology from Marien.

"My dinner."

Friends brought George refreshment from the pub next door. Marien joined in the spirit of the game and sent sharp memos down to Finey in the gutter setting out work required. The artist would solemnly do the work as ordered and send it back inside.

For two days, this situation continued, then Marien, with a nice appreciation for when a joke was going stale, sent down one of his pink "Memo from Editor-in-Chief" forms carrying a formal apology. With honour intact, and to massed cheering, George packed up his gear and returned to normal quarters in the art room.

This sort of zany frolicking had the effect of preventing *Smith's* artists from getting into a mental rut. As a result, their ideas were always full of sparkle, and their art work was obviously produced with zest.

Soon after *Smith's* moved from the Imperial Arcade into its own home in Phillip Street, almost opposite — so help us — the New South Wales Police Headquarters, a man who was to become one of the great figures in newspaper art joined the paper. This was Joe Jonsson, "The Bletty Beloved Swede."

Joe was later to create the popular Sunday strip, "Uncle Joe's Horse Radish." Born on a cold Swedish farm in 1890, he got to know the backside of horses unusually well from long hours plodding behind the plough. He had a photographic memory. One good look at a Court room, a cow, or Parliament House, and he could draw the item in perfect detail from memory. Unlike most other artists, he never had to use reference — it was all in his great big Swedish head.

At the age of eighteen, he left his Swedish home, expecting to find an easier life before the mast. He didn't. To save himself from starving to death at sea, he developed the side-line of painting sea-scapes inside the lids of sailors' sea-chests for a couple of bob a pop. This success bred in him a desire to be an artist, but it was a long time before he achieved his ambition.

Going ashore from a ship in New Zealand, he worked in cold stores for a while, and then in 1917, shot through to Queensland where he engaged in timber-cutting. But he lost interest in that work when a drunken camp cook spent a whole night stalking him with an axe, because he fancied Joe had slighted his culinary skill.

Joe escaped to Sydney, where his experience in dancing around the rigging of sailing ships earned him a job as a high rigger on the White Bay wheat silos. Nothing exciting happened to him there, except, perhaps, for the time he dangled some four hundred feet above the earth, held solely by a thumb which had been jammed between a wire cable and the top of a silo. Joe's thumb was always dicky after that.

While toiling high above Sydney, Joe decided to become an art student, and saved carefully against the day he could go to a school full-time. From somewhere, he got the crazy idea that artists were high-class gentlemen who wore posh suits, highly polished boots, and gloves. He spent a lot of money gathering a stylish wardrobe, which he kept unused in a cupboard in his boarding house.

ENGINEER: *"Why wouldn't the cook be rescued?"*
CAPTAIN: *"He thought I was trying to boss him about when I ordered him to take his seat in the boat."*

At last, the happy day came when he signed off high rigging and was ready for the world of art. With light step, he returned to his boarding house where he found a tearful landlady waiting to tell him that a boarder had cleared out after stealing all the valuables he could find. Joe rushed anxiously to his cupboard. Alas, his unworn posh suits, his highly polished shoes, and his lovely gloves had all gone. From that day until his death in 1963, aged seventy-three, Joe dressed with the greatest disdain for elegance.

As a student, the ex-sailor proved brilliant and, in 1924, was judged worthy of joining the other masters of the black-and-white craft already on *Smith's Weekly*. He was a natural for the team, not only in skill but in uninhibited nonsense. He scored an initial smash hit by introducing a game called "The Endless Swedish Circle." You started by eating raw Swedish herring which tasted so bad that you had to drink some neat Swedish brandy which tasted so bad you had to eat some more herring which tasted so bad, etc. The result was a perfect endless circle from whose trap you could only be rescued by unconsciousness.

By nature, Joe was a gentle soul and desperately kind to lame dogs. But he was prone to perform sudden acts of incredible recklessness. With George Finey, not exactly an unreckless soul in his own right, Joe went aboard a Sydney ferry one evening to cross Sydney Harbour. Both artists had been refreshing themselves merrily at a quayside pub. They took seats outside, but gave these up to some young ladies and seated themselves on the rail.

Joe, quite a gymnast as a result of his sailor days, sought to entertain the ladies by pretending to fall backwards overboard. The screams he aroused inspired him to further backwards bending until, when the ferry was well out in the harbour, he went beyond the point-of-no-return and entered the water. The night was fine, the water calm, and the ladies screaming. George didn't see why he shouldn't be in the fun with Joe and dived in to join him. Whereupon the two artists decided that, as they were half-way to their destination, they didn't really need the ferry anyhow, and set out to swim the rest of the way.

The harbour area in front of the quay became a desperate tangle of ferries and launches, and a myriad of sirens screamed, "Emergency," "Police," and "Man overboard," into the night.

Joe's ferry pulled up beside him and a boat-hook was held out to him. This act enraged the Swedish artist who shouted that he was a qualified seaman to whom rescue by boat-hook would be a complete indignity. Only a lifebuoy would satisfy him. A lifebuoy attached to a line was thrown. Joe then gave a demonstration to hundreds of goggling ferry passengers of the formal method recommended to Swedish seamen for making full use of a standard lifebuoy. He was finally taken aboard and the ferry completed its trip across the harbour.

Meantime, George Finey was picked up by a police launch and taken to a quayside police station where, hours later, he was released in dry clothes. George was startled, on finally reaching his north shore home, to find all lights on and a gay party in progress. Key figure to the fun was Joe Jonsson, dressed in a lady's nightgown, demonstrating the art of saving oneself at sea. In soaking wet clothes, he had gone to Finey's home and then, telephoning friends and associates, organized a welcome-home party for his pal.

Parties were likely to break out at any time among *Smith's* artists in the 1920s. What no one could be sure of was when they would finish, and what damage would be done before they did. One such party, which started in the city and carried on to Joe

Jonsson's home at Wahroonga on a Friday night, continued until Saturday midday, when the liquor supply ran out.

A gentleman present, with a brand-new car sporting a fine cloth hood, volunteered to drive to a near-by hotel for further stocks. Eight party members insisted on getting into the new car with him. It was a funny old ride, made all the funnier because Joe Jonsson, in the centre of the back seat was being sat on by a giant journalist named Paul Goldenstedt. The driver could hear Joe roaring for air and demanding that the car be stopped lest he suffocate. Pitilessly, the driver stopped his ears to Joe's pleas, and noting that the cries died away, concluded that Joe had either passed out or found some means of getting oxygen. When he pulled up at the pub, he found Joe standing on the back seat with his head through a great round hole in the new cloth hood which he had cut with the razor-sharp sailor's clasp knife he always carried.

Joe was a great admirer of the great Australian adjective, but could never get closer to it than "Bletty," though he tried hard enough over the years. When Sir John Longstaff named Joe Jonsson as "the finest black-and-white artist Australia has produced," Joe commented; "Fancy that. And me a bletty Swede too!"

Joe had a humped back, and this, combined with the strength acquired during long, hard years behind the plough, before the mast, and up on top of silos, made him an enormously powerful man. One afternoon, six sailors in a pub down near the old *Bulletin* office in George Street, Sydney, began picking on a group of artists which included Joe. A long-time expert in rough and tumble, Joe threw two of the sailors over the bar, and with hip throws, tossed the other four to the floor, causing his victims to revise their opinion that artists were all sissy fellows.

In the early days on *Smith's,* the artists tended to specialize in certain types of gags. Stan Cross naturally got most of the Abo and bush jokes. Cec Hartt did the Digger stuff, George Finey handled the caricatures, Joe Jonsson did all the horse gags and shipwrecked sailor sequences, Syd Miller was the expert on all animals, bar horses, and Virgil Reilly drew the pretty girls.

Joe's drawings of splay-footed racehorses were beloved of all interested in the turf. When *Smith's* died in 1950, Joe went over to the The Sydney Production Unit of *The Courier Mail* (Brisbane) and created the most successful horse comic strip in Australian newspaper history — "Uncle Joe's Horse Radish" —

FAIR MAID: *"Prithee, Sir Black Knight, why are you stopping in such a desolate part?"*
SIR KNIGHT: *"I cannot return thee to thy father this night; we have run out of chaff for the horse."*

which was carried on by Ian Gall, *The Courier Mail's* political cartoonist, when Joe died in 1963.

Syd Miller's elephants and monkeys were as famous as Joe Jonsson's horses. Joining *Smith's* in 1922, Syd quickly became a favourite with the paper's readers. Endowed with an almost terrifying nervous energy, he could work over ninety hours a week.

Editor-in-Chief, Frank Marien suspected Syd was doing something like this early in the Depression — taking in outside work to make up for a salary cut he had taken along with the rest of the artists. But Marien, to his considerable frustration, could not prove what he very correctly suspected. He continually hurled the charge at Syd who would calmly invite him to prove his shocking allegation.

One afternoon in the Assembly Hotel, next to the office,

Marien and Miller became very pally over a few beers and Syd growing expansive, confessed that he had been doing outside work.

"Ha," Marien shouted, slapping down his glass, "you fool. You should not have told me that. Now I'll have to do something about it."

Syd bellowed suggestions about what Marien could do with the job, the lift, the building, the paper. . . .

Marien stomped out of the bar. Syd Miller had a couple of whiskies sourly on his own, and then immediately caught a train to his north shore suburb, determined that the moment he arrived home he would write a letter of resignation that would straighten the Editor-in-Chief's curly hair.

Awaiting him at home was a formal letter from "F. Marien, Editor-in-Chief" advising him of "instant dismissal." Marien had gone straight from the pub to the office next door, dictated and signed the dismissal notice, and ordered a copy boy to take it by taxi to the distant north shore, to beat Miller to the punch in documenting the severance.

Technically the Editor-in-Chief won that round. He then begged Syd to ignore the dismissal, and the artist came back. But he insisted on a proviso — that he be permitted to sign all his work for *Smith's* with the name "Noel," the *nom de plume* he had been using on his foreign orders. It was a small, but important point of honour. To Syd's further honour, he rated second only to George Finey as a caricaturist on *Smith's*.

The atmosphere of *Smith's* art room could certainly get crazy. But it was always bubbling with fun.

Once when a young and highly promising artist joined the staff, the boy's dad — so Miller insists — called on *Smith's* top brass (in this case Clyde Packer) and asked that he instruct the older artists not to swear in front of his son. Packer passed on the request without comment. If there were any off-colour words the new recruit had not heard to that time of his life, they were introduced to him loudly, clearly, and often.

It is said that the *Smith's* Old Guard art team only took two things seriously — maintaining their standards of wit and work, and the sudden tragic death of Cec Hartt in May 1930.

The folk on the paper, particularly the artists, refused to believe the much loved personality had gone. Adam McCay wrote a curious and touching obituary in which he reported Cec Hartt not dead but just missing. And he ended the story with the lines,

"Perhaps he has just slipped across the road to see his old mate Henry Lawson about something!"

Smith's artists got hold of a funeral urn which, they insisted, contained Cec's ashes. This urn was placed on a special ledge in the art room. And whenever the artists retired *en masse* for a drink, they would ceremoniously "take Cec for a grog." The urn would be placed on the bar of the Assembly Hotel next door, and each man ordering a round would include Cec in. Thus, a row of untouched drinks would line up before the urn until it was Cec's turn to shout. Then each man present would pick up one of the filled glasses and toast Cec; this of course was the drinking routine set by Stan Cross's lay-figure, "Dummy."

BRIDE: *"What is the usual thing to give poor out-of-work men like yourself?"*
WEARY ALFRED: *"Sixpence a week, lady; or a year's subscription for a quid, paid in advance."*

The same happy act of respect and remembrance was repeated day in, day out. One afternoon when the artists had returned from the pub, someone asked sharply, "Where's Cec?" The urn had not been placed back on the little shelf. Clearly it had been left down on the bar. The artists rushed back to the pub. The ashes had gone and were never found again.

This touching story, believed passionately by many people, probably isn't true. Stan Cross insists it isn't. He says, "There was an urn in the office believed to contain Cec's ashes. The literary editor, Reg Moses kept it in his room and it was certainly not taken regularly to the pub for refreshment.

"On one occasion Mo went on holidays and Adam McCay, the leader writer, took over his job and his room. On the anniversary of the late Cec's birthday, two devout female relations of Cec's, a woman and her young daughter, called at the office and asked whether they could say a little prayer before the urn.

BUSH LAWYER: *"Hello, what yer in for?"*
DIGGER *(in clink):* *"Countin' out an officer."*
BUSH LAWYER: *"But they can't shove yer in for that!"*
DIGGER *(well in):* *"Well, where th' blazes am I—out with a flamin' sheila?"*

"Adam McCay hunted in cupboard after cupboard, finding no urn until he came to the last cupboard in the room and that was locked. Assuming the treasured urn was in this locked place for safe keeping, the visitors knelt before the cupboard door, said their prayers, and departed.

"On his return from holidays, Reg Moses was told this touching little tale. Solemnly he opened the cupboard. It contained nothing but a pile of dirty shirts and socks."

(Stan believes the urn went from *Smith's* to the office of *The Australian Women's Weekly* when some of the staff joined that magazine in about 1935.)

Prominent among *Smith's* Old Guard artists was Frank Dunne, who joined in 1928. Although he had lost part of a hand at Pozières, he was still an outstanding draftsman. He was also a first-class painter, even though he was colour-blind. To overcome this difficulty, he would take one of his sons with him on painting expeditions. The lad would indicate what was red and what was green in the landscape and the artist would expertly carry on from there.

Frank took over the Digger joke drawings when Cec Hartt died, and lifted them to a new degree of popularity. He had a rare touch for infusing authenticity into his work, and when he drew a Digger, the study was accurate down to the buttons and the bootlaces.

Editor-in-Chief Marien once roared at Dunne, "You aren't putting enough background into your drawings. Take more care in future."

Frank squared his jaw and took up the challenge. Setting out to draw up a joke involving two tramps sitting on a country hillside, he gathered an abnormal mass of reference. For an entire week, he worked on the one job and meticulously drew in hundreds of thousands of leaves and blades of grass. The result was like a photograph under a microscope.

The artists held their breath for the explosion when the finished job went in to Marien. Under the drawing, Frank Dunne had written, "Is this background thorough enough for your taste?"

Marien almost choked with laughter and kept spluttering with delight: "There must be two million leaves there, a world's record for a drawing!" He directed that the joke, which wasn't really very funny in itself, should be given a big slab of broadsheet space. And he wrote new lines underneath:

1st Tramp: Why did Frank Dunne stick us in this sketch?
2nd Tramp: Because the boss 'as been growling that 'e wants prettier pictures!

Frank Dunne died in 1937 aged only thirty-nine.

Stan Cross was not the only comic artist Western Australia gave to *Smith's*. This State also provided George Donaldson, and in the mid-1920s some critics believed that Don might well develop into "the best of 'em all." Like Emile Mercier later, Donaldson had the capacity not only to think funny, but to draw lines and situations that were desperately rib-tickling in their own right. An English publishing house of high standing produced in the early 1930s a large volume of Empire comic art in which leading Australian newspaper artists were given one page each, except George Donaldson. He got eight pages.

Don made a fine hit with his fellow artists at the first art conference he attended.

Editor-in-Chief Marien: Have you any grievances, Donaldson?

"Listen, if I die you can tell the bloke who belted me I forgive him. But if I live, by heavens, I'll kill the ————!"

Donaldson: Break it up. I've only been here three days and haven't had a chance to find out!

A dramatic story followed Don over from the west. He had been a member of the lifesaving club at Cottesloe and had been reclining dreamily on the beach, when the scream of "shark!" aroused him. Out beyond the first line of breakers, a man was in trouble. Don grabbed a canoe and paddled out to the surfer whom he grasped. A tug-of-war began between Don and the shark. The canoe tipped over. The fight continued with Don edging towards the shore. Other lifesavers joined in. The shark-attack victim was brought ashore, but died later. George Don received a medal.

At the very peak of his promise, he went to Tahiti for an extended holiday, set himself up in a grass hut, and prepared to enjoy himself experimenting with drawing. One evening, after he had lit his kerosene lamp, he realized he couldn't see the light. He had gone blind! He got his sight back in a few days —

sunstroke the doctors said — but he never did recover his health and his great artistic skill never came to full fruition.

Don could also have been a writer of considerable importance had fate been kinder to him. His capacity to devise and write satire was outstanding. Examples of his writing are demonstrated in Chapter 10 — "*Smith's* Satirists."

In the late 1920s and early 1930s, "The Virgil Girl" haunted the daydreams of all young and most middle-aged men in Australia. She, in myriad forms, was the creation of Virgil Reilly, a small, sophisticated artist who gave Australia the equivalent of a Gibson or a Petty girl — a sex symbol just perfect for the time of presentation. Today the Virgil girl would rate as a proper bag with flat chest and, when you got sight of 'em, elastic locked bloomers. In her day, she was a goddess and made Virgil one of the most important and highly paid newspaper artists in Australia.

Virgil, like all *Smith's* artists, could not resist feuding with the Editor-in-Chief, Marien, and played his fair share in the game of getting the master's goat. On one Friday afternoon, Virgil complained he would never be able to finish the mountain of work he was expected to complete that day. Marien swore that he could and he would. There was long and sparkling argument on the matter between the bantamweight artist and the heavyweight boss.

The issue appeared to have been resolved when Marien bustled Virgil into the deserted art room, locked the door, and put the key in his pocket. He shouted through the door that he was off to have his dinner, and that when he got back he expected the artist to have something to show for himself. The dinner was a particularly good one in fact, and when he did get back, feeling well content with the world, he went off to his home in the distant suburb of Miranda, quite forgetting the imprisoned artist.

Around midnight the phone aroused him. The police had news for him.

It appeared that, for a start, Virgil hadn't taken the lock-in very seriously. He had found a bottle of whisky hidden in the art room — no great miracle actually — and had naturally refreshed himself while waiting for his gaoler to come back and let him out.

When it became clear that Marien wasn't coming back, Virgil sat down to devise a means of making his escape in a manner that would teach the Editor-in-Chief not to forget things in future.

The roof was fitted with fire sprinklers designed to go off automatically when hit by flame, and at the same time ring warning bells at Fire Headquarters. Virgil made a pyramid of tables, rolled some papers together into a torch, and began climbing.

The editorial floor and the artists' section in particular remained damp for many a long day.

Lots of people swear this tale is true, and I would not dare the wrath of lovers of *Smith's* artists' legends by probing it too hard at this late date.

In the period of *Smith's* greatest success as a purveyor of comic art — between 1919 and, say, 1939 — it recruited its artists after they had matured. The only male artist to start as a cadet and finish up with the top liners of the Old Guard was Jimmy Russell. Jimmy, of course, is the creator of the nationally syndicated comic strip, "The Potts," a regular star on radio and T.V. panels, and a leading figure in Australian tennis administration.

In his early teens, Jimmy was a message boy employed at Sydney Stadium. From that lowly starting-point, he worked his way to national fame and wealth with a ready wit, a clever pen, and a bubbling personality.

When Stan Cross left *Smith's* in 1940, and went to *The Herald*, (Melbourne), Jimmy succeeded him as Art Editor. Some years after World War II, he followed Stan to the Melbourne paper.

During this war, the word was out that Jimmy would collect something extra hard behind the ear if the Allies lost, because of his two weekly satiric features, "Adolph, Musso, and Herman" and "Schmitt der Sphy."

Lance Driffield got himself known all over Australia in the early 1930s on the strength of one drawing — an advertising poster, showing simply a fuming, bewhiskered cowcocky, carrying a double-barrelled shotgun and shouting, "Hey, who pinched my *Smith's Weekly?*"

That poster in colour went up on almost every railway station in the Commonwealth and had the merit of making the viewer chuckle every time he looked at it.

It is typical of *Smith's* Old Guard art staff that the chap with the biggest shoulders should have the most delicate style. Petrov, then a bulky young man, was a wizard at devising harem scenes out of dots and bubbles and twirls. Design was his delight and his backgrounds — almost invariably interiors — were decorated to the gills with patterns composed of circles and curiously twisting columns. It was all splendid contrast to the more down-to-earth techniques of the Stan Crosses, the George Fineys, and the Joe Jonssons.

Three female artists were included in the Old Guard — Mollie Horseman, Joan Morrison, and Rosaleen Norton. All became notable in newspaper art.

Mollie and Joan arrived in the early 1930s and made a pretty contrast — Mollie, tall, willowy blonde, and gay; Joan, dark, tiny, dainty, and quiet. Frank Marien set them up in a room of their own and put a notice on the door, "KEEP OUT."

This warning proved hardly necessary. The tough *Smith's* journalists and artists treated them as fragile creatures who had to be protected from everybody, repeat everybody. Had the girls not protested bitterly, they probably would never have married.

The actual situation was that they had both been through the fires of the East Sydney Technical College Art School *cum laude* and knew how to stand off wild cats.

Mollie Horseman had finished her effective schooling at the age of twelve and a half in Melbourne when her mother took her to the Continent and enrolled her at a school for young ladies in Germany. Mollie lacked German and her teachers lacked English. She whiled away the hours trying to draw the castles on the Rhine. When she returned to Australia, she could dance the Charleston and speak German in a rough way.

Bravely, she advertised to discover if anyone in or around Sydney was interested in a "German-speaking governess." Norman Lindsay, the artist wanted a governess for his children and didn't care if she spoke Turkish. Mollie entered his employ, and instead of teaching the little ones — though she did spend some time at that — began taking art lessons from Norman. The kids were sent off to school.

One fine day, Norman was most upset when his female professional model failed to appear. Quick as a flash, Mollie, as thin as the average Lindsay lady was thick, volunteered and finished up immortalized in one of the artist's best-known works.

Mollie then decided she would become a real artist herself. She forced her way into the Tech. where she fairly burned up the art classes. As she progressed, she continually heard of a brilliant student who had gone through taking all honours just ahead of her. And when, needing money badly, she got a job at *Smith's* at the age of nineteen, she found herself in the same highly protected room as the "brilliant student" — Joan Morrison.

Mollie drew rollicking stuff. Joan drew dainty damosels, and when Virgil Reilly grew weary of producing endless examples of The Virgil Girl, the Morrison girl was born — a pretty little girl with a rounded figure and soft fluffy hair. When you looked at Joan and at her work, you felt sure she was her own model. And curiously enough, readers of *Smith's,* particularly those segregated in lonesome lighthouses and on whaling ships in polar seas, came to the same conclusion.

Joan received a large fan mail, including lots of offers of marriage from men enamoured of what she drew, and some even came stamping into *Smith's* office when their ships touched port, demanding the right to take her to dinner. Her girl studies were standard pin-ups on ships — naval and merchant — during World War II, and many a sailor insisted he knew the artist intimately.

She eventually married a sea-going captain, Paddy Wilkinson, who had the curious experience of being told by one of his crew that not only did he know "Joan Morrison," but often took her out when in port.

Mollie Horseman and Joan Morrison were reigning supreme in their own fortified room at *Smith's,* when, in 1934, the door opened and a girl of sixteen was popped in to join them. The "child" was Rosaleen Norton, later to become famous as a self-proclaimed "witch" in King's Cross, Sydney, and to bewilder a couple of generations of art critics with her paintings, created when in a trance-like state.

Even then Rosaleen knew how to create an impression. She told Joan and Mollie that her idea of a wonderful week-end was to get a huge box of chocolates and a carton of cigarettes and consume these while lying back in a constantly replenished hot bath. Even in her German days, Mollie had never heard anything like that.

Rosaleen was different. She sure was. Even Frank Marien, who had seen just about everything short of all, swore he had never seen her like. He had employed her as a writer, but she insisted on being an artist so he let her have a go at that.

The girl made her first contact with *Smith's* when, at the age of fifteen, she sent in a short story which caused the paper to comment: "Never have we discovered a juvenile author so gifted as is obviously Rosaleen Norton."

The story concerned a young man who was exploring a strange street by night when he came across a waxworks, admission 6d.

"Dorkins, plant those seedlings immediately—Sir Richard wishes to trample on them."

He liked waxworks and decided to patronize the place. A witch-like woman took his 6d. "in a grey talon," and led him up rickety, worm-eaten steps. . . . The young man ultimately found himself in a vast room lit by candles as black as pitch. Leering, mis-shapen forms were all around him, throwing criss-cross shadows on the floor. "It was like a picture painted by a decadent genius." Were they only waiting for a signal from their master, the devil, to descend from their wooden pedestals and sport in a hellish saturnalia?

Terrified of the atmosphere, the young man sought to flee, but found that he had been locked in.

"Somewhere, a clock struck midnight. A low, clear note of music sounded in the room and that music came from the pipes of a waxen satyr. Carl's brain reeled in an ecstasy of horror. The pieces of the waxworks were descending from their pedestals. . . ."
"The light snuffed out. . . ."

Next morning, two policemen on patrol heard a shriek. Enter-ing an empty, deserted old place that had once held a waxworks, they found "the pitiful remains of what had once been a young man. . . . his eyes had the look of one who had seen things mortals should not see. . . ."

The fifteen-year-old authoress was invited to submit another short story. She responded immediately with "The Painted Horror," a tale even more terrifying than the first.

It concerned a young artist who, painting in his garret, found his hand being mysteriously guided into painting "a gigantic, sickening mass of purplish, bloated flesh, looking as if it had risen from a sea of corruption, topped by a squat, leering, half-human head, and great, thick, blood-bedabbled fingers like writhing worms. . . . The vast hulk crouched on the canvas ready to spring."

The compulsive force fed upon the young artist's brain and soul. One morning, he was found on his studio floor "torn to pieces and chewed." A policeman who found the killing impossible to solve commented, "Funny the way a big canvas in his studio had a great hole in it as if something had jumped right out of it or through it!"

Frank Marien still couldn't believe the stories came from a girl of fifteen. He ordered yet another story and got "Moon Madness," a brilliantly written study of a girl, under the influence of the full moon, murdering her sister as a sacrifice to the marble statue of a young man in an orchard. "There was one shriek from Corinne as Vivienne's teeth met in her jugular. A shriek, short and horrible like a trapped rabbit—but there was nobody to hear it. . . . Only the thin carven lips of the youth seemed to smile as the warm blood of the sacrifice flowed over his feet."

Marien decided that the child, Rosaleen Norton had tremendous talent as a writer and determined to guide her into more normal lines of creative thinking than she had been using in her short stories.

He offered the girl a job as a cadet journalist. She laughed the idea to scorn. Writing held no interest for her, she said; what she wanted to be was an artist. Any jobs going on the art staff? Marien explained that art work on *Smith's* meant funny drawings with a gag to make people laugh. Rosaleen said she would have no trouble doing that sort of thing and offered to produce a sample.

The Editor-in-Chief took her up on that and braced himself to see something unusual. He got a lot more than he anticipated. Rosaleen presented him with a drawing of a number of women sitting on the grass in a circle, biting their babies and laughing like crazy.

Rosaleen in the year or two she stayed with *Smith's* never did get the idea of a funny gag. A year after she started, she drew a study of two flappers standing outside a tiger's cage, watching the

SICK MAN: *"My son, I'll soon be leaving you."*
SON: *"How much?"*

tiger glaring at the keeper. One girl was saying to the other: "Wouldn't it be a thrill if one of the beasts devoured him!"

The restrictions of newspaper art were too much for Rosaleen who left *Smith's* so that she could draw and paint as she pleased. Before long, her painting exhibitions of panthers making love to ladies, and maggots crawling out of rotting skulls made her a much discussed young woman.

After World War II, in her role as a practising "witch," she became one of the best-known personalities in King's Cross.

Numerous artists, now well known, worked as freelances for *Smith's* in the paper's early days. It would be improper not to mention here two at least — Jack Baird and Unk White. It was the paper's loss they did not become staff artists.

When *Smith's Weekly* closed in October 1950, only one of the Old Guard of artists was still on the staff — dear old Joe Jonsson who had loved the paper too long and too well to be parted from it except by its death.

CHAPTER SEVEN

Smith's Artists—The New Guard

"A pure mind will laugh at all things — even a cat's bottom."
—*Emile Mercier*

Mainly because the previous chapter was getting a little lengthy, it is desirable to draw a very faint line through the year 1939 and speak of all artists who joined *Smith's* then or after as The New Guard, as distinct from The Old Guard.

As from the beginning, black-and-white men of great talent continued to make *Smith's* their Mecca, drawing inspiration from the atmosphere, and plump envelopes from the paymaster.

Under the leadership of Jim Russell, who took over the art editor's chair when Stan Cross left in 1940, the new stars carried on the traditions of the old, endeavouring to convulse Australia once every week with their wit and craftsmanship. Like their predecessors, they were highly individual characters who were quick to challenge authority for fun, and Claude McKay who had the ultimate handling of them, needed all his celebrated cunning to save himself from dying the death of a thousand planned frustrations.

The brilliant Emile Mercier, son of a baker in New Caledonia, could never control his natural Gallic naughtiness and delighted in introducing to his comic drawings touches that were likely to offend the gods a little.

When working for Sir Keith Murdoch of *The Herald* (Melbourne), he found he could horrify his employer by doing drawings of dirty dust-bins in back alleys. Em immediately specialized in extra dirty dust-bins with fish heads and other horrid things poking out of them. Most readers found the dust-bins very funny to look at. Sir Keith's teeth were set on edge every time he sighted one, which, Emile cheerfully arranged, was every second day or so.

On joining *Smith's*, Emile tried to find an Achilles heel in

Claude McKay. The boss appeared impervious to all the cunning arrows the artist fired. He didn't seem to see anything wrong in fish heads poking out of dirty dust-bins, dogs being busy round posts, and even — a Mercier specialty — posters in the background. (A typical Mercier poster stuck on a wall in the background of one of his drawings would read: "Larkin and Fartin will fix your faucets.")

It was finally only by chance that Emile got through Claude's guard. He was drawing a cat sniffing at a fish head poking out of a dirty dust-bin, and drew the cat's tail elevated perpendicularly in pleasurable anticipation. More as a doodle than a saucy sally Em added a neat little cross immediately under the base of the cat's tail. The finished job went in to Claude McKay for formal okay.

"For the tenth time, I tell you you're under arrest!"

Touché. Claude was mortally wounded, but was too old a campaigner with artists to scream too loudly. He sought to hide his pain so that the son of the baker from New Caledonia would not know he was on target. However, *Smith's* artists had a brilliant intelligence system and signals came to the art room that "the enemy's" blood pressure was at popping point.

Emile immediately settled down to work on a drawing depicting an extra big cat, with an extra large perpendicular tail, beneath which was a super-sized cross. The whole art staff watched with delight and then listened excitedly for high explosions when a copy boy disappeared into Claude's sanctum with the drawing.

The cat's bottom was a perfect challenge to Claude's taste and editorial instincts. But would he permit an artist to make him cry "enough!"?

The copy boy came scuttling back red-faced from his mission, saying that Mr McKay wanted to see Emile Mercier immediately. Assuming an innocent look, Em ambled in to the presence. Claude, grim-faced, was waiting for him with a lecture on "dirty" gimmicks in newspaper joke blocks. "Go and get rid of that cross and bring the drawing back to me," was the final word.

An Anglo-Saxon artist would probably have considered the joke played out, and obliterated the alleged obscenity with a daub of Chinese white. But Emile was full of pure French blood and subtlety. *The bottom de la cat* offended the master. *Quelle horreur!* But the fact remained that a cat did have a bottom and one could not deny the truth, *non?*

How could both the truth and the master be satisfied?

Emile's solution delighted an admiring art room. Carefully, he drew in a miniature roller blind under the cat's perpendicular tail. The blind, complete with draw-string and decorative tassel, was discreetly drawn down across the offending cross.

Of course Emile knew and Claude was quick to see that the addition of the blind directed more attention than ever to the fact that a cat had . . . Anyhow, Claude was gracious enough to let that new version of the drawing run in his paper. And Emile, ever a gentleman in *victoire,* drew cats with their tails down in *Smith's* after that.

For a period of his career on the paper, Emile, to the surprise and profit of his associates, suddenly bloomed as a horserace tipster supreme. It was all rather queer because he didn't know anything much about horses.

After a period of impressive success, Mercier's unique talent suddenly left him. Only then did he reveal the curious secret of his success as a tipster. He had found by chance that if he lay on the floor of his flat at certain times, and placed his ear to the floor in a certain place, he could hear a man in the flat underneath speaking on the telephone.

The man in the flat underneath happened to be one of the biggest S.P. bookmakers in Sydney!

Scoring a point on Claude McKay in the art conferences he chaired each week, was the ambition of most of the artists who attended. But Claude had a style and dignity that could freeze a bullet in mid-flight, leaving the firer much discomforted.

During the art conferences that took place in his room, Claude was in a supremely powerful position, ensconced at his own desk in his huge sway-back chair. His habit was to press his feet against a drawer in his desk and push himself back in his big chair, puffing at (but never inhaling the smoke of) endless cigarettes, the butts of which he tossed behind him out the window into Phillip Street three stories below. He made a nice study in relaxed control, as he played God over the rough-outs of joke drawings the artists submitted to him in turn.

A point often discussed by the artists in the pub was how Claude would react if one of their number in conference rolled back in his chair, placed his feet against the desk, dropped ash continually on the carpet, and tossed lighted butts nonchalantly out of the window.

Norman Mitchell proved to be the man game enough to make a test. He was, *inter alia,* the star athlete of the *Smith's* art staff, and for years used to ride some fifty miles or so on a push bike each morning before going to work. (That's what he said anyhow, and he claimed he included the steep Bulli Pass south of Sydney in his alleged daily schedule.)

He chose his moment of test with rare cunning. *The News* in Adelaide had offered him the important position of political cartoonist and he had handed in his resignation from *Smith's.* At his last art conference with his old paper, he went into his act — feet against big polished desk, ash all over carpet, and nonchalance.

Claude saw and shot over a quick, icy glare which normally would have been enough. Norman lay back more than ever. Claude switched to deep freeze. Missed target.

The situation was developing nicely when Claude twigged, and ruined it with, "Gentlemen, I apologize. I should have asked before. Would any of you wishing to kick hell out of my desk and ruin my carpets please join Norman and myself?"

It was in this very room that Frank Marien fought many a battle with the Old Guard of artists when he was Editor-in-Chief, and where he suffered a dreadful defeat on one occasion. Marien had been giving his artists a tough time, or so they thought anyhow, and all minds turned to a plan for hitting back.

The publican in the pub next door — at that time mid-1930s — was particularly proud of a number of antique advertising mirrors he had decorating his bars. So when these mirrors began disappearing steadily, his rage was enormous. His angry mind suggested a single thief was at work, but a brilliant one who left no trace. At last, every single mirror in the pub had vanished. The mystery thief had taken the lot.

One afternoon, a *Smith's* artist pretending to be tipsy in the bar, called the publican over and said he knew who had stolen the antique mirrors. "Frank Marien pinched 'em," he mumbled. "He's been picking on me too much lately, the big bullying bugger. You'll find all the mirrors stacked behind the big couch in his room. He's a nut and will pinch anything. But if you want 'em back, you'll have to just barge into his room. If you send your name in, he'll wake up to what you're after and won't see you, see?"

The publican checked with a couple of other *Smith's* artists who, giving the impression of men who were relieved to be rid of a guilty secret, confirmed that the missing mirrors were behind the couch in Marien's room.

At a time when Marien was busy at his desk, the publican was guided to the editorial floor and the Editor-in-Chief's door was pointed out to him. "Remember, your only chance is to barge in and surprise him," he was told.

The publican, a big man, went through the door fast, to the amazement of Frank Marien who was normally well guarded from surprise intrusion.

"Give me my bloody mirrors," shouted the visitor.

Marien identified his vistor on sight and concluded he was fighting drunk on his own wares. He prepared to defend himself and stood clear of his desk.

"You've got them behind that couch," roared the intruder, pointing to the vast leather couch which could seat five men.

"Get out," snarled Marien. "Or I'll toss you out."

The publican jumped over to the couch and pulled it out from the wall. There were all the stolen mirrors — just where the artists had quietly planted them. A perfect *coup!*

The New Guard of artists never dared play such tricks on the publican next door, particularly during World War II and the post-war years, when his goodwill was as essential to them as the oxygen in the air.

In any case, "Smithy" of the Assembly Hotel was regarded as the art staff's patron saint during the dry years.

During World War II, *Smith's* artists staged an At Home every Friday night in the office. It became traditional that the front door should be on the latch and friends of the artists could drift in, bearing, if possible, a fiery offering. Mates on leave from the services were particularly welcome.

The sacred core of these gatherings consisted of two gallon jars of almost priceless beer. "Smithy" filled them every Friday in his deepest cellar, whence they were furtively smuggled out through a toilet, and so to the art room. Artist Les Dixon, who followed Jim Russell as art editor, was the arch-smuggler and never spilt a drop in a brilliant carrying career. From these evenings stemmed the art room "pickle jar bank," a never-failing source of loans to those in need of a pound or two in a hurry. Journalist Isla Brook, and Gwen Philpott, the Editor-in-Chief's secretary, provided suppers for the Friday night affairs by buying loads of pickled onions, rabbits, bread and butter. All persons partaking tossed an offering into a large pickle jar, the girls reimbursed themselves, and the change just sat there adding up.

Quite early in the war, the jar contained a credit of £10. One day, an artist needing a pound took it from the unguarded bank and dropped in an I.O.U. to be honoured on pay day. This act established the pickle jar as a self-operating loan agency which, during its life of ten years, loaned hundreds of pounds to those in need. No I.O.U. was ever dishonoured. Often enough, on a Friday morning the jar was filled with I.O.U.s and in the evening with money. And the bank was always left out in the open art room.

The pattern of Friday night parties was soon set. Discussion first and then singing and acts. Over the years, some of these acts became quite brilliant as a result of talent combined with enthusiastic practice.

Les Dixon invariably sang, in a fine basso, "Trade Winds" and "The Banjo Song," and Jim Russell specialized in The Les Darcy Song (with appropriate actions, of course):

In Maitland cemer-treee
Lies poor Les Darhar-seee.
His mother's pride and joy,
Orstralia's fighting boy. . . .

Bruce Cousin had a version of "Sonny Boy," worthy of top vaudeville. Dear old Joe Jonsson, on special occasions, could be induced to sing, in Swedish, a song which appeared to be about a yellow bird which got a pretty poor deal from another bird. Anyhow, Joe invariably ended the performance with a flow of sentimental tears and cries of "That's a bletty nuff."

Journalists also contributed items to the Friday night fun feast. The poet, Edgar Holt, would dash off a sonnet with both hands on large sheets of newsprint ripped from a reel — one in legible writing from his right hand and the other in mirror writing from his left. As an encore, he would produce a two-handed drawing of the Battle of Jutland — his right hand depicting the position of the British fleet and his left hand the enemy's line-up.

Poet, Bartlett Adamson demonstrated his ability to produce instant poetry, usually of a brilliantly bawdy "billowing beauty of bosoms and bums" (his own line) variety.

But perhaps the most regular entertainer among the artists was Jean Cullen, the fourth and last girl artist to work on *Smith's* during its lifetime. Jean was an attractive young creature, who set herself the curious wartime task of seeing how many American servicemen of officer rank she could get herself engaged to at the one time.

She saw the proposition as a game of skill. The rule she drew up for herself was most searching. To claim a new "kill," she had actually to receive an engagement ring from the victim. She presented her real self — Jean Cullen, *Smith's Weekly* artist — to her quarries, so that no one could say she was guilty of cheating.

The art of the game was to capture men, no two of whom were likely to be in Sydney at the same time. And whenever one of her fiancés was in Sydney, she always brought him along to *Smith's* Friday night party so that all her workmates knew all her future husbands — the whole seven of them.

Jean's bright brain was heavily taxed, making sure she wore the right ring and said the right thing to the right man at any one time. And *Smith's* artists were always geared up, waiting for a loud explosion. Her most admirable capture was a General of the American Air Force, whom she duly paraded on a Friday night, and whose silver stars she made into a brooch.

Jean never did disclose how she got rid of all her fiancés after the war ended in the Pacific. But it didn't break her heart any to wave them goodbye, for she had not been romantically involved with a single one of them. She had merely hypnotized them with her bright personality. Her true love was a young Digger who, on returning from the war, married her and became a regular at post-war Friday night art room dings.

Sadly, Jean died young, soon after *Smith's* closed down.

The most famous party *Smith's* artists ever turned on was on V. J. Day, 15 August 1945. The need to celebrate was obvious, but means of fulfilling this need were considerably less so.

The people of Sydney were so excited that many hotels simply locked their doors to prevent trouble. "Smithy" of the Assembly shut down too, even though he had supplies of beer in his cellar.

He did not dare allow anyone to carry supplies away from his premises. There would have been a minor riot.

It fell to Les Dixon to find a solution, which he suggested to "Smithy" by telephone. Result was that Les dropped a hose out a first floor side window into the backyard of the Assembly Hotel. Reg Smith took the end of the hose into his cellar, and to his everlasting glory, devised a means of pumping beer into it. For a long time, beer flowed continually into *Smith's* composing room, where the artists invited the paper's whole staff to bring a pot, a cup, a vase . . . anything!

One happy aspect of the affair was that there was no tap on the receiving end of the hose, so that *Smith's* people did not dare stop drinking. Only when the Assembly's cellar was dry, was the hose pipe reeled in; only then were the celebrations declared officially over.

A carefree, optimistic team were *Smith's* New Guard artists, and it took something of atomic shock effect to check their stride. A copy boy named Harold stumbled across the perfect formula to bring them to a shuddering halt.

Soon after the war, *Smith's* artists organized themselves into one big party to attend the annual Artists' Ball in Sydney. On the afternoon of the ball, the total art work for the week was cleaned up, checked, okayed, made up into one big parcel, and, as was the standard drill, handed to a copy boy to deliver immediately to Ben Jordan's, the blockmaker's, a short tramride downtown. The finished blocks had to be back first thing next morning. So Ben Jordan's needed to work on them through the night.

Their week's work happily done, the artists refreshed themselves in standard fashion, never a care between them. They had arranged to change into their fancy clothes at the office and proceed *en masse* from there to the ball. So there they were in hilarious rigs, having a last tot in the art room, before marching off to have the night of their lives when the phone rang.

Ben Jordan's, the blockmaker's! Where was all the art work?

Well, the copy should have arrived hours before. It had been given to a copy boy. . . .

Much back tracking was done until it was discovered that the wily older copy boys had handed the carry-the-art-work chore on to a brand new copy boy named Harold. And where was Harold? This proved impossible to answer. No one knew where he lived. And he, seemingly, had vanished somewhere between *Smith's* office and the blockmaker's.

There was only one solution to the situation. Les Dixon took off his Henry VIII bonnet, Joe Jonsson took the pirate patch off his left eye . . . all the strangely clad artists sat down at their desks and began doing the week's work all over again. It was two in the morning before they dropped the new material in at the blockmaker's, and went on to the Ball to be in the fun for the last few minutes at least.

On the following day, there were a number of people at *Smith's* who were eager to hold a postmortem with Harold, the new and missing office boy, if the lad should turn up.

Well, Harold did arrive at the office, a cheerful smile on his face and the big packet of art work under his arm. It was left to Les Dixon to ask the pertinent question of the moment, "Harold, where did you take those drawings?"

Harold replied brightly, "I took 'em home to show me Mum. She laughed all night!"

Harold was then told that his services were no longer required.

The only person to see a pin-prick of light in the gloom was the journalist, Isla Brook who had kept bringing coffee up to the artists while they repeated a week's work.

Isla commented, "At least it has proved the solidarity of the art staff and their loyalty to *Smith's,* in spite of their apparent irresponsibility towards anything serious."

In post-World War II years, the dominant figure in the *Smith's* art team was Les Dixon. Apart from the fact that he was the one man who could supply the beer on Friday nights during rationing and could sing better than the whole mob put together, he was a first-class artist. (Les has been drawing the famous daily comic strip, "Bluey and Curley" for some years now. He inherited the strip on the tragic death in a car accident of Norman Rice who had worked under him on *Smith's.* Norman had taken on the strip on the death of its creator, the much loved Melbourne artist, Alex Gurney).

As a husky young buck Les, who hailed from a most unlikely place called Dry River, got a job as a blacksmith's striker in Sydney. As he struck the anvil, he became fascinated at the likeness between the late Les Darcy and himself. The point of comparison was that Darcy had also been a blacksmith's striker.

He enrolled at the gymnasium of Jack Dunleavy, a quietly spoken trainer of pugs, who ran a gymnasium in Sydney, and asked to be made into a champion. He proved to be a devil at belting the stuffing out of the heavy punching bag. And he felt he moved fairly well around the ring in training.

"Kids! Kids! Kids! I'll be glad when they go back to school!"

Unfortunately his gentlemanly instincts were against his progress. For example, he was sparring in the ring at Dunleavy's one evening when a heavy right to his nose tapped the claret, as they say in the fight business. Les didn't like this very much, but battled on boldly and would have continued had he not heard a knocking on the front door of the gym. He told the man who was hitting him on the nose and spreading blood all over his face that he was going to answer the door and jumped out of the ring.

The front door of Jack Dunleavy's gym sported a little shutter, through which a man inside could peer and judge whether a visitor should or should not be admitted. Les slid back the shutter, placed his bloody mask to the aperture and saw a pale-faced young man standing without.

"What do you want?" asked Les, reasonably enough.

The young, pale-faced man seemed to have trouble finding words to express whatever emotions were gripping him. Finally, he said in a sort of strangled voice, "Is this where you learn how to fight?"

Les told him to wait a minute, closed the shutter, and hunted out Jack Dunleavy to tell him a new pupil was at the door. Jack, considering the depressed times, needed new pupils more than anything else in life and sped to fling wide the port and welcome the new recruit. But the visitor had vanished as though he had never existed.

Sadly, Jack Dunleavy closed the door on nothing and called to Les Dixon, "Come here, son." Les came and stood before the man who had made the great Jack Haines into a star middle-weight.

"Whenever you answer a knock on the door," Mr Dunleavy said, "always make sure you wipe your bloody face first!"

Les continued to train, seeing himself as a future champ. Faithfully, he studied the art of the pugilist, and continued to grow in strength and purpose until Jack Dunleavy said, "Come here, son. I've got you a four-round preliminary at Sydney Stadium next Saturday night." Between that moment and Satur-day night, Les came to the conclusion that his true avocation in life was not prize-fighting, and retired unbeaten from the ring. Later, he also abandoned the craft of striking for a blacksmith and began driving a petrol waggon. Unfortunately, he had a driving accident which put him in hospital for a long time. Instead of feeling sorry for himself, as he had every right to do, he began taking art lessons by correspondence, thus catching up with a long-held ambition.

Now, as the artist behind "Bluey and Curley," he rates as one of the top newspaper artists in Australia.

Eric Jolliffe, celebrated for his brilliant comic studies of Aborigines in the more or less raw and the Outback, joined *Smith's* in 1944 on his march to glory. He had already attracted attention by his interpretation of bush humour, and *Smith's* gave him every chance to gather in a wider audience. Jolliffe had humped his bluey through Queensland and New South Wales, and had worked as a rabbit trapper and shearing-shed hand, to learn first-hand what life in the Outback really meant.

Everywhere he went, he sketched the minutiae that many people ignored — bush shacks and sheds, funny old gates and the tree stumps they hinged on, bark roofs, waterholes, billa-bongs, and cows stuck in bogs. And when he drew a bush gag, he poured such authentic reference into it that he developed into the foremost interpreter of the modern Australian countryside.

The queer thing is that Eric is an Englishman, born and bred, although it's rather hard to tell it by even close observation any longer.

Normally, the primary requisite for a *Smith's* artist was to be an expert at comic drawings. A man had to be something special to get on the staff as a pure illustrator. James Phillips and Hal Quinlan were two of the few who scored. Phillips was a dedicated artist who punished himself in pursuit of perfection. It was not enough that he should purchase sticks of charcoal for sketching. He had to make his own — even searching out the dry twigs most suitable to put into a cocoa tin and consign to the fire. And for painting, he ground and mixed his own colours, experimenting endlessly to get just what he dreamed of. In later years, he was to take two Walkley awards for his illustrating — a rare performance.

When *Smith's* ceased publication in 1950 it was developing a new group of young artists including Bert Smith, Bruce Begg, and Lex Bell. All did well elsewhere, particuarly Lex who, after experience in England and Canada, returned to Australia to become a leader in the commercial art field in Victoria.

H

CHAPTER EIGHT

The Jokemaker's Art

"To create a joke, you first have a good laugh and then think backwards."
— Stan Cross
Dad : Where's the new hand, Dave?
Dave : Out Condobolin.
Dad : Struth, and I thought he had no time for the women!
—*Smith's Weekly*, 1932

If *Smith's* primary purpose as The Public Guardian was to warn the Australian people, with many a dramatic flourish, of the difference between current good and evil, its secondary purpose was to create belly laughs with jokes illustrated by artists.

The comic artists on the staff could have a go at almost any subject that tickled them and submit their ideas in rough-out pencil form to the Editor-in-Chief for approval. But it was public reaction that ultimately set the pace, forcing editors and artists to follow certain distinct lines.

Smith's learnt by trial and error that the Australian masses never tired of gags about : Jacky, the semi-civilized Abo, Dad and Dave, "Pommies," the public service, workmen tricking the foreman, Jews setting fire to the shop, Scotsmen, the darlin' Irish, stokers and seamen, flappers, grog and drunks, the domestic scene, old Digs, and animals of all sorts, but particularly monkeys, elephants, and dogs. It was selections from this list that made *Smith's* world famous for its comic art.

The Scot and the Englishman both got their share of gigging. The former was naturally tickled for his alleged extreme canniness.

A Scot in kilt is crawling along the ground, when a policeman comes across him.

Cop (kindly) : Wot's up, mate?

Old Scot: I've taken poison and I'm trying to get to the chemist's to get the 3d he charged on the bottle.

And neither *Smith's* nor its readers seemed to tire of chuckling at the English new chum working in the bush. The round-

104

NEW CHOOM: *"Oo! no! It doesn't seem right for a single man."*

cheeked lad was usually in a flat cap and leggin's, and presented making a primitive error related to his ignorance of Australian farm life.

> Excited Pom (rushing into homestead) : Come quick, sir, Strawberry's had a child!

Smith's managed to wring out an extra laugh at the expressions assumed by Dad, the new chum's employer, at the choom's innocent gaffes. Imagine the possibilities for arranging Dad's face at this situation:

> Dad : Well, did yer dig out them rabbits in the bottom paddock?
>
> Choom : Aye, sir, but I'm afraid I injured one of the little fellows with my pick!

These days, the rabbits have gone and so has the innocent new chum with the Pommy tag writ large on him. But for those who remember rabbit plagues, the laugh is still a good one.

Smith's always looked with kindly amusement at the solemn eagerness of the English migrant to succeed in the new land he had found. Thus:

Pom (digging ditch) : I wish you would not speak to me when I'm working, sir — you are hindering me getting on in the world.

The purest vein of Australian humour developed by *Smith's* was probably the Jacky type of gag, of which Stan Cross was the undisputed master. Stan not only devised the merriest Abo jokes (never a cruel one from Stan), but presented them with an artistry that is still quite breath-taking.

Traveller : Hey Jacky, where does this road go?

Jacky : How you expect me to know — I'm no plurry road scholar!

Grog and drunks were always popular, both with the paper's staff and with its readers.

A standard pair of soaks — 'erb and 'orace — were endlessly used to wring a giggle out of grog situations. The standard demanded of this dowdy couple wasn't very high.

'erb : Wot's yer favourite film?

'orace : Fill 'em up, of course!

If that's crook, this one's crooker:

'erb : I've never tasted beer in me life.

'orace : That's because yer drink it down too quick!

Having swallowed those two, you may as well have this one as a final chaser:

'erb (overboard) : 'elp. I can't swim. Drop me a line.

'orace : Allri! if you promish to write to me shometimes too.

Smith's, in its early days at least, had something of an obsession about Jew-burns-down-shop-for-insurance gags. Traditionally, the blame is laid on J. F. Archibald, the celebrated old *Bulletin* editor, who helped play midwife to *Smith's*.

The formula was simple:

Young Abie : Can we remove my bike before we burn the shop down, Papa?

Moses : Certainly not, son. We must be honest!

At another time, we have Young Abie and Papa Moses watching someone else's shop burn down, Young Abie is saying:

"Aren't you envious, Papa?"

It is some comfort to know that *Smith's* later made amends for this early anti-Jewish bias. Before World War II, it could not stomach Hitler or his treatment of the Jewish race and reacted by constantly damning the Nazis and insisting on a fair go for Jews in Australia. On searching for a stick with which to beat Hitler, *Smith's* found that Australia had much to thank her Jewish citizens for in services rendered and sacrifices made. To the end of its days, *Smith's* treated Jews with respect.

"Pardon me, but are you a Christian?"
"Lor, lumme, Charlie! Ain't it bad enough bein' a plurry blackfeller?"

But the paper was more at home and more admirable when poking fun at the domestic scene. Here there was never a veiled sneer, just honest laughter.

Angry wife : I insist you sack that red-headed typist.
Husband : But I don't know how I'm going to carry on without her!

(*Smith's,* by the way, never allowed blue jokes into its columns. The above gag was about as advanced and naughty as *Smith's* ever got in the comic field.)

Even flapper gags were kept under tight rein and didn't go much beyond:

Mary : The wedding was quite informal.
Mollie : My goodness! Supposing they have children!

And saucy female philosophy reached its peak in *Smith's* with a lamenting good-time girl complaining : "You can never trust a man. If you find one you can trust, he's not worth trusting!"

Being a man's paper, *Smith's* tended to see that jokes were loaded against the ladies, but not so heavily as to be offensive to females.

"Vot are you doin' that to Ikey for?"
"Shh! Dere's a ice cream man goin' by."

Boy : Pa, what makes a man give a woman an engagement ring?

Pa : The woman, son!

And here's a gag that raised a big laugh against the ladies when published in *Smith's* many years ago:

Cop : In what position was your husband when the bullet got him?

Wife (weeping) : He was second-in-charge of a fruit barrow!

Public service gags in *Smith's* were always variations on the same theme — a theme completely expressed in this one gag:

Chief Clerk of Govt. Dept. : There are six chaps out there wanting a job.

Under Secretary : We can't take them on.

Chief Clerk : But I'm alluding to members of the staff!

Worker versus foreman gags provided another *Smith's* joke theme that never varied year in, year out. Strangely enough the idea was that the worker was forever trying to injure the foremen physically. And here are three gags to demonstrate:

108

Gag 1. Worker (mourning death of mate who has fallen from high scaffolding) : Bill was a good fellow. He kicked at the foreman as he fell past him.

Gag 2. Foreman : Hey, you missed me by an inch with the pick.

Man : Cripes! The boys will never forgive me!

Gag 3. Chap in pub : I hear the foreman fell off the building today.

Mate : Shut up, you fool. It doesn't happen until tomorrow.

Smith's readers could never understand where the ideas for fifty fresh laughs a week came from. There's no harm in revealing the secret now. The weekly flood of gags came from two sources — the comic artists on the staff and the "gag box."

It is part of the skill of a good comic artist to be able not only to draw funny situations, but to think them up from a cold start. An outstanding joke deviser like Peter Harrigan of Sydney, Stewart McCrae of Brisbane, or "Weg" of Melbourne, can sit down cold and spin endless gags to order on any subject thrown up — match boxes, pin cushions, atomic bombs, haircuts, shoeing horses . . . anything.

Smith's artists used to get together each week in gag sessions, formally chaired by the art editor. Subjects would be tossed up and the artists would play with them until the laughs came.

Here's a verbatim report of a gag being forged from nowhere at a gag session.

Artist 1 : Damn birds! One sploshed my coat when I got off the bus this morning.

Artist 2 : Bird-watching is a big business these days. Ought to be some laughs there. Good situations. Fellows up trees.

Artist 3 : Cocky in the cage gags are a bit done over. I've had 'em.

Artist 2 : Ever see the poultry at the Royal Show? There's a lot of interest in chooks. And the champion chooks look pretty pompous.

Artist 1 : What say, for a situation you have a big pompous chook sitting on a top perch and she's just dropped an egg on a chook underneath and couldn't care less.

Artist 3 : The underneath bird could be a poor skinny thing whose always being put upon. The skinny bird could be saying something . . . complaining about the egg on its head.

109

DAD: *"Some blokes can knock a tune out of anything."*

Artist 2 : Nice study — the skinny chook, with broken egg all over its head, looking up angrily at the fat chook above. Could someone call him an egg head?

Artist 1 : No. The skinny chook has got to do the belly-aching. He could say : "Are you trying to turn me into an egg-head?"

Artist 2 : It's got to be sharper than that. Something like "You're a dirty big layabout."

Artist 3 : The skinny one could say, "Don't hit me even in yolk."

Artist 2 : No puns, mate. They're dead. That layabout idea is not bad.

Artist 3 : Well how about "Lay off me, you big mug" or something like that.

Artists 1 and 2 : That's it

The gag line ended up as : "Hey, lay off me, will yer!"

The second source of supply was the "gag box." *Smith's* was prepared to pay for all gags accepted for publication from contributors. Even in Depression times, it would pay 10/- for an average gag, £1 for a good one, and £2 for a winner.

Some contributors with a talent for gag spinning would send in twenty or thirty ideas a week each. They were glad to get a couple over. The most successful contributor of ideas bought himself a fine home from his earnings from *Smith's*.

When *Smith's* staff artists had exhausted their own ingenuity, they would ruffle through the "gag box" and pick out any suggestions they considered worth using or developing. Each artist would rough out in pencil half a dozen gags each week and take them into full art conference, where the Editor-in-Chief would make final decisions about which were good enough for *Smith's*.

It was always important for an artist to remember that *Smith's* was one hundred per cent Australian, and this had to be made abundantly clear to the reader in every issue. Consequently, to be on the safe side, *Smith's* artists mixed in handfuls of "struths," "Cripeses," and "you cows" with their gag lines.

Cecil : Is Bill very sick?

Harold : Cripes, he's so weak they have a trained barmaid in attendance!

And here's a "struth" routine :

Judge : Remove your hat when in Court!

Crook : Struth! Whose funeral's going past?

And anyone who didn't find this sort of thing humorous from 1919 to 1950 was just a silly cow.

CHAPTER NINE

Smith's Celebrated Sporting Scribes

"The pugilist Jamito of Manila is a man upon whom nature has
bestowed only enough forehead to keep his hairline out of his eyes."
— Jim Donald, *Smith's Weekly*, April 1920

Not long after World War I ended, a short, thick soldier and
ex-Victorian pug named Jim Donald marched in on the infant
newspaper, *Smith's Weekly*, and declared that he wished to write
for it.

Jim didn't look very promising material on his battered
surface. In his time he had been Featherweight Champion of
Sweet Fanny Adams. His nose was distributed across his face,
and his eyebrows and ears were gravely gnarled and knocked.
Had he hit his opponents as hard as they had hit him, he would
surely have killed them, every one. And he hadn't killed anyone.

His main claim to fame was that his forbears had been Fenians
in County Clare, and a distant cousin had shot an informer in
Tipperary. Oh yes, and he had been earmarked for the priest-
hood in early life, but had fought his way out of that predica-
ment. Sadly he admitted that his education had been very
limited, but stressed that he had been striving to improve himself with long sessions in the Sydney Public Library, reading
Greek mythology and the Bible.

Claude McKay sat up on hearing that last bit, his quite
amazing instinct for picking hidden talent warning him that a
gold mine was in front of him. The foundation Editor-in-Chief
never did the obvious in anything and he followed that policy
with Jim Donald. It would have been a most logical move to
have sent him off to the Stadium to have a crack at reporting on
matters he knew something about. Claude assigned him to
reviewing films, giving the would-be writer a bigger shock than
ever he had received in war, pugilism, or peace.

It was quickly clear that fate, which had denied Jim the re-
flexes and enough mastery of the sweet science to preserve his

"This must be your lucky day, Tiger! That's the third time the bell's saved you!"

features as they had been originally designed, had made amends by placing in his rugged hand a honeyed quill. Claude switched him from films to fights.

Jim couldn't spell for nuts, but as a writer he was a one round knock-out. In the early 1930s, as a copy boy with the ambition to be a great fight writer myself, I eagerly sought the chore of typing his sacred screeds from the tatty bits of copy paper on which he scrawled them with a blunt pencil stub.

Everyone wondered how I could read his writing, for not even Jim himself could decipher what he had put to paper once the work was done. Wise men decided that my purity of soul was the answer. Only a youth too young to have been in contact with sin, and guided by a band of friendly Presbyterian-type angels, could have held the key, they claimed. Joyously, I pecked out with one finger a typescript of Jim's classic weekly fight feature, "When The Gong Goes." And the author's kindly gruff cry of "You bloody good, bloody boy," each time I handed him the finished copy, was a crown of roses on my brow.

Jim's first fight piece appeared on 31 January 1920, and was a dissertation upon the much discussed question of the hour: "Would Carpentier of France have beaten Les Darcy of Australia?"

"Methinks not," Jim wrote. "I saw Carpentier box Gunner Feathers at Le Havre. He ruffled Feathers, who was slower than a gouty tortoise, with every wallop known and practised since cruel Cain hit affable Abel. Feathers in fact had a chance akin to a celluloid collar in Hell."

No one in Australia had ever written fight copy quite like that before, and certainly no one had brought Biblical allusion into the ring. The moment Jim knew that this new type of reporting was acceptable, he concentrated on developing it, until he became world famous. For years, Nat Fleischer of "The Ring" sought to lure him over to America, but Jim was happy to stay at home. Fight fans often felt that his report of a fight was more entertaining than the bout itself. These snippets from the long yellowed files of *Smith's* show why.

Reporting a bout between Digger Evans and Jackie Green in *Smith's*, (14 February 1920) Jim declared, "When the final bell called cease fire at the Stadium on Saturday, Referee Wallis bestowed the fiat that signifieth victory upon Digger Evans, after twenty rounds. Evans indeed beat Jackie Green, who fought the good fight but was six pounds too light."

Generally, Jim had a kindly heart, but it was noticeable that he could not resist slipping in tart touches when reporting the fistic affairs of "coloured gentlemen." This was his comment on Jamito of Manila, who fought Digger Evans of Australia in April 1920:

> The pugilist, Jamito of Manila is a man upon whom nature has bestowed only enough forehead to keep his hairline out of his eyes. . . .
> The Manilaman's trouble lies mainly in his thinking apparatus. He can't anticipate, nor does he spice his work with that versatility which brings joy to the heart of the critical onlooker.
> Should ever his hands and feet establish a working partnership with his brain, he will be no man's plaything in the ring.

And commenting on a Negro boxer named Edwards, Jim declared, "Alas, he just can't see openings for his uppercut, the reason being that there are too many empty cells in the beehive of his brain."

One of the most popular pieces was written on the bout in 1921, in which the celebrated Jimmy Clabby from America was finally defeated in Sydney: "Everything comes to him who waits. Jim Clabby waited fifteen years for the peddler with the dream pill. On Saturday night at Sydney Stadium, the latter gent kept the long overdue appointment. Enter Francis Burns. When the veteran Yank signed up with Burns, Kismet put the edge on the tomahawk, and the Clabby pitcher visited the well just once too often."

By the late 1920s, Jim had the power to break (with ridicule) and make (with purple praise) any pug, in or visiting Australia. He was ruthless with puffed-up reputations.

A Johnny Reisler turned up from America in 1927, with a scrapbook worthy of a Chinese executioner, looking for fights and was put in against Billy Grime. Here's Jim's view of the match:

Johnny Reisler, the most gifted pantomimist in pugilism, entered the ring on Saturday night, his panto to perform.

His pantomimic play of feature, registering as it did derision, disgust, mock resignation, and a certain sneering contempt for his opponent, was much admired.

But Mr Reisler's ardent emotionalism was outweighed by Mr Grime's six-ounce mitts. . . .

Each Christmas, Jim would write a piece summing up the Australian fight scene for the past year, and this was always gay even though the message conveyed might be gloomy: "In Australia, the year's (1929) boxing crop has failed. Our once fertile field of fistiana is choked by the weeds of wallop. . . . "

He described Ambrose Palmer and Fred Henneberry, who fought so brilliantly against each other, as "greyhounds of the glove with the armament of Airedales." And in colourfully reporting a bout between these gladiators in October 1931, Jim had Australia laughing with this opening, "At the bell, Palmer, all tenderness thrown to the winds, rushed at Henneberry and struck him a violent blow in the stomach."

So famous did the fight scribe become that he was given a godlike reputation as a champion in his own right, independent of the record books. His battered features naturally helped develop the popular image.

As he grew older, there were signs that he was beginning to believe that his frown spread terror, and the sight of his fists raised in fighting pose was something few mortals dared gaze long upon without retiring. This image was completely acceptable to all young men on *Smith's*, including myself, until one tragic afternoon a group of us standing on the footpath outside *Smith's* witnessed an event that gave us food for thought.

A taxi drew up and the great Jim Donald himself alighted, somewhat inspired by alcohol. The cab driver, no youngster himself, came briskly round to the kerb and put out his hand for the fare. We observers gathered from Jim's gestures that he wasn't going to be pushed around by anybody and wasn't going to bow to any cab driver's demand anyhow. In short, he would not pay his fare.

The cabbie, poor chap, clearly didn't know what he was fooling around with, for he began to insist on what he considered his rights in a loud, irritated voice. Ah well, he has asked for it. Jim assumed his most dreadful fighting face and raised the fearsome fists before which a thousand giants had quailed. We young observers trembled, realizing we were about to see a man destroyed.

The cabbie took one swing which clocked Jim on the jaw. Immediately the fierce expression faded from the great warrior's face and he fell to the ground where he lay limply. The driver gazed on the fallen figure in disgust, and then, jumping into his taxi, drove off never knowing what a magic image he had shattered in one swift blow. Fred Flowers, who had admired Jim probably more than any of us, was first to reach the stricken idol's side. Then we all closed in. But we did not catch each other's eyes as we helped the old fighter through the front door.

So important was Jim to *Smith's* as a fight writer that, sadly, he could rarely be spared for general reporting. However, every now and then, Claude McKay or Frank Marien would get one of their wicked ideas for novel treatment of a story and assign Jim to a job normally covered by anyone but a boxing reporter.

Smith's was not very popular at Government House, Sydney, at one period, and this was indicated by the fact that invitations were not sent to the paper for public receptions held there. The paper's staff could not have cared less, but there were apparently some people in authority who imagined that everyone from the Editor-in-Chief to the copy boy was filled with a sense of shame through being ignored.

One year, two invitation cards for a Government House public reception suddenly arrived with a subtle hint that they were by way of a challenge. If *Smith's* reported the reception in dignified fashion, then there might be more invitations in the future.

Here was a situation made to order for a bit of *Smith's*-type fun, and much thought was given to exploiting it to the limit.

Any ordinary newspaper would have sent along two lady social reporters. *Smith's* took the attitude that the reception was really a bun fight — guests were notorious for their pushing and shoving to get at the tucker — and the only person who could cover it properly would be a fight writer.

The job naturally fell to Jim Donald, with Virgil Reilly, the artist, to act as his second and make sketches. Writer and artist went to a suit-hire company and decked themselves out in top hats, cutaway coats, and striped pants, then off they went to "the fight."

Jim described, in boxing parlance, every move of the mob versus the grub — the footwork of the waiters, the determination of the heavyweight eaters, the ruthless brutality of food-crazed flyweights fouling middleweights by stamping on their toes.

It was grand fun. The invitations to *Smith's* stopped again.

Jim Donald did not have his greatest hour as a writer in reporting a fight, but in covering the opening of the first Parliament in Canberra in 1927. *Smith's* had taken umbrage that Parliament was to be opened by the Duke of York at what it considered was to be a private function for a "Social Four Hundred," hand-picked by goodness knows who. . . . What about the working class?

Smith's sent Jim — complete with suitcase containing top hat, tails, and striped pants — to cover the opening and this he did with a gusto that still rings through today. "My pilgrimage to Canberra," he wrote, "opened in the all-night lunch room at Sydney Central Railway Station, where an ingenious old gentleman stole my sandwich while I was ordering another cup of coffee. . . . "

He reported that "came the dawn" and the train arrived at Canberra, where a "barking human sheep dog" called the names of "thrice puissant deadheads, the pure merinos earmarked for the Hotel Canberra." The "crossbreeds" went to the Hotel Kurrajong, and "ordinary senators, ships' chandlers, lesser singers, and riff raff" were assigned to the Acton pub.

With cruel skill, Jim reported the antics of the Four Hundred on the eve of the opening: "Tomorrow is the great day. The

Jim Donald, fight writer (right) cheekily joins the dignitaries at the opening of the first Parliament in Canberra in 1927. Smith's provides appropriate comment.

Jim Donald, accompanied by his aide-de-camp, who is seen consulting Jim's private secretary. Immediately behind is Jim's political adviser, and in the background his naval and air force guard.

Four Hundred are eager and ready to bray. Tonight, as on the eve of Waterloo, the Twin Gods of Gaiety and Guzzle reign."

On the Big Day itself he wrote, "All roads lead to the Capital. The winding herd wind slowly o'er the various leas. Picked troops line the avenues. Policemen, urbane, inexorable, are everywhere. Soon the public stands are filled. Here are the true hosts of the day. It will be their privilege to pay the bills."

On the great day, Jim strutted around secretly among the great, while a special cameraman snapped him near the Duke and other V.I.P.s. Jim insisted that, in raiment, he was outshone only by a Chinese diplomat named "Pong" or "Tong" who cut (koff) "a truly celestial figure." Third in excellence he rated Stanley Melbourne Bruce, whose linen was "whiter than the soul of St Anthony."

Jim was critical of the dress of most of the politicians: "Over the clobber of some of these birds, let us draw a veil of pity and forgive them for they know not what to wear — or how." After reciting how they had all charged madly into Parliament House after the Duke and Duchess, Jim wrote, "When the Royal Couple later emerged, still pursued by the Four Hundred, Canberra had given birth to a nation." Probably not one of the official guests at the opening of the Parliament House at Canberra ever forgave *Smith's*. But the hoi polloi delighted in the report that Jim Donald gave them.

Towards the end of his career, Jim Donald left *Smith's* and joined *The Daily Mirror* in Sydney, in whose service he died in 1952.

The fight game in Australia is not likely to look upon such a battered face linked with such a golden writing hand again.

It was typical of the *Smith's* way of life that, whenever Jim Donald went on leave, his weekly boxing feature was written by the most cultured member of the staff, Kenneth Slessor, the poet. And a brilliant job Ken did, though he complained constantly at the amount of time he had to spend hiding on the fire-escape from men with flat faces who came looking for him.

In 1919 *Smith's* started its turf section, and it wanted to make sure the sport was handled by the best racing writer in Australia — whoever he might be. Claude McKay and Clyde Packer agreed that No. 1 choice was Cliff Graves of *The Sun* (Sydney), a most remarkable journalist who had left school in Adelaide at the age of twelve to join *The Advertiser* (Adelaide).

As a minor turf writer, he had left Adelaide for Sydney to seek fame and fortune. To give himself a touch of glamour in the big city, he had adopted the pen name of "Iroquois," the name of the first American horse to win an English Derby in 1881.

Graves was aged thirty, and in his prime, when *Smith's* discovered he was getting £8 a week on *The Sun* in 1919 and offered him the magnificent salary of £11.10.0 a week. The writer accepted, and *Smith's* triumphantly announced that "Iroquois" was on its staff.

The paper got its money's worth immediately. On taking up his new job in 1919, Cliff Graves promptly tipped the Caulfield Cup winner (Lucknow) and the Melbourne Cup winner (Artilleryman). This was a fabulous achievement, and *Smith's* was ready to believe Cliff could produce the double for 1920.

Graves, who had the pulse of *Smith's* and its readers, correctly tipped the 1920 Caulfield Cup winner (Eurythmic) and then pulled a novel stunt to present his Melbourne Cup tip. He got an artist to draw the back-end of a horse racing down the Flemington straight and wrote, "This is the view that opponents will get of Poitrel in the Melbourne Cup." Many an expert considered that Cliff Graves had missed badly because Poitrel was to carry ten stone, a quite impossible weight, and ten to one could easily be obtained about him.

Poitrel won, giving Cliff the double for two years in succession. In a racehorse-crazy era, the writer became a national hero. Sir Joynton Smith, prodded on by Claude McKay and Clyde Packer, presented Cliff with a new Morris Cowley motor car for his novel achievement.

Soon Graves's salary had soared to some £30 a week and he had became one of the most important journalists in Australia.

In spite of his lack of scholarship, he had tremendous ability as a writer and demonstrated this in a writing match in 1924 with the celebrated Adam McCay, M.A. (Hons), who was *Smith's* leader writer and Literary Editor.

During World War I, Graves had been attracted to a series of articles in *Punch* (London), purporting to be a report of day-to-day life in the trenches as seen by a modern Samuel Pepys. He suggested to *Smith's* that he should write a week-by-week diary of a modest betting gentleman in the Pepys fashion. Literary Editor Adam McCay said the diary idea would be better presented in the form of thoughts and experiences of a precocious office boy who went to the races and risked his miserable weekly wage on good things he heard about here and there.

McKay and Graves locked horns on the matter, and Clyde Packer, playing at peacemaker, offered a novel solution: both men were to go to the races on the following Monday, Adam McCay to write his Office Boy's Diary and Cliff Graves to write his Pepys-style Diary.

On the following Wednesday, Adam McCay, M.A. (Hons), took a quick look at "The Punter's Diary — Being the Experiences of a Modest Gentleman of The Turf," and declared himself outclassed.

On 1 January 1924 the first take of the Diary was published in *Smith's*. The series was to become the best-loved turf feature in Australian racing history. Here's a piece of the first instalment:

Christmas, a time of much merrymaking and the heat, doth encourage a great drinking of beer and spirituous liquors. Of a truth nought to do but treat friends and be treated, and must confess to taking overmuch. . . .

But do find some relief in the racing at Randwick on Monday, though great heat prevailing and do array myself in white, but a storm brewing doth break heavily at the last race, and a grievous wetting, my breeches soaked to the knees, and a sorry sight to return home. The day began well with a modest £25 to £10 upon Maidos and thus do beat the market to my great content and nought better than two to one available afterwards. The jockey doth allow Maidos to drop twenty lengths to the rear, and this angering me so that I do defame him loudly for his lack of judgement in giving the race away.

Perchance, he hearing my cries and moving up in the first round, is third up the straight, and going to the front by the home turn, to win by an undisputed margin and so showing good judgement after all, and my anger turning to praises for the jockey in knowing his mount so well. . . .

Not to bet upon the Christmas Handicap, this being as hard of choice as a Doncaster, and so foiling the bookmakers, but sorely distressed at the win of Solar Rays and should have backed this horse, but hearing that the owner did deny his chance while the trainer doth declare him a good thing, and so put off did refrain from wagering. . . .

That was brilliant stuff for a first attempt. After a few years, Cliff Graves had achieved a perfect style.

I awoke this a.m. with a violent ague of the back, come, I believe, of the great heat whereon casting the clothes from my bed, and presently a cool breeze did spring up and so to taking a chill of it.

This comes of leaving off my stomacher, and this I will not do again, come what weather may, and anon the pain abated by a drug and so forth and to the races at Randwick.

The original garrulous Sam Pepys would have been proud to have put his name to the Cliff Graves Diary.

Cliff finished his full-time active journalistic days on *The Daily Telegraph* (Sydney) celebrated as the doyen of Australian turf writers. On *Smith's,* he established a tradition of fine racing journalism. From his stable came Algie Gray, Roy Abott (now Turf Editor of *The Sydney Morning Herald*), Tom Foley of Brisbane, Bert Lillye, and Ted Wells.

Apart from racing and boxing, *Smith's* didn't take much continued interest in sport, unless something sensational such as bodyline bowling bobbed up, fairly screaming for the *Smith's* type of analysis, and, if necessary, curetting.

The paper only ever used one top-line general sporting writer—the fabled Hughie Dash, who came to *Smith's* following World War II, after leaving *The Daily Telegraph* where he had been a spectacular, if unpredictable, sporting editor.

Hughie was one of a brilliant bunch of journalists — Brian Penton, Edgar Holt, E. R. Jackson, Hugh Dash, etc. — produced in Queensland in the 1920s and 1930s. Most of these men invaded Sydney and won high journalistic honours for themselves.

All journalists who came south from Queensland in the 1920s told a story about a strange copy boy working for the old *Mail*. The lad was to be found every Saturday in the press box at Brisbane race meetings, ready to run errands for his erudite seniors. Among his functions was the carrying of bets from journalists to the ring and bringing back winnings, if any. After a time, it dawned on the journalists that the enthusiastic copy boy was the best dressed figure in the press box. Investigation revealed that, so poorly did he rate the judgement of the turf experts, that he had set up his own book and carried their bets himself to his considerable profit.

The cunning copy boy was Master Hughie Dash, destined to become Press Secretary to the Australian Prime Minister, Sir Robert Menzies.

Hugh was blessed with a most fertile imagination, with which he could fill in any blanks in a story without taking his fingers from his typewriter. He was the joy of any fight manager with a new fighter but no ideas on how to promote the fellow.

Here's a Hughie Dash puff par:

If you watch Charlie X, the new flyweight sensation from Redfern, you will notice him place his lips to his left forearm just before he comes out to cross gloves with an opponent. Charlie, in America with an R.A.A.F. contingent during the war, visited Hollywood and met among other people Miss Marilyn Monroe who, in wishing him luck in battle, placed her fingertips on his left forearm. Maybe for some psychoromantic reason, three indelible red marks appeared where three of the star's fingers touched. . . .

While Hughie was on *Smith's*, he was visited by a constant stream of strange characters, some bearing arms. One underworld figure associated with horseracing, seeking revenge for something Hugh Dash had written, thundered his way into the office. Hughie interpreted the noise correctly and intercepted the invader in a corridor, asking him who he was looking for.

122

"I want that ————— Dash," shouted the man "And I ain't going till I've got him."

Hughie nodded energetically. "If you find the mug, you can give him a belt for us here too. He wrote a phoney story about a decent bloke last week and just about ruined the reputation of the paper. We sacked Dash out of hand. Not a day's notice. . . ."

The man went away happy that justice had been done.

Hughie was game and would usually stand up to anyone who felt himself offended by the writer's inventive and mischievous pen. One man he did dodge was Dave Sands, Middle, Light-Heavy, and Heavyweight Champion of Australia. Hughie, maybe short of a few lines, cheerfully wrote that Sands, who had coloured blood, was causing his handlers a lot of trouble by obeying the instincts of his race and going walkabout at the most unexpected moments. Desperate on the eve of a major bout with Dave Sands somewhere out in the Pilliga, the handlers went to a wise old tribal elder for advice. As a result, smoke signals ordering recall were sent up from outside Newcastle which the champ did not dare ignore without incurring the wrath of the snake totem, or words to that effect.

Maybe Hughie meant it as a great big joke — you could never be sure with him — but Dave Sands took the story poorly and came stalking his man through *Smith's* corridors. Dash, having had forewarning (by smoke signals, he swore), found need to investigate a story way down south of Sydney.

However, Hughie won the affection of most sportsmen, some to a startling degree. A number of us heard a trainer of fighters trying to thank Hughie for something quite wonderful he had done. The trainer offered money, gifts for Hughie's wife, gifts for Hughie's children, all of which Dash nobly refused in front of his fascinated audience.

"Well, look, Hughie," the grateful trainer cried earnestly, "is there anyone you want bashed?"

On leaving *Smith's* in the late 1940s, Hugh Dash went to *The Sydney Morning Herald,* where his style and inventiveness were not as acceptable as they had been on uninhibited *Smith's.* Finding himself withering on the vine, Dash turned to politics and, to the amazement of many, became the Press Secretary to Prime Minister Menzies.

Hughie's idea of public relations was novel, but entertaining. He would buttonhole an acquaintance in the street and cheerfully demand to know:

Did you hear what happened to Bob and Artie Fadden when they got off the train at Galargumbone during the last election tour? No? Well they got off the train at this little station see, and Artie says "Where's the ruddy pub?" Naturally this shocks Bob and he says "Break it down, Artie. You'll lose votes talking that way. You'd make a better impression if you asked where the local church was." And Artie replies, "You're a darned hypocrite, Bob Menzies. Why you don't even know the Lord's Prayer!"

Bob says he'll bet a fiver he does, and Artie takes him up and bets he can't.

So Bob says "Here it is — Gentle Jesus meek and mild. . . ."

And Artie holds up his hand saying "That's enough Bob. You're too good for me. Here's your fiver. . . ."

Hughie Dash spoke with machine gun speed and ended his stories with a roar of laughter which primed and set off the funny bones of all around him.

He died in harness, serving the P.M.

Tom Foley, for long one of the top race commentators of Queensland, was *Smith's* bright young racing man in Victoria for many years before World War II. Tom, who had retired from studying law to become a journalist, returned to his studies in middle age with success.

There was on *Smith's* before and after World War II a most remarkable advertising man named William Gaznier. (He was Advertising Manager during the paper's last few years). He was something of an expert on sport and claimed to be quite a fair practitioner in his own right.

An office cricket match was organized to test Bill's qualities and the best bats were stacked in the opposite team to his. Bill bowled seven and caught the other three. He could play cricket all right. He could also catch fish at office outings when no one else could get a nibble, and he could play tennis and run fast.

Indeed, he was so capable at most things sporting that people on *Smith's* gave up challenging claims he made, except for one. They will not accept the proud father's insistent cry that his baby son could handle a ball so well, even in the play pen, that he would surely be a world-beater at some sport when he grew up.

Ah well, Bill Gaznier's son grew up to be Reg Gaznier, claimed by many to be the greatest Rugby League back Australia has produced.

CHAPTER TEN

Smith's Saucy Satirists

"Smith's is a paper that lives on its wits."
— Claude McKay, continually, 1919-1950

Satire was instinctive with *Smith's* because Claude McKay was a natural satirist who could not resist poking fun at anyone or anything in the sacred cow category.

Claude devised and encouraged ruthlessly a satirical technique called "codding." An issue in which the public was warmly interested was taken each week and joshed unmercifully. An artist was used to add barbs to the written material, and it was rare that *Smith's* failed to raise at least one national laugh per week.

The "cod" was at its best in *Smith's* when written by Reg Moses, one of the funniest, but perhaps least remembered humorists Australia has produced. He came to *Smith's* soon after the paper started, having been lured away from *The Sunday Times* by Clyde Packer, who had previously edited that journal.

"Mo" as he signed himself shyly at the end of all his pieces, was short, tubby, crew cut, and a University man with a classical education. He had worked on papers round Sydney, and in J. C. Williamson's Publicity Dept., where only the most inventive could hope to survive.

Mo got away to a splendid start on *Smith's* in 1920 by codding the Australian tour of H.R.H. The Prince of Wales, with a series of alleged letters from the Prince to "The Folks At Home." The pieces cleverly satirized the social climbers and bureaucrats who sought to gain distinction for themselves by pursuing the Royal visitor ruthlessly. Mo flourished under the cheers he received from readers, and by mid-1921, his pen was hitting gold every week.

In May 1921 Australia was watching with irritation a Royal Commission into allegations of pilfering at Cockatoo Dockyard,

Sydney, where naval ships were being built. The affair prompted this skit from Mo:

The Committee of Inquiry appointed by the Woop Woop Progress Assn to inquire into the state of affairs at the Parrakeet Dock, continued yesterday.

Percival Bergonia, rocking-horse painter, said he was employed on the building of the super-*de-luxe* dreadnought, "Cockle's Creek." It was commenced in 1872, and allowing for reasonable delay, might be expected ready for launching somewhere in the next ten years.

There had been trouble about one of her twin propellers. One Friday morning, the Superintendant of Tinned Fruits had come down to the Dock, unscrewed the port propeller from the tail-shaft, and taken it away with him. Witness had asked him why, and the answer was he had wanted it for an electric fan.

Chairman: Did you see anything wrong in that?

Witness: I told the foreman.

Chairman: What steps did he take?

Witness: He went down and removed the tail shaft and sold it for old iron.

Councillor Miggins: Are you a teetotaller?

Chairman: The witness did not come here to be insulted. You are only playing to the gallery!

Smith's could never resist peering into other people's pay packets, and was always fascinated at the way lawyers presented their accounts in almost petty detail. Mo devised an "Account Rendered," in the form of a "Bill of Costs to a travelling-mother-in-law from her son-in-law in the legal profession."

	£		
To welcoming you on arrival from England	5	5	0
Asking you if you were well and had a good trip	1	1	0
Being publicly embraced	1	1	0
Embracing you in return	1	1	0
Attending you to luggage shed	2	2	0
Consoling you for shameful delay	1	1	0
Beckoning to cabman and instructing him when summoned	2	2	0
Frowning at discourteous cabman on his refusal to accept legal fare	1	1	0
Listening to reminiscences and anecdotes period 1853-1890, say	10	10	0
Seeing you on express to Melbourne	5	5	0
Begging you to take care of yourself	1	1	0
Promising to take care of self, wife, and children	1	1	0

SMITH'S SAUCY SATIRISTS

Promising to write	1	0	0
Embracing you (in carriage)	1	1	0
Additional embrace (through window)	1	1	0
Waving one handkerchief, properly washed and ironed		10	6
Seemly display of grief	1	1	0
TOTAL, say	£110	10	6

Lawyers everywhere cut that item out of *Smith's* and insisted on trying to show it to one another in clubs, pubs, and coffee houses, until the scraps of newsprint fell to pieces.

In legal circles the popularity of that cod rated second only to a joke drawing *Smith's* printed, targeted on the weakness many old cow cockies had for litigation against one another. This drawing depicted two old farmers struggling for possession of a prime cow. One was pulling at the horns and the other blindly at the tail. Neither was getting any advantage. However, unnoticed by the angry farmers, seated on a stool, in full wig and gown, was a lawyer milking the contested cow with the greatest enthusiasm.

Smith's had an antipathy towards envangelists of the hellfire and brimstone variety. This attitude was one more influence attributable to Claude McKay, whose Presbyterian background required that if one took any religion at all, he took it plain and without undue display.

It was not strange therefore that, in 1926, visiting American evangelist, the Rev. W. P. Nicholson, should attract *Smith's* angry eye by continually referring to men who smoked as "stinkin' polecats," and to young ladies as "short-skirted, powder-puffed puppets of the Devil."

Mo went to work on the situation. He wrote a spare sermon in the Australian idiom for the Rev. Nicholson to use in emergency:

PRAISE THE LORD. If that sloppy looking slattern in the shapelesss slip-on doesn't stop slopping her bulk all over the front pew, I'll have her put out.

You jolly well start seeking salvation, my fat sheila, or you'll slip on St Peter's front step, by cripes.

AND GET YOUR HAIR CUT!

Dark haired damsels of dandruff and destruction, laying your tress trails of danger and dismay upon the coat collars of innocent men!

And that frump in the fourth row can stop her brat insulting everybody with its ignorant yowling. . . .

There's only one person in this hall who can do that!

It was difficult for any public figure to carry on once *Smith's,* via Mo, had got the masses giggling at him. The cod, as used by *Smith's,* was powerful enough to change public policies, and the paper was ruthless if it felt the people were not getting a fair go.

Naturally, all patriotic citizens were excited at the prospect of the Duke and Duchess of York — later King George VI and Queen Elizabeth — coming out to open the first Parliament in Canberra in 1927. Royal visits were extremely rare and therefore very much treasured in those days. There was great dismay when officials organizing the visit pompously announced, "The Duchess of York is to have perfect rest and quiet throughout the tour."

The Duchess was young, strong, and in no need of coddling.

Smith's, via Mo, promptly published a list of Standing Orders, by which the Royal Tour was to be conducted. It appointed a Committee to police the Orders. The Chairman was the President of the Cotton Wool Makers Assn Vice-Chairman was Mrs Kirby (a leading funeral director), etc. The committee was given a crest : an oyster silent.

Standing orders were as follows:

1. On arrival at the Sydney Heads of H.M.S. *Renown,* ferry boats, and other craft will be allowed ONE silent cock-a-doodle-doo and no more.
2. Land forces to fire twenty-one gun salute with unloaded catapults and/or pealess peashooters.
3. No banners to bear "Hooray," "Whatho," or "Is She Any Plum Pudd?"
4. All archways to carry the words "Hush, Hush."
5. No ordinary police on duty. Only silent cops.
6. People with hay fever must stay home under their beds.
7. Persons wearing noisy hatbands or loud ties to be removed to the underground railway.
8. No shouting in private or public bars under any circumstances.

Smith's liked to claim credit for the fact that, after that saucy stuff was printed, the Duchess of York was permitted to have fun and was not screened off from the hoi polloi.

The paper had every respect for Royalty, but refused to be overawed by it. The gay Prince of Wales was particularly fair game as far as *Smith's* was concerned, and when, in 1927, the world was wondering why he didn't get married, *Smith's* set out to help the young man. It took the attitude that since the Prince would not, or could not, choose a bride for himself, he was clearly in need of aid. So it launched what it called its Prince's Bride Competition."

"There Must Be A Winner," a banner headline cried. "Maybe It Will Be YOU," echoed another.

The conditions stressed that no foreigner was eligible to enter on the grounds that "we scorn the foreign yoke." However, no colour bar was drawn within the Empire, and any female was eligible to enter by filling in a coupon and enclosing a shilling.

First prize was naturally the Prince of Wales. Second and third place-getters were to have their choice of the remaining members of the Royal family. The next twenty could select from Lords-in-Waiting. Some two hundred equerries and aides-de-camp were to be provided as consolation prizes. There would also be, declared *Smith's*, five hundred O.B.E.s and, finally, ten thousand prizes at 10/- each.

The poor Prince could not have got into more bother than he ultimately did had he let *Smith's* find him a wife.

Censorship was a natural for *Smith's* to cod and, when a popular song came under a deal of official criticism in 1930, the paper insisted that it was indeed time a halt was called to the trend in *risqué* lyrics. It then piously rewrote the popular song book, supplying purified words of the style:

Mademmoiselle from Armentières, parlez-vous.
Hasn't had a conversation lolly for forty years,
Inky Pinky etc.

Another major rewrite was:

I wonder who's her Sunday School Teacher now?
I bet he regrets it, poor cow.
I wonder who's gazing into her pince-nez
As she stands at bay
All through the day. . . .

Caustic criticism was aimed at the smash hit of the day, "Hallelujah I'm a Bum."

It was suggested the sentiment should be changed to:

Hallelujah I'm a Christian young gentleman.
Hallelujah, I'm still a Christian young gentleman.
Hallelujah if you can't be as virtuous as me,
For goodness sake be as virtuous as you can.

Those were grim Depression days and every laugh was precious. *Smith's* played a gallant part in lightening the gloom.

Reg Moses dominated cod writing on *Smith's* from 1920 until he left to join *The Australian Women's Weekly* in 1935. Sadly, he was only to live one more year. His age at his death was forty-six.

His friends and admirers used to argue over which was the best of the hundreds of cods he wrote. There was considerable support for his satire on the contention of a medical witness in the New South Wales Supreme Court that "litigation neurosis" caused people in the box to speak in a disguised fashion.

Mo set up a Psychiatric Court before Mr Justice Looney and jury and provided a report of proceedings:

Mr John Potty, who was sworn with the aid of a Mexican parrot, deposed that he would not tell the truth, the whole truth, or anything like the truth. He said he suffered so much from litigious aphasia that the sight of a final notice from the Gas Company on blue paper made him faint.

In any case, he claimed, there was a distinct hiatus in his osmotic process. It was the same with regard to Mary Queen of Scots and heaven only knew he had tried to help her. But the tram conductor made things so unpleasant he had to get off.

Dr Dopey, acting as interpreter, said this meant Mr Potty was a retired grazier of independent means, living apart from his family.

"Potty" back to stand. Speaking under obvious emotion, he said when he thought of the first number he first thought of and added the engine driver's name, Winooka seemed a sure thing for the cup.

Dr Dopey (interpreting) : He denies he met the accused on the night in question.

The judge issued a decree in all directions with costs against the Master-in-Lunacy.

With the departure of Mo, Kenneth Slessor, *Smith's* Jack-of-all-trades, slipped into the specialist job of cod writing. Like the chameleon, Ken could adapt himself to any condition of heat, cold, or colour. He was the regular understudy for Jim Donald, the famed fight writer, and also the official office poet, leader writer, film reviewer, special writer, satirist, and doer of anything else the gods wished to dump on him. Some say Ken Slessor has been the greatest Australian journalist since World War I.

In August 1939, when the smell of war was in the air, honest but over-stimulated citizens began hearing morse messages and sighting flickering lights that didn't really exist. *Smith's* felt the situation needed quietening down and tossed the chore to Ken, who promptly wrote a learned piece on secret service operations:

One of the first things you notice about spies is the way they send messages to one another. Most of the spies I know send messages in buns. They use a special oilproof paper that stands up to any amount of biting and does not clog the teeth.

I once knew two spies who kept up a correspondence in buns, goulashes, and sponge cakes for the best part of a year. He used to send her passionate messages in buns. She responding in sponge cake.

After that, he switched to waffles and she used to roll up tiny messages in his cigarettes. Often, when smoking, he'd go pale on account of having inhaled a tiny message.

What finally drove him out of the Secret Service was when she took to hiding maps and things in his toothpaste. He used to rush around the place roaring with his mouth filled with foam and confidential reports about the Salvation Army. . . .

(Not long after that gay piece was written, Ken Slessor was appointed Australia's first Official War Correspondent in World War II. He found little to cod in Greece, Crete, the Middle East, and New Guinea.)

The fabled Lennie Lower came back to *Smith's* from *The Daily Telegraph* (Sydney) in 1940. He had been with the paper, or rather, its young brother, *The Daily Guardian,* years before, when he had distinguished himself by writing his two best-sellers — *Here's Luck* and *Here's Another.*

Lower had a magic gift for writing humour. He only needed to have a go with pencil and paper and whatever went down sounded hilarious. He could write good stuff in and out of liquor, whether wide-awake or half-asleep. All he needed was a theme to work on.

In July 1941 he saluted Russia's entry into the war on our side in typical Lower fashion with the headline, "Hooray For The Hammer and Shicker!" He took the attitude that now Australians were fighting side by side with the Reds they'd better learn something about their new Allies quick smart. "Russian books, for instance," he declared, "are tense and bright." Thus:

Ivan was drunk. He was very terrible when he was drunk. He was going home to choke his father. With his heavy boots and his bloodshot teeth, he trudged through the village, mouthing curses through his black, lank, frozen beard.

His wife was the local blacksmith. Smirna was her name. Yes, that was her name. He wondered why he had never thought of that before. He belched slightly. It was snowing again.

It must have been the lard sandwich he had at Krakavol at the Fair. . . .

They didn't write cods better than that.

Lennie was determined to get into the war effort and enlisted in the Second A.I.F. on numerous occasions. Time and again he was seen by members of *Smith's* staff, waving from the back of an army three-tonner as he was taken yet again from the Martin Place Recruiting Depot, Sydney, out to the Showground. Unfortunately, he had physical weaknesses which made him unsuitable for army purposes.

In 1947, Lennie entered hospital for a throat operation, but didn't stop writing for an instant. He enjoyed the whole show, and each of his many mates visiting him, secretly slipped a small bottle of brandy under his pillow and removed the empty he found there. It was grand fun, until in July, following a haemorrhage, Lennie collapsed and died. He would have been forty-four had he lived two more months.

During World War II, Ronald McCuaig, the poet, joined *Smith's* and proved a first-class satirist. *Smith's* appointed him as its War Correspondent, but the authorities refused to let him get into the action. McCuaig cleverly responded with home-front communiqués which needled the officious Blimps mercilessly.

After the war another poet, John Quinn, who had made himself a fine reputation with a first book of war poems, showed a nice sense of waspishness in satire. When Quinn went to *Woman's Day* in 1947, Edgar Holt recommended artist-author Bernard Hesling as his replacement.

"I'm sure we'll find him conscientious," Edgar told Claude McKay as they walked down Martin Place to lunch.

Claude stopped in his tracks, his eyes widening in simulated alarm, "For heaven's sake, not too conscientious. I hope."

Hesling proved a good buy, decorating his merry writings with his own curious humorous drawings.

Here's a taste of 1947 vintage Hesling, sent in to *Smith's* from a holiday boarding house:

> I am writing this at Mon Repos on my holidays. The fish are biting as only catfish can bite.
>
> I can hear the screams of happy holiday-makers drifting up from below. One happy holiday-maker has been screaming now for forty-five minutes. Someone is saying that the bait was in that yeller tin and if it ain't then the baby must have 'et it. . . .

The last of *Smith's* star cod writers was Alex MacDonald, who had developed his funny bones writing radio scripts for Roy Rene ("Mo"). *Smith's* was fading when Alex arrived, but he gave it a shot in the buttocks with a brilliant weekly radio review column, which set new standards in Australia for fearless and delightfully readable criticism. On the death of *Smith's*, Alex was to win glory as a humorous writer on *The Daily Telegraph* and then *The Daily Mirror* in Sydney.

A *Smith's* man, who perhaps could have become one of the best satirical writers in Australia had he persevered with the medium, was the comic artist George Donaldson. George had a magic touch all his own for needling the vanities and weaknesses of humans via the short story.

One of his quaint tales which delighted the nation in 1940 opened up with a gentle, little soul named Mr Lamb taking a short cut home across a dark paddock when he was attacked by thugs. The thugs got Mr Lamb and put in the boot in traditional fashion, but the victim noted through his fears that the men were wearing thick sponge rubber cushions on their toe caps. With one last "panther-like rush," the bashers closed on Mr Lamb, kissed him on the forehead, and disappeared into the night.

Mr Lamb went thoughtfully home to his boarding house, in which lived the dreadful landlady, Mrs Skinnerlouse, of whom the poor little chap was terribly afraid. He didn't have his rent ready and expected a proper tongue-lashing. Entering the place, he happened to put his hand into a pocket and discovered a huge bundle of notes obviously placed there by the thugs.

When Mr Lamb sought to pay his rent, Mrs Skinnerlouse looked most hurt and cried, "Don't dare insult me by offering me money!"

Next day at work, Mr Lamb was called in by the normally grim boss who begged him to accept a partnership in the firm. "And please forgive me for putting the proposition so bluntly, my dear Lamb."

It was all very confusing, for Mr Lamb who was one of life's fall guys, used to being pushed around by one and all. But more bewilderment was to follow. In the evening paper, Mr Lamb read (World War II was on) that Hitler was bombing London with kapok. England was counter-attacking with shrapnel shells filled with frankfurters.

Poor little Mr Lamb imagined he had gone mad and rushed to a doctor who smiled sadly and said, "Scientists have just proved that man is truly immortal and has a future life. No doubt about it whatever. For every good deed a man does, he will get paid ten thousandfold and will enjoy his reward for ever. Humanity's become hopelessly demoralized. The whole social system of the world is in chaos. Doing good things has become a racket!"

CHAPTER ELEVEN

News Hounds and Other Literary Gents

"Never investigate a good story too far or you'll kill it!"
—Claude McKay, continually

To survive as a journalist on *Smith's,* you had to be a good hunter of news or a spectacular writer, or, best of all, both.

An example of a good early model news hunter-writer was Harry Maddison, *Smith's* long time Melbourne man, billed by the paper as "The Gimlet of Gun Alley."

Harry had graduated from being an ace crime reporter on Melbourne dailies to being a specialist on *Smith's.* He was a quiet little chap who wore quiet little brown suits. But murderers liked talking to him and telling him why they done it. He was also good with hangmen and other normally shy types. Detectives felt a need to tell him secrets they hadn't even told the superintendent. His only rival was Vince Kelly who served *Smith's* in New South Wales, Victoria, and South Australia, and became Australia's No. 1 crime writer and author of fifteen books.

Whereas Harry and Vince hunted down their stories as a chicken hunts a worm, Adam McCay, doyen of the early *Smith's* writers, was an example of the pure writer who could wring an excellent story out of the air while he sipped a glass of fine sweet sherry.

Adam was ordered, in February 1920, to take a smack at New South Wales Premier Holman, and, being a highly professional hired pen, went straight to work:

> It is not true that Mr Holman murdered his aunt's cook for the sake of her silver-backed brushes. There is no proof that, lunching at Parliament House, Holman stole the spoons.
>
> But Holmanism in the Nationalist Party has been perpetually associated with fraud, jobbery, falsehood, corruption, and waste. First step towards clean Government in New South Wales is to get rid of the gang led by Holman.

That's what's called distinctive writing. Adam applied it regularly against Holman until not only did Holman's Liberal Government fall, but the Premier lost his seat and cried at a public dinner, *"Smith's Weekly* has left me without a shred of reputation or a penny to jingle on a tombstone."

An M.A. (Hons. 1), Adam was one of the last of the great bohemian journalists of Sydney. To be with him in a pub was a delight, for his scholarship was profound and he employed his research as a means of entertaining. He discovered the Borgia method of cooking a duck when he stumbled across the recipe hidden in an ancient Latin book. One took the duckling and tied it by the foot to a stake circled by faggots of dry sticks. Beside the creature was a bowl of water. When the faggots were set ablaze, the heat would cause the duck to sip the water, thus keeping its flesh tender as it slowly roasted to death.

Adam also had a recipe for drowning lobsters in claret to get a delicate flavour right down into their nipper tips.

In trams, he was likely to burst forth full voice with a rendition of "Mine eyes have seen the glory of the coming of the Lord" — a relic, he claimed, of having been reared in a manse in New Zealand. And in pubs, he was always likely to indulge his taste for composing saucy verse. His particular delight was to scribble an opening line on a sheet of copy paper and toss it in challenge to any other poet in the group to carry the poem a step forward.

On one notorious occasion, his opening gambit was, "The loveliest whore in Darlinghurst was in the family way."

The following line supplied by the man to whom Adam tossed the paper ran, "In spite of her diamond pessaries and jewelled whirling spray."

That poem went on and on until it reached the classic proportions of "Eskimo Nell." Alas, there is no place where such a poem can be permanently recorded with safety.

Ever ready to add a saucy line to such poetic ventures was Bartlett Adamson, among whose claims to distinction was that he had never worn a necktie since birth.

He was a left-wing poet by inclination (which didn't interest *Smith's* one scrap) and a crime analyst by professional necessity In a famous feature entitled "The Man in the Mask," decorated each week with a drawing of a character peering with sinister gleam through slits in a piece of cloth, Bart recited terrible tales of mayhem.

To Bart, all bushrangers had been forced into their unhappy

mould by a cruel society and most cops were dingoes. His poetic nature would drive him into fruity flights in describing how Australian bandits always died game, while the police, hiding like curs behind trees, shot them down.

This sort of stuff had a tremendous following in *Smith's*. In its time, it was equivalent to modern private eye shows on TV, minus only the cop wrapping himself round a hot blonde at the end of each instalment.

Smith's normally recruited its writers trained and polished from the dailies. Occasionally, it would pull someone in from outside the craft. But that someone had to be a rare soul of great talent.

Claude McKay had a good eye for picking 'em. Soon after World War I, McKay's attention was attracted by articles on education appearing in the Sydney press and he traced them to a schoolteacher public servant named Lew Deer. He kept an eye on Deer who rose to be Chief Inspector of the New South Wales Public Service Board, and, in 1922, invited him to resign and join *Smith's*. Deer found the offered terms attractive, and, on becoming one of the *Smith's* team, wrote a spectacular series of stories exposing the New South Wales Public Service as "a haven of mediocrity," a "sepulchre for brains, energy, enthusiasm, and initiative," and "a paradise of the incompetent."

The shake-up which followed in the Public Service did New South Wales a lot of good and won many permanent readers for the paper.

Another inspired pick from the ranks of the schoolteachers was Isla Brook, B.A. (Melb.), who called in at *Smith's* Sydney office during World War II, looking for a job. Claude McKay said, "You're hired. Go out and interview someone on the basic wage."

Many hours later, Isla returned to report that there was no one left on the basic wage.

"A wonderful story!" enthused Claude. And it was too. Without knowing it, Isla had been the first journalist to discover the fact that every worker in Australia was on a margin of some sort, the situation having developed under cover of war. In one day Isla learnt to do what some journalists cannot do in a lifetime — identify a spark of interesting fact in a bucket of dull words.

Within a couple of years, she was one of the leading women journalists in Australia, her Sydney Diary being a major *Smith's* feature. Later she was to cover a Royal Tour for *The Courier*

THE THIRSTY SEVEN: *"Spare us something for a feed (hic)!"*

Mail (Brisbane), and become a star reporter on *The Australian Women's Weekly* before marriage took her overseas.

Her courage was notable. She was prepared to go into many situations a man would duck in search of a story.

Immediately after World War II, a tip came to *Smith's* that a Sydney night club was providing special small rooms complete with single bed for the convenience of couples who might care to dine in especially private circumstances. The cosy rooms were being used to discomfort clients, forcing them to order more and more expensive drinks.

Isla insisted on testing the allegations, and took a male artist to make sketches. Her story of how all night long people kept suddenly unlocking the door and charging inside, plus the art-ist's sketches, was a minor classic of investigation and exposure. The evening became most uncomfortable when the waiters grew suspicious. But that suited Isla just fine. It helped the story.

This capacity to investigate was a mark of the good *Smith's* reporter, and for most of its years, the paper maintained a special Investigation Department staffed by journalists with a bent for sleuthing. Departmental founder was Captain John O'Donnell, a giant of a man who had won himself a name in the First A.I.F. for having helped quell the notorious Battle of the Wazir in Egypt when the troops attempted to raze a brothel area.

O'Donnell delighted in playing dumb sucker to confidence men, trick salesmen, go-getters, snide business agents, and imposters, thus gathering material for spectacular *Smith's* exposure stories. Every day he and his men scanned the small ads in the daily papers, sniffing for indications of smart operators fishing for dupes. They were true makers of news.

Such was O'Donnell's acting skill that none of the people he exposed in the paper suspected he was other than a goof until they read his story. Those who rushed screaming into the office after his blood would find O'Donnell, huge and smiling, waiting behind his desk for them. If they became too threatening, O'Donnell, still smiling, would take a large baton from his bottom drawer and place it without comment on his blotting pad. That always ended the tantrums.

Once you'd been through O'Donnell's school, you could regard yourself as a hardened journalist. Reg Harris, Quentin Spedding, Gus Walker, Bill Rodie, Clem Cleveson, and Blaine Fielder all graduated *cum laude*.

Harris, Spedding, and Rodie all became noted public relations men in later years. Rodie, before coming to *Smith's,* had been a romantic adventurer from New Zealand who had wandered the south seas with Errol Flynn, pursuing a try-anything-once policy.

Four white dots under his right eye showed where the prongs of a fork had hit bone when the wielder had intended to drive them through his eye. In the depths of the Depression, he took a job as footman in Government House, Sydney, and on leaving, wrote a cheerful series of articles on hard times in a palace.

Either *Smith's* had an attraction for men with a talent for public relations or it bred the skill into them, for besides those mentioned above, it processed Alan Hulls and Norman Elison, both on *The Referee* side of the *Smith's* family and both now of Sydney, and John Handfield, founder of *Image Australia,* Melbourne.

Smith's had a number of good finance writers in its time, but the best all-round newsman of them all was G. B. Jackson. A Sydney university man and a State hockey player (in spite of the fact that he had only one lung operating), Gordon delighted in tracking down doubtful doings. After World War II, he broke the great land sales scandals in New South Wales single-handed, smashing the man-made bottlenecks which were frustrating land-hungry people in their attempts to get land deals concluded. His courage in criticizing company performances was matched only by Claude McKay's courage in printing the criticisms. One bad judgement, and a monumental writ could follow.

Smith's finance page, as written by Gordon Jackson between 1930 and 1950, gained a big reputation for its accuracy and outspokeness. Just how big this reputation was no one realized until the paper was dead.

In the very last edition, Gordon Jackson slipped a little panel into his page stating that he intended to start an advisory newsletter, and anyone interested could contact him at his address. The response almost broke the back of the postie at Clontarf, Sydney. Following his newsletter success, Gordon obtained a seat on the Sydney Stock Exchange and still graces it.

Some writers more or less touched *Smith's* for luck on their way to successful writing careers. Ernestine Hill, on arriving in Sydney from Queensland in the 1930s, worked on *Smith's* as a typist. The paper discovered her writing talent and encouraged her to become a professional, which, of course, she did with notable success.

Kenneth McKenzie, the poet and novelist, also served a stint with *Smith's*. And Henry Lawson wrote just one poem for the paper. It appeared on 7 June 1919, and it was horrible. Called *The Township* it started:

Let us sing in careless measures
of the days of long ago,
Like the trot, trot, trot of horses,
In the time of Cobb & Co. . . .

It never got any better.

Soon after World War II a young man wearing a large aggressive moustache was brought more or less struggling into *Smith's* Editorial Floor, and the word went round that he was to be made into a journalist. This was David McKay, Claude's second son, fresh from overseas where he had been driving tanks through jungles.

David had had a shot at Agriculture at Sydney University and found it not to his taste. He had tried practical farming and, after a fight with a crazed bull, had gone searching for pastures new. Journalism didn't seem to appeal to him much, mainly, it seemed, because he was being prodded into embracing it. But there was one thing he was prepared to do without quibble—drive journalists out on their assignments in his green MG. He could claim he was studying solid craftsmen at work close up. To his disgust he found that the solid craftsmen had no stomach for being driven through fog, rain, and over muddy roads at, say ninety m.p.h.

David abandoned the cowards and their craft and concentrated on speed driving to such effect that he became Australian champion and a world figure in car racing. Then, his spirit content, he turned back to newspapers, and, as motoring editor of *The Daily Telegraph,* Sydney, invented a new approach to motoring journalism — why the hell shouldn't it be as interesting as any other news?

Smith's, which always made a point of doing something unusual if possible, employed probably the youngest War Correspondent in the world when it sent Warren McIlraith, eighteen, into Spain in 1936 to report the civil war there.

Warren, son of Frank McIlwraith who had been *Smith's* London man for many years, was such a success with his battle-field reports that he was brought out to Australia and eventually became chief sub-editor of *Smith's,* staying with the paper until it died.

Smith's finished World War II with only a handful of tired old journalists on the staff. Eagerly it took in new blood released by the services and reserved occupations. Men like Dave Barnes, Eddie Dunstan, Douglas Blaikie, Hugh Dash, Alex Macdonald, and John Quinn put new sparkle into the paper. Dave Barnes could make a story out of a bent pin, and tap dance like a professional. Eddie Dunstan was a wizard with pictorial layout and human interest stories. Douglas Blaikie, a former *Daily Telegraph* (Sydney) court reporter back from the wars, could handle any sort of story from murder to a baptism. Clive Robinson was an infantryman with a mission to win justice for prisoners of war.

Smith's thrived on the new men.

Bart Adamson was still there. And George Goddard. And two men who were part of the spirit of the *Smith's* Editoral Department though they were not formal journalists — Percy Ford who drove the lift, and Philip Gidley King who screened all visitors who wished to speak with "The Editor" and channelled them in the proper direction. They had one thing in common — both had lost a leg in World War I.

Percy Ford was full of paragraphs which he recited to the

reporters as he raised them aloft. Here's one that found a place on the Digger page:

Percy's small son Billy had become intrigued at his father's lack of a leg and demanded to know where it had gone.

Said Percy, "A naughty Turk took it from me, son."

Young Billy thought deeply about that and then cried, "Why didn't you belt that Turk with your crutch, Dad?"

Percy taught many scores of legless Digs to drive his lift, fitting them to take the test that would enable them to graduate as lift drivers themselves.

When Philip G. King came to work on the Editorial Floor to release younger men for World War II his dignity and cultured bearing made him an outstanding figure. He had the charm of a diplomat and handled all visitors, even the ratbags which all newspapers get, with a fine old-world courtesy.

When his secret came out no one was surprised. Phil was the direct descendant of Governor Philip Gidley King. He had been born at famous Goonoogoonoo when it was one of the biggest sheep properties in Australia. Extraordinary people tended to join *Smith's* staff, if only for the reason that they enjoyed the company of other extraordinary people. And if they had a talent — to draw, to write, to drive a lift, to handle people — they were welcome whether they were heirs to governors or to swagmen.

But sometimes it took a candidate a long time to get the message over that he was worthy of being enlisted.

Editorial eyes, honed razor sharp to miss nothing in the passing scene, noted in 1935 a new printer's devil constantly racing up the iron fire escape from the composing room one floor below. The lad carried handfuls of proofs for editors and sub-editors to deliver final judgement on.

He had big brown innocent eyes, his dark hair was parted almost dead centre (an infallible sign of purity in the 1930s), and his shirt was ever of a whiteness that would have competed with the driven snow. The boy gave the impression that he was entering into some sacred place when he set foot on the Editorial Floor. This fact, added to the courtesy he displayed towards his intellectual betters, won him some good marks among the writers.

A particularly pretty trick he had was the rolling of his little blue printer's apron into a thin rope round his waist so that editorial eyes would not be obliged to gaze upon inkstains.

Sadly he used to tell those who would listen how much he would like to be a journalist too. How droll! A minnow wishing to be a Triton. Other kids in the composing room hated the humble job of running round with proofs. The new boy took the entire function on his back.

Smith's in those days constantly cried, "Every Reader is a *Smith's* Reporter" and paid handsomely for paragraphs at $2\frac{1}{4}$d per line. There was a regular column to fit almost any subject — Wild and Wide, Secret History, Strange But True, Nature Notes, Laughter and Tears, Unofficial History of the A.I.F., and so on.

Because the Depression was still being felt, paragraphs poured in by the thousand each week but relatively few finished up in the paper. Bartlett Adamson and Ken Slessor usually did the final selection from proofs which were delivered to them by the willing boy below.

Keen contributors made their main target the feature, "First Impressions" — a witty, pithy, humorous, sometimes invective-loaded account of a person or event in the news expressed in as few words as possible. For example when Mussolini was pushing his unwelcome way into Abyssinia a First Impression which attracted much attention in Smith's was "MUSCLE-INI."

The lead First Impression on top of the column was worth £1. The next few returned their writers 10/- each, and the remainder were worth 2/6.

Frank Marien, when Editor-in-Chief, insisted on making the final selection of these witticisms himself, and the boy from the composing room used to lay the proofs carefully on the big boss's desk, stand meekly aside with hands tucked in rolled apron while judgement was made, and then dart back beaming to the nether regions.

A day came when Marien was heard roaring with a mixture of rage and laughter. He had discovered that the fast-footed proof carrier from the composing room was one of *Smith's* highest paid contributors.

Young Fred Flowers had decided to become a journalist in the second week after he entered the composing room. On finding that there was no known way to make the switch, he set out secretly to write his way to glory. By day he worked in the composing room. By night he attended a technical trade course. Late at night and at week-ends he worked on paragraphs, sometimes polishing one small item for twelve hours.

His pars, under a multitude of names, somehow always got on to the first page of final proofs which went before Slessor and Adamson. And, as all literary men know, if a par is on the first page it has a better chance of being read and selected than if it is on the last page.

Young Fred, along with the rest of the contributing field, concentrated particularly on First Impressions and the big money. By watching Frank Marien's reactions as he read proofs he was able to assess what tickled the master most. Among other things he noted that Mussolini angles, if apt, were sure fire stuff.

"Muscle-ini" was one of Fred's £1 winners. It was a curious, though secret fact, that every week, the first items on the first galley of First Impressions Fred laid on Frank Marien's table were Fred's. And usually one of them took the £1 — until Marien twigged. Fred, you see, could set type with the best of them.

Although the bright young man with the innocent eyes didn't know it, *Smith's* hierarchy was tremendously proud of the initiative he displayed and predicted a fine future for him in newspapers. A study of his ancestry revealed that his grandfather had been Fred Flowers, one of the founders of the Australian Labor Party and for many years the distinguished President of the New South Wales Legislative Council. (His father was Bill Flowers, in his time a well-loved Publisher of *Smith's*.)

Claude McKay and Frank Marien decided that the boy should first finish his apprenticeship in the composing room before switching from type to typewriter. Young Freddy went along with this, but refused to stop writing and wrote many features for *The Referee*, *Smith's* sporting brother. As a sideline, he also became an ABC broadcaster on The Voice of Youth Session and sports programmes.

Time came when he was too senior an apprentice to trot around with proofs. How could he keep the gods upstairs alert to his presence? Trust Fred to have a special answer to that. At the Ultimo Technical College he turned all his set projects into advertisements for *Smith's*. Folders, blotting paper, and so on all carried a whole-hearted brightly written plug for the paper. A copy of each of these efforts was placed on important editorial desks. By whom? By Fred of course.

The day came when Fred Flowers was a graduate compositor and a top-liner too. In his best suit he marched straight up to Claude McKay reporting for journalistic duty, sir! He almost instantly became a third year cadet. Then, just as quickly came September 1939, and World War II. Fred went.

On his discharge in December 1945, he went to Adelaide as *Smith's* South Australian editor and later became *Smith's* Victorian editor.

When the paper died, Sir Keith Murdoch of *The Herald* (Melbourne) grabbed him within hours of the death knell ringing. From there on all Fred's paths led to glory. He covered Queen Elizabeth's first tour of Australia and New Zealand, was selected Australia's Associate Nieman Fellow at Harvard for 1954-55, became Assistant Chief of Staff of *The Herald* (Melbourne), manager of radio station 3DB (Melbourne), and, in 1959, Sales Manager of The Herald and Weekly Times Limited, Melbourne, a senior post he still holds.

And that's one of the nicest success stories associated with any *Smith's* man. What a happy song and dance the old paper would have made of it, had it lived!

CHAPTER TWELVE

Hangman, What Are You Thinking Now?

Parson : I have something to tell you.
Condemned Man : Well (chuckle) break the noose gently.
— *Smith's Weekly*

Smith's always strove mightily to give its readers something quite different from the fare served up by the daily press. To do this it sought out, often with great patience and skill, what it called "The News Behind the News." The dailies of yore let the world know the simple facts — for example, that a murderer had been hung at such a time and such a place. *Smith's* felt its readers would be interested in knowing how the hangman felt as he pulled the lever, and what the condemned man thought as he stepped on to the trapdoor. This type of story was extremely hard to get, but *Smith's* reporters attacked with such determination and unabashed cheek that as often as not they brought back an exclusive piece well worth any man's fourpence.

All Australia was excited about the hanging of Melbourne murderer Angus Murray, set down for April 1924. The dailies in this case were marching every inch of the way to the gallows and missing apparently nothing.

Vainly *Smith's* Melbourne editor, Harry Maddison, "The Gimlet of Gun Alley," and one of the most brilliant crime reporters the Australian press ever produced, hunted for an exclusive *Smith's* angle. It occurred to him that while the whole world knew everything about the man to be hanged, from the colour of his eyes to the size of his appetite, not a thing was known about the second most important character in the drama — the hangman.

Maddison set himself the difficult double-barrelled task of (a) discovering the hangman's identity, and (b) probing his mind on how he felt about his task. Through important contacts he had in various Government Departments, Harry Maddison learnt that the official Victorian hangman was a man aged thirty who lived with his wife and children in a nice little house in North Melbourne. The chap had been a lieutenant in the First A.I.F. and earned his living as an engineer.

Harry took to shadowing the hangman who was gaunt and tall and of melancholy mien, just as a hangman should be, and learnt much about him, including the fact that his civil job returned him £2.9.0 a week. The man received a fee of £10 per hanging and 7/- per flagellation, he being the official flogger as well as executioner.

All this was fascinating enough but lacked the exciting morbid flavours that would stem from a mind-probe. Patiently Maddison took to riding in the same train as the hangman night and morning, and sitting first near him and then right beside him. Never a word spoken, mind you.

As a further refinement of approach march tactics he walked close to his quarry to and from the railway station, until he became accepted as just another antelope in the herd, and not a news hound on the prowl.

With nice judgement he opened a conversation with his man one evening on the train and was not rebuffed. It was natural the pair should stroll away from the station still chattering. Harry had the next step all carefully planned. As the pair drew level with the pub, the journalist took the hangman gently by the arm and steered him through a door, muttering words to the effect that he was enjoying the conversation so much he would like to continue it over a convivial glass.

Convivial glass indeed! Harry Maddison imagined that any hangman would be a heavy drinker because of the need to blot out all sorts of dreadful memories. He was prepared to souse his quarry and then milk him mentally for a front page special. The tall, gaunt hangman said he would take a shandy, and when he had slowly sunk that he declared "one is my issue," and prepared to go.

Harry Maddison was so disappointed that he snapped, "One shandy only. Oh, that be hanged for a yarn!"

The word "hanged" proved most unfortunate, for it had the hangman out of the door and away like a guilty soul fleeing Judgement Day.

Maddison's careful planning had failed dismally. He was left with a little bundle of facts which had some novelty, but they were not front page stuff likely to have people saying admiringly, "Cripes, I dunno how the old *Smith's* gets these stories!"

On the eve of the execution the paper printed what it had

CONDEMNED MAN *(tripping over rope)* TO HANGMAN: *"Struth, d'you want ter kill a bloke!"*

gathered, and that appeared to be the end of the tale. But *Smith's* was a paper to which the most amazing things were likely to happen, and in this matter there was an unexpected jackpot.

Maddison was sitting in his Flinders Street office on the afternoon of the day upon which Angus Murray was hanged, when he was told that a gentleman wanted to see him. Gloomily Harry said, "Send him in," then jumped up in amazement as through the door came his friend, the hangman, still tall and gaunt but no longer of melancholy mien. The man declared he had read *Smith's* story on himself and wished to say thanks for the write-up.

Chattily the fellow went on to say that he had had a very busy day in the punishment field. He had despatched Angus Murray at ten o'clock and then "administered a flogging" at one o'clock. The hanging had gone off without any fuss. Would Harry like to know what Angus Murray had to say as the noose was looped over his head?

Harry said he sure would like to know.

Angus Murray had said, "Carry on, Dig, not too tight!"

The hangman said that he did the work only for the extra income it brought him, and did not permit himself to have any

147

feelings. He had whipped thirty men, he declared, and added, "If I gave way to my feelings I would be as sorry for them as I would be at having to beat my own children."

But, really, the whole business of hanging and flogging wasn't really as cruel as some people made out — when handled in expert fashion, of course. "We don't use leather thongs any more," the expert declared cheerfully. "Our cats are made from light whipcord that has been soaked in water and partly dried. It hasn't the weight to do any real damage."

Thus *Smith's* got another successful exclusive which added to its reputation for novelty.

It was not surprising that when the paper got the tip through its elaborate intelligence network in May 1931, that the Assistant Chief Executioner of Great Britain was visiting Sydney *en vacance* it put its star investigator, John O'Donnell, on the trail. A hangman of such distinction must surely be an unusual mortal. What went on in his mind?

The quarry, when cornered, proved to be quite a surprise. He was a mild, tubby little chap with gold-rimmed specs, and a powerful sense of pride in his profession. He was, he claimed, in world class at his craft, having spent seventeen years "in the business," and he suggested his presence in Australia might quite likely give local governments a chance to get rid of any backlog of executions that might have built up. His fee was £20 per execution, plus fares to and from his ship.

O'Donnell told the man that New South Wales intended to abolish capital punishment, and the visitor was horrified. "You'll get your prisons filled with rogues and villains living at their ease," he predicted bitterly.

The British executioner kindly supplied some inside facts which, while not of actual use to the average man, were certainly interesting. Execution drops were calculated with mathematical precision (a hangman can never be an uneducated man, and do the work properly) according to height and weight, and range, in the visitor's experience, from six feet three inches to eight feet five inches.

Reading from his official log-book, the English hangman related how one Frederick Seddon (poisoned women with poison off flypapers) needed a fall of seven feet ten inches, whereas Edmund Tumbridge (pushed sweetheart into river) departed perfectly with seven feet three inches. And guess what the time lapse was between cell and death which created the record for the quickest execution in England? This was the case of Patrick

Herbert Mahon, deceased. Executioner was the distinguished visitor himself. Time was ten seconds.

Smith's was correct in estimating that details such as these were worth 4d, for sales on that story were excellent. But the paper did not stop at probing the minds of hangmen. It sought to learn (and tell its readers) what persons closely associated with celebrated criminals thought.

Early in 1923, *Smith's* became alert to the fact that Ned Kelly's mother, then aged ninety-five, was still alive but ailing. What did mother think of son in retrospect? (Ned had been hung in 1880). Bart Adamson was rushed away from Sydney office to quiz the old lady who was living quietly in Victoria. Bart, a great giant of a poet, with a voice like the bass pipe of an organ, was the paper's best man for inspiring confidence in old ladies.

The old lady proved to be very frail but remarkably bright. Her thoughts on Ned, when gathered together, made the following picture:

Ned was a great son. He was the only dark one of the family. All the rest were red-headed. They took after their father. But poor Ned was black like meself.

Constable Fitzpatrick was the cause of all the trouble. Ned would have made a great general in the World War just ended.

Mrs Kelly was proud of the final advice she had given Ned just before his execution: "Mind you die like a Kelly!" And did she have any final thoughts? "If I were young again, I'd give the world to own a motor-car, and the faster it went, the better I'd like it." Maybe the daring dash in Ned came from the parent who had given him his black hair.

Smith's intense interest, on behalf of its readers, in what celebrated people thought, led it to take a lively interest in Mr Squizzy Taylor, leader of the Melbourne underworld and the nearest approach to an Al Capone Australia ever developed. By September 1922, Squizzy had been in hiding from the police for a year, and most people were interested to know if he was still in the country. Popular opinion was that he was hiding out in Melbourne.

Jim Donald, the boxing writer, was ordered to go from Sydney down to Melbourne and ferret out the answers. There was a theory on *Smith's* that Jim, because of his squashed nose, would be acceptable in the lowest company and would be able to discover things a nice-looking reporter would never have a chance of learning.

Jim returned with a big claim for expenses and a fabulous story about how he had set up a secret interview with the legendary ex-jockey — Squiz was then five feet two inches and aged forty-five — and then the man who had organized the affair and was to have been the guide had been arrested and . . .

Smith's didn't take this defeat as most other papers might have done. It dusted off one of its poets, Bart Adamson who, if he didn't have a squashed nose like Jim Donald, did possess a sparkling imagination which could squeeze the best out of a story. Bart disappeared from Sydney aiming in a southerly direction and eventually returned with a story that could well be used as the basis of a modern James Bond thriller. He told of a complicated series of manoeuvres in Melbourne which resulted in his being ordered to stand alone, on a dark corner of Spring Street at a certain time on a certain night.

And so he stood there for ages with no one else in sight but a hopeless drunk. At the chilly hour of 2 a.m., who should come to life and sidle up to him but the drunk who had really been a secret guide in disguise, checking to make sure that Bart was alone. The drunk took Bart through a maze of streets and then handed him over to a beautiful young woman, who took him to an S.P. shop, where he was picked up by someone else, who took him for a long trip in a horse cab to a strange house, where he spoke to a queer old crone, who told him to shoot through back to Sydney and quit minding other people's business.

A guide, who allegedly led Bart back to the civilized section of Melbourne in the dawn light, assured the reporter that, although he had not been aware of the fact, he had had an interview with the Crime King?

What, what, what?

Yep, the old woman had been Squizzy Taylor in disguise.

Ah well, no one could say that Bart didn't come back with a story, which he did not hesitate to write. Squizzy saw it and wrote a pained letter to the paper asking why it didn't give him a wrap-up instead of a rap down. This proved to be a foolish move on the bandit king's part, for from that time on, *Smith's* took an abnormal interest in him and would eagerly print snippets of news supplied by characters who brought them from goals, sly grog joints, and houses of ill-fame.

After the police caught Squizzy he served a term in Pentridge Gaol, Melbourne, with *Smith's* making friendly and cheering comment from time to time. When Squiz was due to be released, *Smith's* felt it had the right to an exclusive interview and had a man at the gates with a pencil a'quiver as Taylor marched out.

Apparently Squizzy had been practising what he would say if ever he met a *Smith's* man, for he fired off a quite brilliant stream of abuse and threats. From what the reporter could gather, one of his paper's friendly stories had cost the criminal all his good conduct remissions. (It was probably the story about Squiz cleverly organizing tobacco supplies and messages to and from the outside world.)

In spite of the fellow's rudeness, *Smith's* continued to take a lively interest in his activities, following him in and out of jobs, on and off racecourses. Indeed the paper chased him right beyond the grave. When Squizzy was shot to death in a gun duel with Snowy Cutmore, who also expired from his wounds, *Smith's*, on 5 November 1927, sought to answer the bannered question, "Did Squizzy have a kink?"

It was reported with enthusiasm that all of Squizzy's remains did not go underground by any means.

The brain of this remarkable criminal was removed and sent to the Melbourne University Medical School, where scientific tests revealed that the man had been suffering from a brain disorder.

In saying its last farewell to Australia's Public Enemy No. 1, *Smith's* got in a final good hearty kick, "He had a heart as black as ever beat under the Southern Cross!" It never did pay to be cheeky to *Smith's,* whoever you were!

News behind the News in *Smith's* was not confined simply to what went on in and outside the brains of hangmen (local and foreign) and such types as Squiz Taylor of Melbourne.

There were times when *Smith's* was capable of making the News Behind the News out of news that probably didn't exist. On 10 August 1929 the paper came out with a front-page headline capable of making the tastebuds of the average Australian adult male of the time shudder and shake, "SEVEN YEARS HELL AS NAKED DRUDGE FOR ABORIGINES."

Never did a headline promise more. The story which followed that big, black exciting type was something less than might reasonably have been expected.

Smith's limpingly lisped that "persistent rumours had reached police" that what the headline claimed was true, and there was a chance it could be, by jingo! A ship called the *Douglas Mawson* had been wrecked in the Gulf of Carpentaria in March

1923, and who was to say a woman off that might not have been captured by natives and shockingly used?

Defending its headline desperately, *Smith's* insisted that the case could happen in real life, and recited the instance of one Mrs Barbara Thompson who, in the previous century, had been captured by natives in Queensland and become "the envy of the men and the bitter sport of the women." Maybe *Smith's* was extra hard-up for a front page that week.

The paper always took the liveliest interest in Nellie Melba while she lived, the main reason being that Claude McKay had been closely associated with her. *Smith's* was not prepared to let Nellie die a normal death, and in a News-Behind-The-News special in 1931 attributed her passing to the Curse of the Pharaohs.

How's this for a purple patch on a deceased diva?

Egypt, the old midden world, has laid its curse on the surging spark that was Melba in whom life throbbed and shouted. . . . Could she have sung once more, her lips would have said only the words that Anthony said once to Cleopatra, "I am dying, Egypt, dying." (She might also have said "Bull, by cripes!")

Said *Smiths's*:

Melba and her friends attributed the illness to an infection received in Cairo. But what the nature of this curse is that has come out of mysterious Egypt to drain the life force from the greatest soprano in the world, no man can say.

It is obvious that *Smith's* loved a touch of mystery and supplied it wherever possible to the undoubted delight of its large audience.

Why did Alfred Winbush, son of a wealthy English country family, choose to live in humble circumstances, often in penury, in the Australian bush when he might have collected £10,000 by just saying the word?

Smith's asked this fascinating question in May 1927, causing readers to catch their breaths in excited anticipation.

The secret lay in a little tin box in the form of documents. As Winbush lay dying he cried to a friend: "Burn the papers for heaven's sake, burn them!" The friend took them out of the tin box and burnt them.

"And so," said *Smith's* sadly, "the secret died with the burning."

With a bit of pushing here and there many *Smith's* stories could have been presented on stage as melodramas, which probably isn't so strange, considering that the paper was conducted by editors, most of whom had spent part of their lives in show biz and left big parts of their hearts round the footlights.

CHAPTER THIRTEEN

Unofficial History of the A.I.F.

Old Dig (in flooded trench) : If a bloke don't get pneumonia here, there's something wrong with his ruddy lungs!
—*Smith's Weekly*, 1930

The survivors of the First A.I.F. came marching home as *Smith's* was born in 1919, and the paper cheered itself hoarse from its cradle. The politicians and the masses cheered also and swore that the Diggers would be generously rewarded for their sacrifices and gallantry. Nothing would be too good for the widows and children of the 60,000 dead they cried. Nothing too good for the sick and the wounded.

Instinctively the paper seemed to realize that when the flags had been folded and packed away, and the politicians and civilians had dried their eyes and laundered their hankies the fine promises made in moments of emotion would fade, fade, fade.

Smith's developed an obsession about protecting the Digger and what it considered to be his rights, and throughout its thirty-two years of life never missed a single week in beating the drum to remind the nation of its everlasting responsibilities to its fighting men.

The paper had a considerable stack of sacred symbols and of these the Digger was ever the most admirable and untouchable. As *Smith's* pictured him, he was a diamond-dusted combination of Australian manhood, Australian courage, Australian humour, Australian sacrifice, and Australian mateship.

Every single week the paper honoured its concept of the Dig in poetry, prose, black-and-white art work, and gags. It hired Banjo Paterson to strike his lyre in his honour.

In time it created what was generally called "The *Smith's Weekly* Soldier." And there was a very curious phenomenon associated with this figure. It looked completely different when viewed from different angles.

Many senior army officers saw the *Smith's Weekly* soldier as "an undisciplined larrikin who would not button his tunic, delighted in insulting his officers and dodging his proper duties, and made a virtue out of going AWL and resisting Military Police."

Such officers cursed *Smith's* for having created such an image, which they claimed, many young Diggers in the Second A.I.F. insisted on imitating to the detriment of good order and discipline.

People looking at the *Smith's Weekly* soldier from another angle saw a most admirable personality. An easy-going, fun loving, joke-spinning, intensely individualistic chap who had a mind of his own and a healthy disrespect for pomposity and red tape. (After all we were a civilian army, weren't we?) He was always right in the front line when there was fighting to be done, even though he was a bit careless about returning from leave on time. And, of course, situations of the most extreme adversity always brought out the best humour in him.

When *Smith's* adopted the Digger as its favourite son it also adopted the attitude that he could do no wrong, and anyone who said he could was a bloody, lying cow. *Smith's* angrily spat, from a great height, on anyone who had hurt the Dig, was hurting the Dig, and might, in the future, do him some mischief.

The paper's blind admiration for its Digger symbol was often quite ludicrous in the early 1920s, particularly when viewed with a modern, sophisticated eye. Diggers with complaints rushed to *Smith's* with them, and were warmly received in an atmosphere where the Dig was always right, irrespective of the facts. From a modern viewpoint it was all unbelievably naïve.

In its issue of 19 April 1919 *Smith's* screamed with horror at what the prison authorities had done with a Digger incarcerated in the Darlinghurst Gaol, Sydney. The Digger prisoner had been forced to work in the gaol kitchen ALONGSIDE GERMAN PRISONERS! Worse than that — HE HAD BEEN DETAILED TO ACT AS A WAITER TO GERMANS!

Smith's fairly wept. "It is infamous that this good soldier should, for his lapse, be forced to act as waiter to a gang of blackguardly Huns. The gaol authorities took it upon themselves to humiliate him to the dust." The modern mind immediately seeks to know what particular crime had put the "good soldier" into prison where he could be humiliated "to the dust" by working beside blackguardly Huns.

Tucked away quietly in *Smith's* story we find the answer. All that "good soldier" had done was get himself convicted for

These men are convicted of having served their Country.

inciting troops to mutiny on the troop carrier *Somali*. As far as the paper was concerned, that mutiny business was beside the point. No Dig was low enough, whatever he did, to have to work near a Hun.

Smith's sure did hate Huns and could work itself into hysterics over anything German. It regularly exploded with rage at "William Hohenzollern, Greatest Criminal in History" and charged and recharged him with the death of 7,857,087 soldiers and 9,185,523 civilians. This perhaps was a reasonable enough attack, considering the emotional climate of the immediate post-World War I years. But the paper surely could have been a little more merciful than it was in attacking the Australian Government for permitting a Hun to be quartered with wounded Australian soldiers in March 1920.

The German in question was Father Jergen, a minister of religion who had been interned during the war for alleged "disloyal utterances." When, with the war over, the internment camp had been closed down, Father Jergen had been in need of treatment for an eye complaint and pyorrhoea.

Smith's claimed that the authorities had sent the man to the Fourth Australian General Hospital (military) at Randwick, Sydney, in which Australian soldiers were receiving treatment.

Smith's did mention that Father Jergen had been isolated under armed guard in a small wooden building well away from the hospital proper. However, it still demanded to know, "What is the Government going to do about it?"

While it is possible to laugh at *Smith's* for this style of uninhibited screaming, you must raise your hat for what it did for the Digger. It provided the pioneer thinking behind much of the modern repatriation programme of which Australia is so proud these days.

It identified and appreciated "shellshock" early in 1920 when many an expert considered that any man whose nerves broke down under continued battle strain was a bit of a dingo, and more deserving of a kick in the tail than sympathy. Having decided that "shellshock" should be treated as war wounds and not treated with scorn, *Smith's* took dramatic action to demonstrate its belief.

Sir James Joynton Smith announced that he was handing over his home at Coogee, a mansion capable of containing forty bed cases, "where those suffering from war strain would get the attention they needed." To this generous gift, Sir Joynton added £15,000 "to get the place going." All added up it was a more concrete demonstration of goodwill towards the Digger than was shown by the majority of people who criticized *Smith's* for its noisy championing of the returned soldier.

Early in 1920 *Smith's* set up what it called "The Soldiers and Sailors Parliament," with a laywer, W. Bede Dalley at its head. Dalley and assistants provided free advice to Diggers in need of it and wrote dramatic stories for the paper whenever they encountered cases of dirty deeds against Diggers or their dependents.

From the cases which came before this "Parliament," *Smith's* got a unique insight into Digger problems. The paper saw as early as July 1920 that returned soldiers would not have the life expectancy of civilians, even though they appeared healthy enough on discharge. Those years of strain and exposure to mud, cold, flies, and bullets had subtly undermined health, *Smith's* claimed.

Critics sneered at this attitude in 1920 when *Smith's* began demanding what it called a "compassionate pension" for sick returned soldiers who could not prove their condition due to war service. The paper also argued that the old Digs were more likely to contract tuberculosis than ordinary people, and demanded special consideration for them if they developed it post war.

By 1934, it was clear that *Smith's* had been right in claiming that the returned soldier had left many years of his life in the trenches. In that year Diggers were dying at the rate of 2,000 a year at the average age of forty-five, while the average non-returned man was living to an average of over sixty years. By 1936, *Smith's* was able to point out that 8,000 Diggers were dying each year still at the average age of forty-five.

"The biblical three score years and ten missed the A.I.F.," cried *Smith's*. "Yet these men were the finest specimens in a virile race!"

Smith's and such organizations as the R.S.L. and A.I.L.A. can take credit for having forced the Federal Government to grant T.B. pensions and early retirement pensions to Diggers, irrespective of whether they could prove their troubles due to war service or not.

The paper would have died happy had it passed away knowing that it had been the inspiration behind the formation of the Legacy movement. It did not play a specific part in the birth of that magnificent organization but it did begin advocating the special care for the children of dead Diggers as early as 1919. And, perhaps, its advocacy played some unconscious part in moulding the thoughts of the men who actually launched Legacy.

In pre-Legacy days, *Smith's* fought for the wives and children of deceased Diggers, providing them with legal advisors and financial aid. In February 1920 *Smith's* went to war on behalf of Mrs Katherine Baxter, whose husband and two sons had all gone to the war and been casualties. Her story was that, in the absence of her menfolk, she had taken the lease of a Sydney residential in April 1917, and had run it for two years. Strikes and the great flu epidemic had damaged the business and caused the rent to fall into arrears. Owners of the premises had repossessed them, leaving the poor woman poverty stricken. The woman had been advised she had no redress. In desperation she went to *Smith's* which, on investigation, found she was protected by a moratorium. This assistance from *Smith's* was worth £1,000 to the woman.

Victories like that were commonplace for *Smith's*, which always maintained a permanent staff of investigators and advocates to handle Digger problems.

Smith's had a special eye for the Digger who was given a soldier settler block of land and, as early as 1919, was suspicious that the Federal Government was trying to do the settling too cheaply. It engaged the poet, Major "Banjo" Paterson, in that year, to watch the interests of the Digger on the land and keep the public informed of the problems of settlement.

Paterson had no difficulty in finding targets to fire at. In May 1919 the Federal Government decided after a short test that Cecil Grice, ex-schoolteacher with four children and a "stainless war record," was no good as a farmer, and kicked him off his soldier block.

The Government learnt that its actions were being closely and critically observed when *Smith's* opened fire on that deal.

Smith's warned that Digger settlers were being given impossible problems to solve. It said that blocks were often too small to be economic, and capital assistance was too niggardly. All this judgement proved to be sound by 1935, when Digger settlers by the hundred found that, after fifteen years of toil, they owed more than when they had started, and that interest was piling on interest to suffocate them.

Closer settlement stemmed from this mess, and while government officials would probably claim credit for having nutted out the idea, soldier settlers almost to a man gave *Smith's* the credit.

Occasionally Banjo Paterson would scribble a few verses in praise of the old Dig. They were pretty poor Paterson, but popular enough in the immediate post-war. Here's a lump of *Cassidy's Epitaph* :

> Here lies a bloke who's just gone west,
> A number one Australian.
> He took his gun and did his best
> To mitigate the alien.

(According to Banjo this Cassidy grogged on terribly and enjoyed a punch-up with anyone who would be in it, because life without drink or fight was no good to him. Nevertheless he was a real Dig.)

> But when St Peter calls the roll
> Of men of proved tenacity,
> You'll find the front rank, right-hand man
> Will answer: "Here . . . Cassidy."

This was an early prototype of one aspect of the *Smith's Weekly* soldier (June 1919 to be exact). And it could be that Banjo was responsible for a tremendous amount of heartbreak among brass hats in World War II.

Smith's printed tens of thousands of Digger stories. The one of which it was most proud was published in July 1923, and attracted world attention. The paper discovered that one Trooper Rolph was doomed to spend the rest of his life lying in a tepid bath in the Randwick Military Hospital because he had lost his skin and it would not grow again. Rolph had been severely hit by mustard gas. For some unusual reason the chemistry of his skin had been utterly destroyed. He had to lie in a tepid bath because the water supported part of his weight. He could not bear the agony of lying on a bed.

The story of "The Man In The Bath" as printed by *Smith's* was reprinted round the world as an indictment against gas warfare, and the horror of it touched millions. Perhaps the case of Trooper Rolph of World War I played some little part in preventing gas being employed in World War II.

Smith's story was read to Rolph as he lay in his bath and he insisted on dictating a letter to the paper. He said that he had been greatly heartened to discover he had not been forgotten by the world. For a long time he had been praying for death, he said. But, having heard *Smith's* story which posed him as an example of pure Digger courage, he felt that it was proper he should battle on as an example to others who could possibly benefit from anything they might see in his case.

Many of *Smith's* critics felt the paper was impertinent for the way it pried into the private affairs of individuals in distress. Yet, strangely, *Smith's* prying often produced dramatic and worthwhile results. The William Dobell case, mentioned elsewhere in this book, is perhaps the classic example of all.

Down the years, *Smith's* zealously guarded the rights and reputations of Diggers both alive and dead. It fought grimly and bitterly for proper recognition for "John Monash — The Greatest Digger of Them All."

"When the Prince of Wales drove through Melbourne," *Smith's* snarled, "John Monash, who had commanded the Australian Army Corps in France, stood on the kerb and watched."

Monash was grateful to the paper for its attempts to keep the Digger image clean and bright. By 1930 the Depression was making men bitter, and there was a sourness developing against the Diggers for the hard-earned privileges they were receiving — preference to returned soldiers in employment, war service homes, finance, and so on.

Irritated by this trend, *Smith's* offered its front page to Monash to defend the Digger. The great general went in to the attack hard, blasting at "catchpenny scribblers" who had been seeking to brand "the greatest shock troops in the world as boastful and lecherous."

Monash wrote a series of articles for *Smith's* and insisted that the paper expressed Diggers' opinions "in great measure." That statement remained the paper's prime sword and buckler against those who sought to damn it for creating an artificial atmosphere around the returned soldier.

Smith's gave its front page to the defence of Monash. With equal willingness it would give the same place, same space, to the lowest private if he had been wronged. In February 1932 the paper devoted its front page to the case of a soldier who, for the previous sixteen years, had been branded a deserter.

"Deserter!" *Smith's* commented, "Bitterest word in the dictionaries of war, the brand of Judas, last taunt in the shameful brotherhood of cowardice and treachery. For sixteen years it has wrung in the ears of a soldier's wife and a soldier's mother. The soldier had gone missing in France and had been proclaimed a deserter by a Board of Inquiry."

The important point was that, after sixteen years, proof had turned up that the soldier had been killed in action, he had not been a deserter; he had been a hero. *Smith's* saw that the record was rectified. It was the only Australian newspaper that made any fuss about the matter.

It let out a roar which must have been heard in Siam when, in 1925, it discovered that a Soldiers' Memorial of five stained glass windows for St Augustine's Church of England, Hamilton, Brisbane, had been MADE IN GERMANY!

"Insult to the dead!" thundered *Smith's* which claimed that the biggest stained glass firm in Brisbane could not get enough orders to keep its designer busy. (The German windows had cost £630).

The R.S.L. was brought in on the affair, and *Smith's* was able to announce triumphantly, "No German war windows for Queensland. *Smith's* wrecks repulsive idea."

Smith's felt that Australia had done more than her fair share in the winning of World War I, and considered that all the Allies should be grateful to her. Consequently when France slapped a supertax on Australian butter *Smith's* was livid with indignation at such meanness. "France Sells Its Soul For A Pound Of Butter," it told the world, and it further made its point by writing an open letter to France:

> For 500 years and more you have hidden yourself behind the image of a pretty girl—*La Belle France*. Now behind the music we hear the cash registers clicking and the dirty little fingers grubbing.

We have seen at last the real France, which has traduced the dead Australians who lie beneath the peasants' feet in Flanders. *La Belle France* — the pretty fiction of petticoats and lace — looks ugly when she haggles over the bodies of dead Diggers!

When defending Australia or the Diggers, *Smith's* was not afraid to fight dirty.

From its beginning, it invited old soldiers to send in original stories about their wartime experiences. Quickly a fascinating weekly feature evolved — little Digger anecdotes spiced with joke drawings by Cecil Hartt, "The Digger Artist."

In October 1924 the feature was given the inspired title "Unofficial History of the A.I.F." and, under that bright banner, became probably the most widely read weekly section of the paper.

Many famous Digger artists drew for that page. Frank Dunne followed Cec Hartt and became, perhaps, even better known than Cec as a depicter of the Dig at work, play, war, and AWL. Charlie Hallett, Lance Mattinson, and Norman Mitchell all starred as "Digger Artists."

The one essential of a *Smith's* Digger joke drawing was that it should demonstrate one of the Digger's virtues — his indifference to danger, orders, officers, rank, and discomfort; his scorn of the foe, overwhelming odds, military police, and so on.

The most commonly used formula was that of a grinning Dig giving the retort discourteous to a sour-faced officer thus:

Officer (to Dig shaving in open): Well, my man, do you always shave outside?

Digger: My oath! You don't think I'm fur-lined do yer?

Old soldiers loved that sort of fun. It made them feel they had been real devils over the other side, and it delighted them to show the jokes to their wives and children.

Before any other newspaper *Smith's* had been able to realize that the Australian soldier had gone away to the Great War not as a formal warrior but as a free swinging civilian in uniform, having a world tour and a fight at the same time; and that the same chap had returned home still a civilian at heart but with a nostalgia for his gay soldiering days.

The paper catered with enthusiasm for the nostalgia factor. Probably few of the countless anecdotes published under the "Unofficial History of the A.I.F." were gospel true. But they had the right flavour to waft the old Dig reading them, back into the *estaminet* near Amiens where he had winked at. . . .

Here's a typical Unofficial History anecdote:

After the Armistice the troops were sent to Le Havre in a car-de-luxe of the *'8 chevaux ou 40 hommes'* brand. The weather being cold, the food crook, and the journey taking anything up to four days, the troops arrived at their destination in a somewhat peevish mood.

Our crowd was reported to have busted open some railway trucks at Abbeville and helped themselves to cognac, and the O.C. No. 5 Company at the Australian delousing camp was deputed to intercept the train at Revelles and search it. He carried out his duties faithfully by telling the O.C. train his orders and saying "I shall be back in twenty minutes with my staff and I will search thoroughly. If I find any cognac, heaven help anyone found with it."

When the search was made the honour of the A.I.F. was vindicated. Next morning the O.C. No. 5 found a bottle of cognac on his bunk — Base Wallah.

Every nostalgic ingredient short of Mademoiselle from Armentières was in that mix. And there was free grog all round, even for the officer!

On occasions *Smith's* would have a smack at the true history of the A.I.F. or at "How our sixty-three V.C.s—one-ninth of those issued — were won." On such occasions there was no romanticizing around. Someone of the calibre of General Gordon Bennett would be called in to give his name to one more recital of how the Second, Third, and Fourth Battalions of the First A.I.F. went into the attack on Lone Pine, Gallipoli, with sixty-five officers and two thousand and eighteen men and came out victorious but with only eight officers and six hundred and sixty men remaining. It made magnificent reading. It made old soldiers proud.

Smith's had good reason to believe that it had settled for all time the much argued question, "Who really did shoot down Baron von Richthofen alias the Red Knight, ace pilot of the German Air Force?" Richthofen, with seventy-eight kills to his credit, had been shot down in April 1918. History was tending to give the honour to Canadian Air Force Captain Roy Brown.

In August 1934 the war diary of an Australian infantry officer, Lieutenant Travers, M.C. was found in an old deed box in a store house and handed to *Smith's*, "the Diggers paper," in case there was anything in it worth printing. The diary contained an eyewitness account of the shooting down of Baron von Richthofen and stressed that the Red Knight's plane had been hit by Australian ground fire. And where was Captain Roy Brown at the time? According to *Smith's*: "Like the snow shoe rabbit — invisible but for his little pink eyes."

The paper published details from the diary. Lieutenant Travers, M.C. saw the story and came forward. *Smith's* began a sifting of evidence and spoke with scores of witnesses. Finally it sent all the details it had gathered to the British Legion Journal in England for independent judgement. The Journal set up a panel which ruled out the claims of Captain Roy Brown and judged that Baron von Richthofen had been shot down by Gunner Robert Bule, No. 3801, Fifty-third Battery, Australian Field Artillery. This assessment has never been seriously challenged since.

The coming of World War II was like a shot in the arm for *Smith's* which was automatically accepted by the 1939-45-type fighting Australian as his official journal. The paper set about banging the war drum with a zest that stirred the blood of old and new Digs and irritated to screaming point politicians and high service officers.

The paper reported in the second month of the new war that the young Diggers were the "same old breed" as the first lot, and therefore the country was safe. Political leaders were given a belting for "lagging behind the beat of the nation's pulse." A *Smith's* reporter who rushed up to Bathurst Gaol to check if internees incarcerated there were "comfy," caused editorial pleasure by reporting they were having a pretty cold time.

Having trained for the entire peace period between the two wars at shouting "Hooray for the Diggers and damnation to his enemies," *Smith's* was immediately in fine voice when the shooting started.

When the first contingent of the Second A.I.F. sailed in late 1939, *Smith's* engaged ex-Prime Minister Billy Hughes, "The Little Digger" and Australia's Elder Statesman, to write its front page farewell.

While the boys went to fight overseas, *Smith's* devoted itself to fighting for them at home, which meant belting verbal hell out of anyone who even looked like impeding the war effort.

Over in America, Colonel Charles A. Lindberg, first man to fly the Atlantic solo and an old favourite of *Smith's,* made a suggestion which the Diggers' Paper interpreted as meaning that the United States should get together with Germany and "clean up all the small and decadent countries of the earth."

Smith's put up a headline: "What A Louse Was Lindberg." Under that it made a suggestion that America "should remove

Lindberg with a fine tooth comb and, after that, crack him!"
When this paper fought a war it fought a total war, by cripes.

At home it took umbrage at the attitude of the religious sect,
Jehovah's Witnesses, which preached against the war. The paper
demanded that the organization — "a world-wide, high-power,
sect of religious cranks," it called them — should be banned.
Week after week the paper attacked with skill and tenacity until,
finally, the sect was banned for the duration.

In October 1940, in a moment of patriotic fervour, *Smith's*
decided that Billy Hughes, then aged seventy-six, "The Little

Billy Hughes.

Digger" himself, was the man to lead Australia to victory as in
World War I. A reporter and photographer went to Billy's home
at Linfield, Sydney, to ask the elder statesman how he felt about
such a proposition.

Billy was quite enthralled that anybody should be entertaining
such an idea, and after a decent period of koff-koffing and ah-
humming declared, "I will not count any task given me too great
or too small."

No one could prove from that statement that he was angling
for the Prime Ministership. But I know he was ready to jump at
it because I was the reporter who did the quizzing.

Billy felt it would be a good thing if the photographer took some shots which would demonstrate that, though he had been touched by seventy-six summers, he was still a very active operator and not likely to fail physically under stress.

The elder statesman collected an ancient canvas bag containing three irons and a tatty old wood and, leading the photographer and me out on to a tennis court, began posing in what he apparently imagined was a demonstration of war-winning vigour. He waved a tennis racket to indicate his all-roundedness and photographer, Bill Brindle, the calmest man in the business, shot picture after picture without the suggestion of a smile.

Smith's duly came out with a powerful piece headed, "Nation Looks To Billy Hughes For Guidance." It said that Mr Hughes stood steady to serve his adopted country "with all that was in him." It quoted in heavy type, "I will not count any task given me as too great or too small." With these bold utterances went a series of action pictures which carried their own message. Alas, for once *Smith's* had misjudged the desires of the Australian people, and Billy was not called upon to lead the nation.

Throughout World War II *Smith's* cheered for the Digs and jeered at those it felt were not doing the right thing by the boys. It took a man-sized dislike to Mr Frank Forde, Minister for the Army. That good man delivered himself into the paper's cruel hands by permitting himself to be photographed, visiting troops in New Guinea in shorts, safari jacket, and with his topee on back to front. What the artists did in caricaturing that curious rig made Australia laugh and the poor Minister squirm.

The Federal Government would not forgive *Smith's* for its gadfly tactics and would not permit the paper to send a war correspondent to the front areas. Cheekily *Smith's* appointed the poet, Ronald McCuaig as its "Official War Correspondent, Somewhere in Sydney." Each week McCuaig, who could write delightful light satire, turned in a mock report which neatly peeled the skin off the politicians who held him in chains.

However, *Smith's* didn't really need an official correspondent in the field. All the young men on its staff had gone off to war, and almost everyone of them sent in stories regularly. It was a miracle that not one of the hundreds of stories posted to *Smith's* from the field was blocked by censors. These staff men serving in the slit trenches and in the cockpits of planes were able to report the war more intimately than did the official newspaper correspondents who were obliged to spend most of their time hanging round base headquarters waiting for official handouts.

Smith's got stacks of exclusives. One of 1942 vintage which was reproduced widely overseas goes as follows:

Here is told the amazing fact of a Digger who, to all intents and purposes, had passed into eternity; who returned from the brink of the grave into which he was being rolled. It is the closest thing to a resurrection from the dead in the 1942 years that have passed since the first Christmas.

It is related by a member of *Smith's* editorial staff who is an officer of the A.I.F. Names quoted are those who played parts in this real life drama, and are not fictitious.

THE MOST AMAZING STORY OF THE WAR!

Just before Christmas 1942, there wasn't any peace and goodwill round Sanananda way. There was mud, heat, mosquitoes, hate, and the strong, sweet smell of death.

"A" Company, Thirty-six Bn. attached to the Seventh Division, A.I.F., had attacked an unsuspectedly strong Nip position just forward of Kessel's. A well-placed Woodpecker and two LMGs had driven our boys back with heavy casualties. Seven men were posted missing, and as the withdrawal had been for only a couple of hundred yards there was little hope for them.

Three days later a corporal of "A" Company volunteered to make a lone patrol into the Nip lines to locate the Woodpecker and LMGs. He couldn't find them, but he returned with information that an Australian body was lying in a Jap slit trench under the corpses of two very high Nips. Accompanied by a strecher bearer he went out and carried the body back to his own perimeter.

Padre N. G. Anderson, chaplain of the Thirty-Sixth Bn., formerly Presbyterian minister at Moruya, New South Wales, was asked to perform burial rites. He ordered his batman to prepare a grave inside the wire. The grave was almost ready when the Padre arrived. The body lay beside it. No dead man is a pleasant sight after the jungle heat and the flies had worked on him. The one beside the grave was unusually horrible. The head was swollen to almost twice normal size. The eyes, wide open, stared fixedly. The body, clad only in tattered green shirt, was thin as a wafer and grey as dawn light.

Padre Anderson felt under the shirt for the identity discs that should have been on the chest. There were none. Placing a hand under the hip, the Padre rolled the body on to its stomach. As he did so he had a queer sensation that all life had not gone out of it.

"Do you think this man is really dead?" he asked his batman who was busy digging.

"Looks as if you're going troppo, too, Padre," the sweating batman commented.

Still the padre was not satisfied. He sent for the battalion M.O., Captain W. J. Pullen. The doctor took one look at the grey still form and shook his head. However, he placed his stethoscope against the shirt.

"Good God," he shouted, "the heart's still beating." Hurriedly the body was carried from the graveside to the company first aid post. After half an hour the soldier had been cleaned up and his main wound located — a bullet had entered his right ear and stopped at the base of his skull. He was given a few hours at most to live.

Nothing more could be done for him. A small group stood beside the stretcher discussing his identity. He certainly wasn't a member of "A" Company. General opinion was that he was from Seventh Division Cavalry.

In the middle of the discussion a tiny voice squeaked "I'm one of you!"

Everyone spun around. The body still lay stiff and grey. The glazed eyes still stared into space, but the lips were moving very, very slightly.

"What's your name?" asked the Padre.

"Gordon!"

That was the name of one of the "A" Company men posted missing after the attack three days earlier.

"What's your number?"

The squeaky voice whispered an NX number. It was Gordon's number.

But Gordon had weighed more than thirteen stone, and this man wasn't more than eight. Several men from Gordon's Company were called in and also his company commander. All agreed the man was not Gordon. The voice squeaked out the nicknames of numerous numbers of "A" company while the eyes still focussed on the canvas roof of the tent.

"What happened to you?" the man was asked.

"I went in with the attack. Then I remember coming to consciousness with Nips tearing off my boots and pants. They ripped off my steel hat and hurt my head. I groaned and they bashed me with the helmet until I passed out again. The second time I came to I was alone and very thirsty. There was a Nip slit trench near by. I crawled to it hoping there was water in the bottom and fell in. I was so weak I couldn't get out. A 25-pounder barrage from our guns came over and shells fell all around me. Then came a mortar barrage. Two Nips jumped into the trench on top of me. A mortar bomb hit the lip of the slit and killed them both. Their bodies saved me."

"Do you know where the machine guns are?"

"They were moved this morning."

"In which direction were they taken?"

"How was my body lying when I was discovered?"

"Head north, feet south."

"The guns were taken west. The Nips stepped across my slit trench from right to left."

The voice stopped. For the first time the eyes closed. Obviously death was near. Next morning the Digger's heart was stronger than ever. He was moved back to an advanced dressing station where he was again placed to one side to die quietly. His heart beat even more strongly.

From the ADS he was sent back to a main dressing station where the bullet was removed from the base of his skull. Within a few days he was recovering rapidly, and soon after he was evacuated to the mainland.

Eighteen months later, in Martin Place, Sydney, Padre Anderson met the man he set out to bury on the Sanananda Trail. "The body" was thirteen stone again and perfect in all respect except for a deafness in the right ear.

"Did you know I almost buried you?" asked the Padre.

"Know it! I heard every word you said to the gravedigger. I couldn't speak then, but I wasn't worried. I only hoped you'd get it over quick. Then the things the flies put on me wouldn't worry me any more. Guess it was the merriest Christmas I ever had!"

After World War II, *Smith's* sought to do for the new batch of returned Digs the watchdog job it had done for their fathers. It set up a very large team of special advisors and advocates, and any Digger who wanted his case fought with Repat or in the private world had only to call on the paper, and he got expert action without having to spend a penny.

Clive Robinson, who had been one of *Smith's* bright young men in the infantry, returned to civilian life with a curious obsession. He contended, and he would argue the point endlessly, that all Australian injured by ill usage while prisoners of war under the Japanese should receive compensation. And dependants of prisoners dying from ill-usage should also be compensated, he said.

At editorial conferences Clive's advocacy of the point became a joke. He should have lost faith in his strange idea but wouldn't, or couldn't.

An early president of the Eighth Division Association was a lift driver. Clive haunted the unfortunate man's lift urging him to back the compensation idea.

Claude McKay, *Smith's* Editor-in-Chief, finally broke under the pressure. At any rate, in Editorial conference one day, he suddenly got an odd look in his eye and suggested that Clive go and have a chat with "Young Joe Starke," the Sydney barrister who had been closely associated with the League of Nations in Geneva before the war and had established himself as an authority on International Law.

Joe listened to the proposition and to Robinson's amazement and delight said that under the Geneva Convention, injured P.O.W.s would have a very real claim for compensation.

Did *Smith's* start roaring with its front page when it got that message! Digger organizations took up the cry, and it is now history that the Federal Government arranged compensation as Clive Robinson had always claimed it should.

The Eighth Division boys held a very gay dinner to celebrate the victory, and Clive Robinson of *Smith's Weekly* was the guest of honour. Everyone present sought to give Clive a drink, and being a do-or-die infanteer he battled on bravely. He now claims his memories of that evening include a distant voice moving that Mr Clive Robinson be paid one per cent of all compensation received and massed voices shouting "aye." But he never has been able to find the man who moved the motion or anyone who remembers voting for it.

CHAPTER FOURTEEN

"Have You Eaten the Forbidden Fruit, Sir?"

Greek : How you enjoy da Queensland mud crab?
Dad : The inside was bonzer but, cripes, the crust was baked a bit 'ard!

— *Smith's Weekly,* 1921

If, at the start of World War II, you came across something extra odd in Australia like, say, a Japanese running a hospital for sick goldfish in Brisbane, there was only one thing you could do about it — Tell *Smith's Weekly!* While all newspapers these days are engaged in a desperate pursuit of the offbeat story, *Smith's* had the field almost entirely to itself between 1919 and 1939.

That goldfish story, for instance, was a *Smith's* exclusive (8 April 1933). Mr A. Suzuki, official interpreter to the Police Courts in Brisbane, conducted the hospital. He maintained special water tanks packed with water plants imported from Japan and, said *Smith's,* ninety-eight per cent of the seven hundred and fifty sick Brisbane pet fish which passed through annually, in time went back to their own private bowls and pools full of rude health.

Smith's, you see, had a rare capacity for caring about anything odd — animal, vegetable, mineral, or human — and eagerly publicized such things.

In the early 1920s a passing cow calved in the back yard of the Crown Hotel, Rocklea, Brisbane, and then went on her merry way, leaving a baby bull calf to get on in the world as best he could. Licensee Jack Abercrombie found the little fellow and, with the kindly instinct of a publican who was not a sinner, gave him a drink of beer. By July 1925 Brownie the Rocklea bull was worthy of a story in *Smith's.* Mr Abercrombie, through the paper, proudly challenged any three men in the world to match his pet at beer drinking. Brownie could swallow five gallons in five minutes from either pot or bottle, boasted Mr Abercrombie.

Smith's called for brave men to beat the beast but no one, alas stepped forward.

Smith's loved printing challenges of any sort. In 1927 it sponsored the claims of Mr Robert Capper Bray, J.P., of Coff's Harbour, New South Wales, to be Australia's Champion Eater.

Mr Bray, a businessman and lay preacher of Coff's Harbour, could, according to an admiring *Smith's,* eat at a sitting a suckling pig (crackling and all), half a butterbox of corned beef sandwiches, fifteen plates of ham and eggs (with two eggs per plate), nineteen helpings of chicken, ham, tongue, and salad, with a case of grapes to top off the repast. All these items Mr Capper Bray had eaten at a Coff's Harbour ball. He could have eaten a further twenty plates of chicken, ham, and tongue but the supply had run out.

Smith's insisted that the gastronomic giant was slim, of medium height, and only forty years old. "He can go for days without sleep or food," said *Smith's,* "and ordinarily he isn't a big eater, but he has never known what it is like to have enough to eat. . . ."

Smith's looked as though it had dug up a genuine challenger when it produced Mr Percy Danby of Parkes, New South Wales, who weighed twenty-six stone but, sadly, the match never did come off. The paper at first thought it had uncovered one of the biggest men in the world in Percy but, on investigation, found that Tom Jennings of Tasmania was far bigger at thirty-two stone ten lb.

One thing *Smith's* could never do was let a situation like this rest.Was the Tasmanian the heaviest man in the world? A worldwide round-up conducted by the paper pointed to Mr Leo Whitton of Canada, fifty stone, as No. 1 weight carrying mortal. And the heaviest man in history? *Smith's* settled for David Lambert of London (died 1828) fifty-two stone eleven lb.

The paper regarded unusual people and their private affairs as a natural diet for its readers and it was quite ruthless in publishing the facts. In 1930 someone in the office decided that the young men of Australia would surely be interested in a "form guide" of the unattached heiresses in the country. As a result the private details of most of the nation's wealthy, single young women were tabulated and analysed — hair, skin, figure, income, and any other important item.

Here are a couple of sample pieces:

If it be true that a little widow is a dangerous thing then Mrs Cleve Kidd, only daughter of the late Mr N. V. McKay of Sunshine Harvester fame, is a positive menace. Income £1,000 a week. Hair auburn. Skin dazzling white. Hobbies — bridge, tennis, golf. . . .

Australia's largest heiress is Miss Isobel Reid. Weight twenty stone. Good singing voice. Some skill as a vet. surgeon. . . .

This was the unexpected sort of stuff that delighted *Smith's* admirers. And it was something the daily newspapers either wouldn't use or couldn't think up.

In February 1934 every daily paper in Australia was recording the fact that Krishnamurti, the young Hindu who had visited Australia in 1925 claiming to be a reincarnation of Christ, was back on a second visit. *Smith's* readers were conscious that the paper had blistered Krishnamurti savagely in 1925, calling him a "notorious nigger moron" and claiming he was the foolish tool of "cranks, dupes, and humbugs."

How would *Smith's* handle his second arrival in Sydney? The paper went for a long shot and decided to question the young prophet on his sex life, if it could get him to receive a reporter. The idea worked beyond expectation.

On a veranda of a house at Mosman, Sydney, the reporter found Krishnamurti sitting quietly in the sun, and fired at him the question:

"Have you ever eaten the forbidden fruit?"

The young Indian didn't even blink as he replied, "Of course. I am only human. Sex is only natural. Our whole structure is based on it." He said he wasn't married and that he would never marry because once you married you possessed, and possession was the end of love.

In 1934 all that was a king-size scoop in Australia. Having found that Krishnamurti no longer claimed divinity, but merely the status of "prophet," *Smith's* became kindly disposed towards him as it was towards most clergymen, particularly those with a touch of the rebel in them.

If the paper had a pet parson it was surely Padre Herbert Hayes of Mernda, Victoria, the *enfant terrible* of the Anglican Church in Victoria.

The good Padre, a charming, bubbling, chubby man held views which were certainly controversial. He supported nudism on the grounds that people wore clothes only as a punishment for what went on in the garden of Eden.

Smith's was quick to give him space to put forward his views. The church authorities frowned mightily. Padre Hayes produced a book of poems which *Smith's* publicized on its front page, quoting one poem — "A Bishop's Punishment" — at length:

> Squeeze his mitre
> Tighter and tighter.
> Burst all his veins
> Squeeze out his brains.
> How his eyes stare,
> Through bloody hair.
> Imps burn his nose,
> Red as a rose.
> Pound his fat belly
> Into a jelly.
> With a rusty pin
> Score all his skin.
> Strip him quite bare
> Singe all his hair.
> Roast his entrails
> Tear out his nails.
> Pluck out his tongue
> Let it be hung
> To be used as a bell
> In the service of hell
> And if nothing is worse
> Let him read this grim verse.

This publicity did not endear the cheery Padre to the Church dignitaries and, in the following years, after a deal of bickering the Padre stood trial before an Ecclesiastical Court on charges of "conduct disgraceful to a clergyman and productive of scandal and evil report." In this modern age it is doubtful if church authorities would have taken the Padre's whimsical approach to matters spiritual and temporal as seriously as they were taken in 1935.

There was in *Smith's* a trace of snobbery in that it was fascinated by anyone connected with the nobility and with great wealth. But there had to be an odd angle. As a result, *Smith's* during its lifetime printed a multitude of stories about persons in Australia of noble or near-noble blood who had fallen on hard times and of individuals of lowly station who believed that they were heir to huge fortunes.

The pattern of the high-brought-down-to-lowly story is typically demonstrated in the tragic tale of Miss Pansy Caroline Fitzgeorge, whom *Smith's* discovered in 1943 living in a single room in North Sydney.

The poor girl claimed to be the cousin of King George V and told *Smith's* she had journeyed to Australia to get this fact officially recognized by the Duke of Gloucester who, she heard, was to visit the country. She was so poor that she could not afford tram fares to work and had to walk to and fro across the Sydney Harbour Bridge every day.

Smith's, always excited at such a situation, insisted that Miss Pansy Caroline Fitzgeorge tremendously resembled the Royal Family and had "the blue eyes of the Prince of Wales." Pansy, by the way, reckoned she was in direct line from Adolphus, Duke of Cambridge, seventh son of King George III. There is no evidence that *Smith's* publicizing of her penurious plight assisted her in being accepted into the ranks of royalty.

In 1933 the Brisbane office of *Smith's* produced the next best thing to an alleged royal lady in distress in the form of a grand-daughter of one-time English Prime Minister, William Ewart Gladstone. The lady, Mrs A. C. (Margot) Webb, whom *Smith's* found living on the dole in Brisbane, insisted she had been a childhood playmate of Queen Mary. She claimed to have just walked from Rockhampton to Brisbane, humping her bluey with her adopted son. No money for fares.

Smith's dropped a noisy sentimental tear in reporting the departure from this earth of playwright Noel Coward's Uncle Percy in Perth. Uncle Percy died a pauper on 3 October 1933, and one of the few interesting things that could be said about him was that he had slept out in all weathers for many, many years.

Besides giving generous publicity to poverty stricken claimants to noble blood and/or high station, *Smith's* took the keenest sympathetic interest in any person or persons laying claim to huge fortunes. For example, in 1927 the paper got most enthusiastic about the claim of a Pentridge Gaol (Melbourne) warder, William Bailey, who insisted that he and his old dad were entitled to the £17 million estate, popularly known as "The Bailey Millions" in England. Bill Bailey said that he and his dad were from an old Limehouse coster family and directly related to the Duke of Westminster.

Anyhow, Mr Bailey worked his way over to England to claim the money, and after only a fortnight in England returned to Australia with a most odd tale. He claimed that on finding that the Duke of Westminster had control of the Bailey Millions he had gone to the Duke and said, "Well, Uncle Richard, I have come about the money which was supposed to revert to Dad."

To that address the Duke had allegedly replied: "Your father was not in the country to get it. I got it and you've got to get it."

"HAVE YOU EATEN THE FORBIDDEN FRUIT, SIR?"

With those words the Duke gave his Australian visitor a five pound note "for refreshments" and departed forthwith for the races at Longchamps.

From 1927 until 1935, *Smith's* kept the Bailey claim alive, and in the latter year a New Zealander, Mr G. A. Smith, inspired by the newspaper's stories, went to England at his own expense to battle for the rights of the Victorian Baileys. Mr Smith, according to *Smith's* excited reporting of his movements, took with him some seventy documents with which to claim the Bailey Millions which had risen to £20,000,000 by that time.

When *Smith's* closed in 1950 the money had still not been brought to Australia.

The paper also gave comfort from time to time to Australian claimants to the Hobbs Millions, the Rose Millions, and the Everingham Millions, all allegedly waiting in England for their rightful owners to step forth.

The paper got a fine old thrill in 1936 when it received a letter from a Dr Ladislau Weissberger, barrister of Oradea, Rumania, who, having heard of *Smith's* reputation as a discoverer of forgotten fortunes, asked for a mite of assistance.

Could *Smith's* please supply any information about the £150,000,000 left in Australia by the late Leopold Weissberger who had died in Goulburn, New South Wales, on 9 June 1888? It all sounded pretty silly to *Smith's*. Nevertheless a check was made with the Public Trustee in Sydney.

"Yes," the Trustee said, "the late Leopold Weissberger of Goulburn did leave an estate when he died in 1888, and there had been no next of kin."

What was the estate worth now? The *Smith's* reporter held his breath until he got the answer, "Just on £5,000!"

The Public Trustee sighed and said the story of the £150,000,000 fortune had been originated by a Dutch journalist visiting Australia in 1905. The Dutchman, seeking a sensational story for European consumption, had multiplied the Weissberger fortune 30,000 times over. Publication of his fancy tale had resulted in four hundred claims being made on the Public Trustee, Sydney, by Europeans. All had been rejected.

The processes that went on in men's minds constantly fascinated *Smith's*. Late in 1935, someone at *Smith's* posed the question, "Just who does this Mussolini think he is?"

Frank Marien, Editor-in-Chief, said, "Let's ask him and see what happens."

A cable was sent immediately to Mussolini in Rome asking, "What kind of a man are you?"

Probably no one expected Il Duce to even see the rather cheeky cable, let alone take it seriously and answer it. Still you never could tell. The idea paid off magnificently. Mussolini did get the cable and took it seriously. He quickly cabled out an article entitled "The Potent Me." This is how he saw himself:

I am a solitary soul driven by destiny.
I am no demi-god, just a man of courage.
I must be forever marching forward.
I love my Italy with an idolatrous love.
When I feel I have the crowd in my hand they are
as plastic as clay.
As a soldier in World War I, I was in my true element.

For a national leader to write such a special story for a small newspaper at the other end of the world must surely represent one of the rarest scoops in newspaper history. But it was the sort of thing more likely to happen to *Smith's Weekly* than any other Australian paper because *Smith's* set out to make such things happen.

All *Smith's* editors applied the code, "There's something interesting enough to make a *Smith's* story happening outside the office somewhere. Go out and find it." And so, when journalists had no specific targets to chase, they prowled the streets of the capital cities, looking in doorways, and striking up conversations with characters who looked unusual.

Immediately after World War II a *Smith's* reporter was doing just such a prowl round Sydney when, in a rough street down near the wharves he noticed a painted-over shop-front bearing the legend "Danish Kirke." This rated as strange enough to probe. He knocked on the door and a grey-haired, gentle-voiced man responded.

The converted shop was full of old pews. On one was a pad. "My bed," said the gentle man, whose name was Pastor Ligaarde, when asked what it was.

The pastor's vestry was a tiny lavatory attached to the shop. There hung his robes of office, from the cistern. The man told a strange, touching story. He had been sent out from Denmark before the war to care for the spiritual needs of Danes in Australia and those visiting Australia. Sustenance had been sent him from Denmark.

Then the war had come, cutting off his contact with home. As his funds ran low he left the house he was renting and moved into the shop he used as a church. There he slept on a pew. And he lived on little more than crusts that he might pay the shop rent so that there would be a spiritual haven for Danish seamen visiting Sydney on merchant ships.

Pastor Ligaarde was starved and weary when the war ended but the Danish Kirke in Sydney was still there for whoever might need it. He tried to establish contact with Denmark but got no replies to his letters.

"Yesterday," he said to the *Smith's* reporter, "I decided I had suffered more than any one man should suffer for a cause. I decided I would take a civilian job and earn money to buy decent food and some clothes. I wrote out a reply to an advertisement for labour I found in *The Sydney Morning Herald.* I addressed it and put a stamp on it. And I was about to post it when I felt an urge to look in the Bible. I opened the Bible blindly and placed my finger anywhere.

"Beneath my finger were the words 'have faith.' So I tore up the answer to the advertisement and have been here waiting. Now you have come!"

Smith's reported all this on its front page under the simple heading, "THE FAITH OF THE PASTOR." The story spread round the world within days. The King of Denmark himself cabled aid to Pastor Ligaarde in Sydney. Assistance came rushing in from many well-wishers who knew true spiritual courage when it was demonstrated. The Danish Kirke in Sydney was saved and still flourishes.

That *Smith's* should have been something in the nature of a divine agency startled the whole staff, but when the shock wore off the general effect was very pleasant.

When the paper scored a success, as in this case, it was never shy in awarding itself a medal. However, when it made a gaffe it was usually almost abnormally ready to shout the fact to the world; not in the form of an apology, but mainly for laughs. (It was a standing offer to any reader that if he could find an error in any *Smith's* drawing he could have the original free on application).

And because it was prepared to bare its own bosom and expose its mistakes it reserved the right to point out in black type the mistakes other newpapers made. In the Australian newspaper family, *Smith's* was often a most unloved relation for this puckish behaviour. It couldn't have cared less!

In December 1944 *Smith's* published an odd little story sent in by a contributor. It related how a high society woman of Elizabeth Bay, Sydney, had given an afternoon tea-party to some elegant friends to celebrate the fact that she had got hold of a tin of genuine pink salmon — something not seen since the early months of the war.

The rare salmon had been served in dainty sandwiches which proved riotously successful. In going to the kitchen to refill the plate the hostess found the family cat dead near the empty salmon tin. Horror! Botulism surely!

A doctor was called in, and stomach pumps employed on all guests who had eaten the salmon. Of course the party was ruined and the stomach-pumped hostess was mourning this when there was a knock on the kitchen door. A neighbour stood at the portal. He said apologetically, "I trust you did not get too great a shock when you saw your poor dead cat. I saw the poor thing knocked over in the street and was bringing it in to you when I realized you were having a tea-party. So I just left it inside the kitchen door. . . ." That was *Smith's* story.

In the very week of publication of that crazy tale *The Age* (Melbourne) published a variation on the very same theme under the headlines: "Tragedy Gives Way To Comedy. Mushroom Luncheon Has Dramatic Sequel. From *Age* Special Correspondent in Washington."

The Age story told of a Mrs Adele Greenwald, a housewife of Woodmere, near Long Island, U.S.A., who had been growing mushrooms in her cellar. She also had a little dog named Honeybunch and a negress maid named Onyx.

Well, that Mrs Adele Greenwald was proudly serving out mushroom stew to some guests when the maid Onyx entered, greatly distressed, crying, "Lawdy, lawdy, our little dawg Honeybunch has just died. . . ."

Honeybunch was lying dead near the mushroom pot. Doctors called. Stomach pumps. Later a knock on the door. A neighbour with a tale of seeing Honeybunch knocked down by a car. . . . *Smith's* called upon the whole world to witness *The Age's* embarrassment and its own.

Two weeks later *Smith's* was happily pointing the finger at *The Brisbane Truth* which carried the story of a family in a Queensland country town which had eaten "with gusto" a rare tin of salmon and had given the scraps to the cat. Later the cat found dead. Doctor phoned. Stomach pump. . . .

Almost at the same time *The Sun* (Sydney) published an exciting short story from which the following extract tells its own tale: "Fear gripped at Mrs Bellamy's throat as she dropped the tray on the kitchen table and looked in horror at the lifeless body of her pet spaniel Poogie. . . ."

Same tale, different animal. *Smith's* demanded to know, "When will this slaughter cease? Honeybunch has gone. Now Poogie. Two nameless cats are dead. . . ."

Before January 1945 was out *The Advertiser* (Adelaide) had killed a cat with salmon and *The Bulletin* in "Ginger The Family Mouser" had done the same thing. *Smith's* made them pay.

Smith's got bored of poking fun at this dead cat fiction after one last pointing of the finger of scorn in March 1945, when *The Sun-Pictorial* (Melbourne) awarded a ten-guinea short story prize to a literary concoction entitled "Cissie And The Cat." *Smith's* concluded the witch hunt with the cry, "Anyhow, we had it first!"

Animals appealed to *Smith's* which, at times, considered their affairs to be as well worth reporting as those of humans. The paper sent a reporter way out west to Eumungerie, in New South Wales, to check up on the alleged exploits of an unusually gentle bull it heard was living there. And happily the lead was found to be sound. Hubert, the town bull of Eumungerie, proved to be quite a character.

Eumungerie was just a little place, but cosy and folksy. By tradition, families in the town kept their milking cows in what was called the town paddock, a piece of public land hard by the railway station. One sunny, summer afternoon, half a dozen cow owners including Stewart McLennan, the local oil agent, were leaning over the fence of the town paddock when someone suggested that if they all chipped in they could buy a bull and raise a lot of calves cheaply.

And that was how a small, cheerful, uninhibited and very naïve shorthorn bull named Hubert came to live in the Eumungerie town paddock. And a happy lad he was. Not only did he attend to the interests of the six men who owned shares in him but he spread his affection among all the other cows in the paddock. And one way and another the cow-owning families of Eumungerie were very happy with the situation.

One night Hubert heard a strange bull bellowing in the distance. Had he been a hardened campaigner he would have roared back defiance or made no sound at all. But, as far as town folk could judge, he seemed to regard the distant bull as an old pal lost and in need of comfort. Hubert, so the *Smith's* reporter was told, made sounds which could only be translated as, "Come on

179

N

The survival of the fittest.

old chap and share my happy lot," and he kept letting out bleeps much in the fashion of a radio beacon guiding lost aviators home.

Whatever the case, the strange bull was most interested and marched some three miles directly overland to Eumungerie, knocking down fences with total disregard to property. When he arrived at the town paddock he was revealed as a red-eyed giant. He began pushing his way through the fence, the meantime making saucy suggestions to the cows. Little Hubert should have been annoyed by all this. But not a bit of it. While startled townsfolk watched from behind trees, Hubert actually helped the visitor to knock down the fence and enter the harem.

It took the bull a day or so to wake up to the fact that he was no longer the number one nigger in the paddock. He protested to the new chap who promptly stopped dallying with the girls, dropped all pretence of being friendly and belted into the small complainant with practised skill. Hubert who had never fought anyone but ladies before, and then only in fun, was bumped out through the fence of the town paddock and in shameful shock took to his heels.

The townsfolk were unhappy to see Hubert depart in this way. But they had something more important to worry about. The new king-size bull wouldn't let anyone into the paddock to collect a cow for milking. And he wouldn't be shooshed off either. He liked the way of life he had found in Eumungerie.

Riders who went out after Hubert couldn't trace him in the scrub. But by night a plaintive moaning in the distance was thought to come from the exile. From the way the new ruler of the town paddock sneered back, poor old Hubert was making the moans all right.

What was to be done about this impasse?

It was Hubert himself who produced the answer. Out there alone in the scrub he apparently thought the whole thing out and concluded that death would be better than the dishonour he was suffering.

Smith's man was assured that Hubert's hooves could be heard drumming two miles away as he came in to do battle in the town paddock at Eumungerie. If the big usurper of Hubert's harem heard the sound he read no menace into it for, the story went, he was standing dreaming dopily as small Hubert came tearing through the wire, nostrils flaring and horns ready for mayhem.

There were some observers in Eumungerie who insisted that Hubert, showing wisdom far beyond what one would expect of a beast, selected a particularly vulnerable part of his rival as his target. This may or may not have been true. But the result of Hubert's charge was that the invader was struck at full tilt in a place a stud bull values highly. That one blow restored Hubert to his former kingdom. His enemy, moaning piteously, staggered away from Eumungerie, and his complaining could be heard long after he had vanished from sight.

Wonderful to relate, Hubert settled back to being the lovable character he had been before the episode described above. However, *Smith's* reporter was assured, whenever a distant bull bellowed "Anyone want a kiss?" (or bovine words to that effect), Hubert invariably answered in such a fashion that the question was not repeated.

Now that story was probably grossly exaggerated. But it was a happy story and *Smith's* gave the heroic Hubert the benefit of any doubt without seeking a statutory declaration from him.

As Claude McKay wisely said on many delicate occasions "Never investigate a good story too far — you might kill it!"

Smith's, you see, didn't have to believe completely in a story to print it.

If a bright-eyed soul came into the office, as did Ernest Wright, in 1935, and declared, "I wish to announce that Armageddon is nigh," *Smith's* would accept the statement then print it as news.

Prophet Ernest Wright said that in the year 1947 the world

would go off its axis. Sinners would suffer. But good folk were not to worry because the spin would readjust itself and a perfect climate would become a permanent fixture throughout the world. And, as a special bonus for the good people, the average life span would be extended to a thousand years.

Ah, well, there wasn't any television in those days!

CHAPTER FIFTEEN

The Wilkinson Case

> "*Smith's Weekly* wishes to clear the name of the late Frank Wilkinson and to withdraw the imputations made against that name in these columns. . . ."
>
> —*Smith's Weekly* 13 August 1932

Although *Smith's* formally died in October 1950, in the opinion of many the seeds of death were sown in 1932 when the paper printed a story which, in later apologizing, it was to describe as "wicked beyond expression." This was the notorious and heartbreaking Wilkinson case.

Normally the public is quick to forget a newspaper gaffe, but it never did forgive *Smith's* in this matter. From 1932 onwards *Smith's* reporters seeking interviews were looked upon often with suspicion and distaste by many who had previously been ardent admirers of the paper. And the story of the Wilkinson case was passed on from generation to generation making the sorry error a perpetually damning one.

The Wilkinson case developed out of a dreadful double murder which took place in bushland in an outer Sydney suburb on the night of 5 April 1932. The details of the killings as they were steadily revealed through the daily press resulted in the public becoming emotionally charged to an abnormal degree.

This is the outline of the story as the public knew it up to the moment *Smith's* became involved.

On the pleasant evening of 5 April 1932, a young courting couple, Frank Wilkinson, twenty-six, newspaper compositor, and Dorothy Denzil, twenty-one, nursemaid, went for a spin in the young man's little red Alvis motor car. At a quiet place, just off the road near Liverpool, they got out of the car, placed a rug on the ground, and settled down to chat in the moonlight — sweethearts planning their future.

Perhaps they didn't hear, or if they did hear, they were not interested in the sound of an old truck chugging along the road near by. Driving the truck was a cheap hoodlum thief named

William Cyril Moxley with convictions in New South Wales and
Queensland. Moxley was going timber cutting. He saw the
parked Alvis. In his truck he had a mask cut from a hessian bag
and a shot gun ready for use in case he should come across an
opportunity for a holdup. Moxley crept up on the young couple,
aimed the shotgun and demanded money.

Bravely young Wilkinson charged and began punching. He was
stunned by a blow from the gun butt and then collapsed from a
number of punches. Moxley turned on the girl and, stripping off
her stockings, used one to bind the unconscious Frank Wilkinson
and the other to bind her. He also tore up the rug to make
further bonds.

Placing the young couple in the Alvis he drove to a deserted
house on the outskirts of Liverpool. Placing Wilkinson in a shed
he took the girl into the house and there ravished her. When he
had had his way with the girl, Moxley once more loaded the
couple back into the Alvis and drove to a patch of thick bush
where he behaved with the most horrifying callousness.

He wished to get rid of the evidence! Taking Frank Wilkinson
from the car he propped him against a tree and dug a shallow
grave near by. When the digging was completed he took his
shotgun and blew off half of the young man's head. He buried
the remains, after mutilating what remained of the face beyond
recognition.

Now came the turn of Dorothy Denzil. Moxley drove her some
distance from her sweetheart's grave, propped her against a tree
and dug her grave hard by. When he was ready he shot her
through the head, mutilated her face so that she could not be
identified by her features, and buried her.

The double murder had been completed. Moxley's only worry
was that the little red Alvis was running short of petrol. He
drove to a near-by garage and bought some. Later, because he
had sprained a thumb punching Frank Wilkinson, he went to
Western Suburbs Hospital to have the pain eased.

When Frank Wilkinson and Dorothy Denzil did not return to
their homes, relatives and friends became alarmed. Police began
investigating. Had anyone seen a little red Alvis? The garage
man who had sold Moxley the petrol came forward. Other people
had seen the car in the Liverpool-Milperra districts. Police concentrated on a search in that area. They also started looking for
the monster Moxley who had been described by the garage man.

About a week after the search for the missing couple began,
police found bloodstains and shot gun pellets in a tree in lonely

bushland near Liverpool. They looked for disturbed earth and found it. Dirt was shovelled aside. A man's hand!

The face of the man in the grave was beyond recognition. Indentification of other parts of the body proved that Frank Wilkinson, twenty-six newspaper compositor, had been found.

Within twenty-four hours the faceless body of Dorothy Denzil, twenty-one, had been found in its sad, shallow grave. Meantime the hunt was on for Moxley. The little red Alvis was found in a garage the killer had hired in the inner suburb of Ashfield. Parts of the car had been sold to junk yards.

On the run, William Cyril Moxley proved to be very cunning, dodging groups of police by minutes at times when they were closing in on his hideouts. At one stage of the hunt police discovered that Moxley had been living on raw meat he had stolen from a railway truck.

The searchers had Moxley locked in on the south side of Sydney harbour and anticipated making an arrest from hour to hour. With amazing daring the killer stole a push-bike and, head high, pedalled through the heart of Sydney, paid his toll on the Sydney Harbour Bridge, and rode over to go into hiding in the depths of lonely French's Forest.

On 21 April 1932 — sixteen days after the killing — Manly Police Station was informed that a man resembling Moxley had been seen riding a push-bike in the French's Forest area. Three policemen were sent to investigate. They found the marks of push-bike tyres running down a bush track and followed them until they sighted Moxley sunning himself as he relaxed against a rock.

The hunters ran forward. Moxley heard them and, fleeing wildly, jumped over a twenty feet drop. A constable gamely jumped off the same ledge and landed on the killer's back. Moxley fought desperately but could not escape.

Taken to Manly Police Station for questioning Moxley yawned and said "Not now. I'm very tired and sleepy."

Later William Cyril Moxley confessed. He pleaded insanity, insisting he had been driven by compulsions beyond his control. When he stood trial for murder the prosecution had little difficulty in proving him legally sane. The horrified public adopted Moxley as a symbol of evil, a ravisher of innocence, a demon. It bitterly resented his apparent indifference to the enormity of his crime. And it grew to hate his skinny face, thin nose, curly hair, and ears which stuck out wide from his head like the handles of a double-handled jug.

On 17 June 1932 Moxley was sentenced to be hanged by the neck until he was dead — a most popular sentence indeed.

The monster appealed. Appeal dismissed. Execution date was set for 18 August 1932.

An emotionally exhausted public was waiting for that date to give it whatever comfort lay in revenge when, in its issue dated 30 July 1932, *Smith's Weekly* came out with a fantastic front-page story. A deck of headlines shouted:

Moxley: Astounding Turn in Events!
Underworld Got Wilkinson.
Gang Sentence of Death.
Sacrifice of The Girl Victim.

Smith's made four amazing statements at the top of the page:
1 Frank Wilkinson, victim of the brutal Moxley, was an associate of gangsters.
2 It was by appointment that he met Moxley the night he was murdered.
3 Because he had broken the code of the underworld he was sentenced to death by Gangland.
4 Moxley carried out that sentence in the fiendish manner now known to everyone.

Smith's declared:

The story herewith presented, can be vouched for in every particular. It is a complete unravelling of the dread mystery in the fearful Moxley murders. It is the real story behind the crimes which brought death to Frank Wilkinson and Dorothy Denzil, and buried their bodies in the bush.

The murder of Frank Wilkinson was planned long before. He went to his death by appointment with Moxley. Frank Wilkinson himself was an associate of gangsters. His death was merely one more savage crime in the sequence of killings among a foul breed of gangsters in Sydney's underworld. Wilkinson, one of them, was sentenced to death by gang law, with Moxley as gang executioner.

The worst horror of the whole ghastly story is that Dorothy Denzil was innocently dragged into the company of this vile fraternity by the double-dealing Wilkinson. He suffered death; but he also brought a light-hearted and unsuspecting girl into the terrors of unspeakable outrage, followed by death itself. . . .

Why did Cyril William Moxley murder Frank Barnaby Wilkinson? An unequivocal answer can now be given. . . .

Smith's claimed that Wilkinson had been an associate of an underworld character named "Barney" Dalton and had been present when Dalton had been shot dead in a Woolloomooloo street by a rival gangster who had been in company with Cyril Moxley at the time.

Dalton, according to *Smith's,* had intended to shoot the man who in fact gunned him down and Wilkinson and another man had been supporting him. After the killing, the man who had fired the shot and Moxley had gone into smoke. Frank Wilkinson, who had witnessed the shooting, had been warned that "the gun would get him if he opened his mouth."

Smith's reported:

As a pawn, not a knight, on this horrible chequer board Wilkinson defied or dared the gangs, and he even ventured to extort small sums of money as the price of his silence. They watched him. They satisfied themselves that Wilkinson was secretly meeting detectives and giving away the movements of the underworld. . . . They branded him as treacherous and dangerous, and revenge upon him was planned. He must pay the forfeit — Death.

. . . With the valour of ignorance, Wilkinson proceeded to hunt for Cyril Moxley (to blackmail him) and Wilkinson was allowed to learn where he could see Moxley to make a demand for money. . . .

Smith's went on to tell a weird tale of how Moxley had been given until the night of 5 April 1932 to produce the money demanded by the "blackmailer" Wilkinson.

Moxley came to terms with the blackmailer. He arranged that Wilkinson should drive to his camp and receive his hush money. With a criminal's callous sense of his duty to the gang, Moxley armed himself with a double-barrelled shotgun. Thus equipped he went to his camp, there to wait for Wilkinson. Already murdered by gang law, Wilkinson in that ride in the Alvis took his death ride.

According to *Smith's,* Wilkinson accosted Moxley who said he couldn't raise the blackmail money. Wilkinson threatened to go to the police with information. Moxley went to his tent, got his gun, and shot Wilkinson twice. He was not aware that there was a girl in the car until Dorothy Denzil attacked him for killing her boy friend.

Moxley struck savagely. He stripped the unconscious girl of stockings and underclothing and bound her hand and foot. . . . about an hour passed . . . a ghastly interlude.

"Wilkinson lay dead. He was done with all the glamour of underworld crime and all the stupidity of bravado. . . ."

This amazing exposure of the dead Frank Wilkinson went off like an atom bomb in Sydney. In the hundreds of thousands of words that had been written on the crime, the hunt, the arrest, the trial, the appeal, not one had suggested that Wilkinson had been other than a nice young man of good background. If anything, the dead young man's image had been rather idealized. And here, suddenly, he was presented as a police pimp, an associate of gangsters, a blackmailer, and an underworld "heeler" who had been put on the spot.

To cap the list of ugly allegations against Wilkinson, *Smith's* said it was asserted in "Gangland" that he had been driver of the getaway car used in the Mudgee Mail Robbery in which £3,000 had been stolen from a train at the foot of the Blue Mountains by a daring gang.

The Sydney daily newspapers, alarmed at the very thought that they could have been scooped on such an amazing story by a weekly paper, rushed to check *Smith's* facts. They went to the Police Commissioner, Wilkinson's employers, his friends, his family, and even his old Sunday-school superintendent. Not one single allegation could be supported by anyone the daily paper reporters contacted. Indeed everyone from the Police Commissioner to the Sunday-school superintendent guaranteed that he had been the finest type of young man.

Believing that *Smith's* had made a tremendous error, some of the daily papers attacked the story violently and supported their criticisms with long lists of character references attesting to Frank Wilkinson's unblemished good name.

Although the edition of *Smith's* bearing the sensational story bore a Saturday dateline, it was out on the streets first thing Wednesday morning to catch readers going to work. By midday *The Sun* in Sydney, was blasting *Smith's* apart and there was every sign of panic in that paper's office. If this story was wrong it was probably the worst case of character assassination in Australian history!

To the frustration of its critics *Smith's* had not mentioned in its exposure story the authority on which it had based its dramatic allegations. The secret was that the information had been supplied by a former police constable who had gone to *Smith's* and volunteered it.

At first the paper had considered his story to be fantasy. But after cross-examining the informant for hours on end, the paper's star investigators became convinced that he was reciting a true story far stranger than fiction. The informant signed a statutory declaration and declared that he was very much aware of the penalties for false swearing.

When the daily papers attacked, claiming *Smith's* had published a gross fabricated libel of a decent dead man, the paper turned to the former policeman. To the comfort of everyone on the paper he stood rock firm by his original allegations. In fact he stood so firm under a further extensive cross-examination that *Smith's* was convinced for the second time that the late Frank Wilkinson really had been a criminal blackmailer who had been executed by gang decree. In its next edition *Smith's* came back fighting. It hurled defiance at the daily papers which had attacked it, charging them with "throwing a false glamour on the underworld and lionizing gunmen."

This time *Smith's* disclosed the identity of its informant and explained in detail why it considered he had been speaking the truth. "To swear falsely what this man affirms would be wicked beyond words and deserving of severe punishment. For this man voluntarily to place himself in such a position is scarcely possible. A newspaper could not lightly repudiate his sworn evidence on which he welcomes the fullest inquiry."

Smith's insisted the man's statements had been positive, whereas statements by the daily papers and the police attacking the story had been "purely negative." It was to be expected, claimed *Smith's*, defending fiercely, that the police would not admit Wilkinson had been an informer for "police never disclose the sources of their underworld information." And it was not unknown for persons of apparently decent character to be found to be associated with the underworld. (*Smith's* quoted the case of an American journalist who was found, after he was shot dead, to be connected with gangsters, and of an Australian who was a parallel case.)

Smith's demanded "The Fullest Inquiry" and said its ex-constable informant was eager to submit himself to "a searching tribunal."

"*Smith's* readily submits its narrative of last week to the test of truth and public benefit!"

A long statutory declaration by the ex-constable allegedly detailing minutely Wilkinson's connection with the police and the underworld was also printed. It was primly pointed out that one paragraph from the original declaration had been omitted because it touched on a matter that was sub-judice.

At the end of this second bite of the apple *Smith's* mentioned something ominous. It said that when the ex-constable had first come forward to volunteer the information about Wilkinson he had confessed that he had been dismissed from the police force.

Before a further week was out *Smith's* knew it had indeed published a story "wicked beyond expression." An investigation by the Chief Secretary of New South Wales left no doubt about it.

For some unknown reason the ex-constable had told the paper a cleverly fabricated mass of lies. Immediately *Smith's* knew that it had been misled into doing a wrong, the paper did not spare the rod from its own back. On 13 August 1932 the proud *Smith's* humbled itself before the world. It sought "to withdraw unreservedly the imputations it had made against the name of Frank Wilkinson, and to express its deep and sincere regret over the whole tragic matter."

It went on to admit that the evidence had been overwhelming, that its informant had deliberately sworn falsely to it. And it led its front page with the line, "Frank Barnaby Wilkinson was an honest, law-abiding citizen." It said, "Towards the undoing of that wrong, *Smith's* will spare no effort. We have faced many issues, and faced them always from a sense of duty. Convinced now that we have been misinformed, we face that fact, too. We take everything that has come to us, as everybody must who would live courageously."

Smith's sought to get the message over that it had printed the story only because it had believed it was printing the truth in a matter of great public interest. But the public did not grant forgiveness, and Smith's tacked into a stiff wind of resistance from those who would not forget for the remainder of its days.

It was a sad thing that a paper which sought to be loved by all but scamps should be so long and savagely punished.

In its thirty-two years of life *Smith's* made only one other massive error. On this occasion its facts were completely correct but its taste was completely wrong. Sadly, in this case, it caused hurt where it had always striven to do the most good — among returned servicemen.

In 1931 in Victoria a most beloved General of the First A.I.F. died. He had been a spectacular warrior about whom many stories were told by his admirers. It was said, for instance, that he had sent a signal to higher command that his troops could capture a certain village if given a crack at it. Back came a message saying he was mad to contemplate such an attack.

The story went that he had morsed back: "There have been many bloody silly things done in this war, and I'm going to do another bloody silly thing, but I'll win through." He captured the town of Villers-Bretonneux! That's how the legend ran and, when he died suddenly, there was much sorrow among the Diggers who had fought under his command.

Then *Smith's* heard a whisper — that the General had died by his own hand. This proved easy enough to check with official sources. Why hadn't it been publicized? Apparently the papers had generally agreed that no good purpose would be served in spreading such a story.

Smith's didn't agree with this attitude. It printed the story: "General . . . chose the Death of a Roman Soldier." The paper said that sooner than face an imagined dishonour he had taken the Roman soldier's honourable method of self-destruction, cutting the artery above the elbow. "A camouflage thrown over the events that led up to the fatal sequel made it appear that the great soldier had died from natural causes as the result of a haemorrhage," said *Smith's*. "It was more to his credit that his fine sense of honour should have been so wounded that he preferred death to the suggestion he had badly advised clients into making investments. . . ."

This sad revelation was published in admiration and the best of faith, but it caused violent anger among the General's old followers. Some hotheads were eager to burn down *Smith's* Melbourne office, or, at least, break all the windows. And some of them assembled outside the building in threatening fashion. Fortunately the passion eased off before violence was done.

Smith's long-range campaigning on behalf of the Digger resulted in the mass of readers giving the paper the benefit of the doubt in this matter. But as far as the Wilkinson case was concerned, mass forgiveness was never granted.

CHAPTER SIXTEEN

Crime and Punishment and Stinkin' Crook Luck

Employer : Can you do hard labour?
Ex-convict : Cripes, three of the best judges in the State reckon I can!

— *Smith's Weekly*, 1923

In spite of the tough appearances of its exterior, *Smith's* suffered from a great innocence of soul. One consequence was that it had a morbid interest in crime and wickedness with the proviso that no violence was associated with same.

The paper even had a sneaking admiration for smart crooks, particularly con-men, and liked to give them a kindly cheer along their way. (Or maybe it was that being a rebel against stodgy convention, *Smith's* had some fellow-feeling for minor rebels against society.) Elsewhere we have noted how *Smith's* took a matey interest in Squizzy Taylor, Melbourne's underworld king of the 1920s, until that harassed soul demanded to be left alone to go to hell in his own way.

Another sinner whose activities *Smith's* followed with unrestrained delight was Mr Ernie "Shiner" Ryan. And "Shiner," for his part, developed quite an affection for *Smith's* and would tell the paper little secrets he would not think of telling the police.

"Shiner" commenced his career of crime in 1901 at the age of sixteen and graduated into the big time when he was associated with the big Everleigh Railway Workshops payroll hold-up in 1914. In 1923, for one reason or another, he was incarcerated in the Adelaide Stockade from which he vanished in a manner that would have brought cheers from Houdini. One morning warders found his cell locked and empty.

"Shiner" was later captured but would not tell the authorities how he had worked his escape trick. But he did tell *Smith's*, which was able to declare with unrestrained delight, "How Ernie

'Shiner' Ryan Broke The Adelaide Stockade. *Smith's Weekly* Gets News Where Third Degree Fails."

And "Shiner" got a very generous plug for divulging his secret: "Not since Edmond Dantes escaped from the Château d'If to become the Count of Monte Christo has an escape from prison been shrouded in such mystery as the getaway of Ernie 'Shiner' Ryan from Adelaide Stockade. Ryan is a misfit genius!" With many illustrations *Smith's* demonstrated how "Shiner," working from inside his cell, had opened the lock from the outside with the aid of some balls of wax, string, and a bent fork.

When World War II broke out *Smith's* was still giving "Shiner" an admiring plug as an "Australian record holder." "Shiner" was fifty-four years old, and his sentences tallied forty-three years, according to *Smith's*. At the time that story was printed, the central character was doing a five-year stretch in Fremantle Gaol.

"When caught in Perth, 'Shiner' claimed that he had never been in trouble in his life before," *Smith's* reported with delight. Then, to remove an undeserved stain from Ryan's character the paper said: "Detectives have regarded 'Shiner' as Australia's No. 1 gunman, but while he often flourished guns, he seldom fired them and, it is on record that the use of his gat never caused an injury."

In its early days *Smith's* boldly dabbled in crime, or its reporters did, to prove in dramatic fashion that there were loopholes in the laws badly in need of plugging.

In 1923 it took up drug running and white slaving to give the authorities a jolt. One day in September that year a boy of sixteen called at the paper's Sydney office, placed a large box of white powder before a reporter, and said the stuff was cocaine which he had bought over the counter from a chemist in Elizabeth Street.

How had he induced the chemist to hand the cocaine over? He had just asked for it, that's all. The reporter didn't believe the lad's story, but he did have the contents of the box checked. The box contained enough cocaine "to kill twenty men."

Smith's sent men to the chemist's shop in Elizabeth Street and all were given cocaine on demand. The paper discovered many points in Sydney, including wine bars, where the drug was readily available. The stuff was coming into New South Wales via Queensland.

To highlight the fact that the smuggling of cocaine was easy,

COP: *"No one is to enter the room containing your husband's body until the detectives arrive."*

WIDOW: *"Can't I invite the lady next door? She was awfully good to me when I was sick!"*

Smith's arranged for a large consignment to be left tied to an anchor chain on a ship lying in Sydney Harbour. One evening *Smith's* reporters "commandeered" a naval launch from Garden Island, headquarters of the Royal Australian Navy, and collected the packet of drug from the anchor chain. They then found a distributor and sold the packet to him.

As a result of *Smith's* disclosures the public learnt two things— that cocaine was being widely peddled in Australia, and that under obsolete poisons Acts in some States, police had no control over wholesale traffic in the drug.

Laws were altered to halt the traffic, but unfortunately a strong market had been created among addicts, and large quantities of cocaine were already in the country in criminal hands.

Then started the evil years of drug running which caused particular violence in Sydney's underworld. Drug runners used street women to distribute cocaine. These women often gathered very large sums of money in one evening. The money attracted a curious type of criminal who sought to scare the women into

194

handing over the drug money by threatening to scar their faces with blade razors — the dreaded razor gangsters.

To protect the women peddlers from the razor gangsters the drug runners hired gunmen. And so in the back alleys of King's Cross and Darlinghurst there were screams in the night as the razor men chased the girls, and loud explosions as hired gunmen opened fire on the razor gangsters. There were many scarred faces and dead men before the end of the cocaine era.

While dabbling in the cocaine market, *Smith's* found that the smuggling of opium into Australia was being carried out on a large scale. With its usual enthusiasm it imported a consignment and sold it to an eager buyer.

The story of that escapade was decorated with a drawing of the face of the man who bought the stuff plus the fellow's name and address. This dramatic type of original storymaking and hard factual reporting earned *Smith's* a tremendous reputation among readers who liked a touch of real-life spice in their newspaper diet.

The paper was quick to get the message in the circulation graph which responded so briskly to the tune of a newspaper playing Private Eye. It crowned its underworld-type endeavours in 1923 by giving its readers a Christmas box recital on how to run a white-slave market in Sydney.

The investigation of opium-dealing in Sydney's Chinatown alerted *Smith's* reporters to the fact that a ready market was available there for white girls. *Smith's* set out to prove the exciting hypothesis, "It is just as easy to sell a white girl in Sydney's Chinatown as to get rid of a parcel of opium!" And it proved the point to the satisfaction of the most doubtful reader.

Smith's did not rely on second-hand evidence. Reporters took a pretty young girl down to the Chinese quarter and whispered here and there that she was for sale to the highest bidder. Numerous offers were made but refused on the grounds they were not high enough. Finally in a room above a shop three wealthy Chinese merchants bid against one another for "the goods." As *Smith's* was to report piously: "The most disgusting exhibition of bargaining ever heard!"

The reporters found some excuse for keeping the girl — maybe the reserve price was not reached — and restored her safely to western society. To give their report an extra kick they later returned to Chinatown claiming that they had for sale three French girls smuggled in from Noumea via Newcastle. This time they had no goods to display but carried saucy pictures as samples. Had they really been selling three French girls from Noumea they could have made a neat fortune.

Smith's commented, "The facts unearthed by this paper indicate that there is a regular white slave traffic in existence in Sydney."

From time to time *Smith's* sought to dig out examples of wicked behaviour with a sexy twist, but it was never comfortable in this muddy field and reported any such antics it unearthed with little conviction.

In 1927 it labelled Melbourne "wicked" on the strength of a police raid on a party at St Kilda where "old boys from Flinders Lane were found gazing on French girls in the nude." According to *Smith's* report, plainclothes Constables Marshall and Walshe popped in to the party uninvited while a departing guest was being let out.

In the dance-room the police were surprised to find a gathering of elderly gentlemen all in evening suits and a group of young girls most of whom were garbed in kimonos only. The next room searched provided a greater surprise. In front of an admiring male audience were four French girls posturing in the nude. When questioned by police they did not understand what was being asked of them and the language of signs did not advance the *entente*. None of them appeared to be over eighteen.

Smith's let the story end on that dull line. It did not even attempt to point a stern moral, or call upon the police and Parliament to halt such things in future, or warn the nation that the business and sacred home life of the nation would be eternally undermined if more French girls were permitted to enter the country. Sex in the saucy criminal sense simply wasn't for *Smith's*.

In sharp contrast to the above reporting of bare facts is the zest the paper put into the announcement in 1933 of the fact that "Barney" Bernard, "Prince of Con-Men and Gentle Grafters" was back in Australia after many successes overseas. (*Smith's* was a great supporter of the theory that Australian con-men were the finest in the world.)

The paper labelled "Barney," a Sydney lad, as "the lightning wooer" and guaranteed that he "could sell a trousseau to an octogenarian old maid." The fellow always lived in the best hotels abroad and employed a butler, *Smith's* reported admiringly. London and European society fawned upon him.

"The world's cleverest and most plausible scamp!"

All this adulation might have appeared more appropriate if *Smith's* hadn't revealed "Barney's" No. 1 trick for making money.

"Barney," dressed in the height of fashion, would enter the gentlemen's toilet at the very best overseas hotels with his right arm in a sling. Courageously he would perform such acts as were necessary without assistance, up to the point where he had to perform the final act of a gentleman before rejoining the ladies. He could not adjust his tie!

Well, having attracted attention by his one-arm act, he would select someone with a sympathetic look in his eye and courteously ask, "Would you please straighten my tie?" One gentleman will always help another. And while the Good Samaritan was straightening the Eton or Harrow old boy's tie as requested, "Barney" would deftly pick his pocket.

What "Barney" did in the dunny hardly seems to qualify him as a world-class crook, but *Smith's* liked his nerve. Second to "Barney", *Smith's* rated "Art the Barber," an Adelaide-born operator who specialized in "barbering" hotels — he hopped into rooms when guests were absent and pinched things. "Art" had been a Great Public School boy in Adelaide and consequently had a special insight into the ways of the great and wealthy, according to *Smith's*.

He had learnt his "barbering" techniques from one of the all-time greats of the game, "Bluey Louis" of Melbourne. It was he who, posing as a young doctor at a Coogee Hotel, had stolen the family jewels of the wealthy McIsaacs family. But his greatest hour of triumph was when, during dinner time, he entered the Windsor Hotel, Melbourne, and "did" the rooms of Nellie Melba and Sir John Forrest, Premier of Western Australia.

"Art the Barber" told *Smith's* — which reported with enthusiasm — that whereas the take from Nellie's room had revealed her to be a mean old buzzard, the valuable items Sir John Forrest had left lying around had revealed him to be a person of wealth and taste, albeit a careless one.

Gentlemen of the underworld (non-violent section) regarded *Smith's* as a kindly recorder of their deeds and would often come forward to volunteer information. The volunteering was particularly enthusiastic in the 1930s when Vince Kelly was *Smith's* star crime reporter. Vince had an abnormal ability to make friends. Indeed to some observers he seemed to be little short of a hypnotist. Sir Thomas Blamey, the Victorian Police Commissioner, and Bill McKay, the dour New South Wales Police Commissioner, were his intimate friends. So too were public enemies No. 1 like Squizzy Taylor of Melbourne and Guido Calletti of Sydney.

Vince could knock on any of these doors and be greeted with an enthusiastic handshake. When he left Sydney in 1934 to become *Smith's* editor in Melbourne, Sydney detectives at the C.I.B. created history by chipping in and giving him a formal send off.

And not to be outdone, a group of the elite of Sydney's underworld showered him with gifts. One of the toughest gangsters of them all slipped Vince a polished granite paper weight in the shape of a heart which he had made with his very own hands. Cops and robbers therefore trusted Vince completely.

One of the most sensational stories in Australian police history broke in 1936 when it became known that Detective Superintendent John Brophy, Chief of the Melbourne C.I.D. had been shot four times. The Police Department issued a statement that the woundings had been an accident which had occurred when the Superintendent had been cleaning his service pistol.

An eager press sniffed out the fact that the top detective had a bullet in the jaw, two in one arm, and one in the chest — the buckle braces had stopped the last slug from hitting his heart. It was obvious the shooting had been no accident. The press put unbearable pressure on Police Commissioner Blamey to tell the truth. Something had to give. Blamey and Brophy decided that the best solution would be to tell the lot to Vince Kelly, Melbourne editor of *Smith's,* and rely on his good sense to get the story over without any distortion.

On 30 May 1936 *Smith's* printed one of its greatest scoops — the answer to the Brophy mystery.

Superintendent Brophy had gone out to a remote spot at Parkville on a special inquiry. He had expected to meet someone who would tell him something of importance to the police. "I ran into more than I expected," he told Vince Kelly. Two masked men came out of the darkness and opened fire on Brophy who fired back twice.

Another Vince Kelly scoop was the answer to "What happened to Walter 'Warrigal' Norton?"

Warrigal, a cheerful scamp had absconded from bail in Sydney and had been recaptured in Western Australia in most curious circumstances. That's all a thirsting press knew and it was all it could find out.

On being brought back to Sydney, Warrigal was placed in Long Bay Gaol where he made a special request—could he please have a word with Vince Kelly? Vince was advised and hurried to the Bay.

"I just want you to have my escape story exclusive, Vince," declared Warrigal.

It was a colourful tale which Vince, a born crime reporter, handled with warmth and a sure touch. Warrigal had been just a f.a.q. crook, according to Vince. While out on £120 bail in Sydney he had decided to get out of the country. He had dressed himself up in plus fours (1931 style) to resemble a playboy of the times, spread the word he was off to Queensland and then gone to Perth. In the West he changed his name and took out a passport with his own picture in it.

His troubles were over. There was nothing to prevent him taking out a steamship ticket and leaving the country. However he developed a fear that any ship might just be the one to have a Sydney detective aboard. Overseas ships picked up passengers on the east coast before reaching Fremantle.

The *Orontes,* due to sail in a week or two seemed an appropriate ship. Cunningly Warrigal sent a signal to certain friends in Sydney asking if any Sydney cops would be on the *Orontes.*

The answer was, "Yes. Detective Sergeant Comans will be going on the *Orontes* to Colombo to pick up a girl held there."

Warrigal checked whether any of the Sydney detective population was on an obscure craft called the *Barraboo.* When advised that the answer was "nil" he booked on her and confidently marched aboard her in Fremantle, just as she was about to sail out over the Indian Ocean.

Fate had a shock waiting for him. That girl in Colombo had taken poison and when the Sydney police heard this they had decided to delay the passage of Detective Sergeant Comans, whom they took off the *Orontes* and put on a little-known ship called the *Barraboo.*

And so when Walter "Warrigal" Norton walked up the gangplank of the *Barraboo* he found himself looking at Comans. He made the mistake of saying "Hello, Jim," to the detective. Up came the gangway cutting off Warrigal's retreat. The escapee then rushed to the purser and demanded to be placed ashore on the grounds that his brother was dying and needed him at his bedside.

The story apparently went over with the purser who had Warrigal's luggage dropped to the wharf in a sling. Warrigal felt he couldn't wait for formal methods of departure and went over the side on a rope. And that's the exclusive Vince Kelly got from his mate Walter "Warrigal" Norton.

Vince has written fifteen books, mainly on crime, and most have been best sellers, or at least have sold very well.

Smith's had one other outstanding crime reporter in its time — Harry Maddison, one of its Melbourne editors before Vince Kelly. Harry, a small quiet man, was a most colourful writer with a rare skill for devising an angle by which to get into impossible places and interview people no other pressman could hope to get near.

In 1932, the most talked about criminal in Australia was the monster-killer-rapist William Moxley who had been found guilty of the murder of a courting couple outside Sydney. The Moxley killings had been front page news everywhere for many months, from the discovery of the bodies to the passing of the death sentence. There the picture had stopped dead. No newspaperman could get to Moxley in his prison cell to ask how he felt, what he thought.

Harry Maddison, then on *Smith's* Sydney staff after transfer from Melbourne, thought of a remarkably simple way to interview the condemned killer. He sought out a close female relation of Moxley's and discussed the case at length with her. He concluded by suggesting that she visit Moxley in prison and volunteered gallantly to be her escort.

Until now Moxley had been hoping to escape the gallows on the grounds of insanity. Harry Maddison was able to demonstrate in *Smith's* that Moxley was far from being the insane wretch he wished the world to think he was.

He reported that Moxley greeted his female relative coldly with "So you managed to get here all right!" Moxley, shaking his fists, had then shouted "I won't be slaughtered like a string of sausages. They won't hang me!"

While Maddison sat quietly by, taking mental notes, the monster Moxley had calmly outlined a plan of appeal. He would use the fact that he had been shot in the head when a child as a key defence point. The wound had made him crazy and not responsible for his actions. Moxley considered he could use as prime evidence the fact that he shot a brother dead by accident as a child.

This story was a tremendous scoop when published on 25 June 1932. It is indicative of the overwhelming public hate of Moxley at the time that *Smith's* was not criticized by any authority for springing Moxley's appeal plans. It was Harry Maddison and *Smith's* at their creative best.

CHAPTER SEVENTEEN

A Fair Go For All—Including Dawgs!

Man (to new neighbour) : My wife said you'd lend me your lawn mower.
Neighbour : Certainly I will.
Man: Fair go, you horrible cow!

— *Smith's Weekly*, 1932

Having assigned to itself the ambitious title of "The Public Guardian," *Smith's* fought desperately throughout its lifetime to ensure that everyone got what it considered the average man would call a fair go.

The catchcry "Take it to *Smith's*" was shouted across the nation and aimed at the ears of those who felt they were being done dirt by hog, dog, devil, politician, wife, mother-in-law, the legal system, and whatever other agencies might wound the human spirit and purse.

Soon after World War I *Smith's* offices were inundated by returned soldiers who "Took it to *Smith's*" in the shape of lost jobs, lost wives, lost gratuities (taken by business sharks), and lost property. In most cases the paper could offer little more than the sterile advice "You'll have to consult a lawyer." And when the Digs said they couldn't afford to do that the paper was acutely embarrassed as it couldn't afford to finance private court cases and it didn't like turning into the snow those whom it had invited to seek its aid.

To resolve this situation *Smith's* took a step so brazen by modern standards that it is difficult to believe it actually happened. It set up its own private court — The Court of Public Opinion with one Jack Drayton, as Chief Justice, a wise, tough old journalist who had spent most of his working life in the Western Australian goldfields.

A man with a complaint would visit *Smith's* and state his case to Drayton who would then investigate. If the evidence seemed sound Drayton would call in the accused — usually a business agent — and listen to his version of the tale. If Drayton found evidence against the accused he would make a judgement, impose a penalty, and grimly warn, "Pay up or we publish."

So feared did *Smith's* become among the snide operators, in Sydney in particular, that most of them paid up quickly. Sometimes, even if a man or organization did bow to *Smith's* judgement the paper still handed out the punishment of publishing names and addresses.

Here's an extract from the 17 February 1923 edition of the paper. Headlines cried:

> Court of Public Opinion.
> A verdict for Complainant.
> Last week ——————————— Limited, Wentworth Avenue, Sydney were cited before *Smith's Weekly's* Court of Public Opinion to answer a charge laid by L. F. Cook, Archer Street, Concord.
>
> Mr Cook purchased from this company a second-hand car for £50 deposit and promissory notes for £75. He found the car was not as stated in the advertisement. . . .

Smith's court ruled that the company should pay to Mr Cook a total of £61.8.6 including £7.12.0 for insurance, two engineer's reports £2, two and a half wasted gallons of petrol 7/6, and mechanic's fee 15/-. The company agreed. "Judgement," declared *Smith's*, "is therefore entered by *Smith's Weekly's* Court of Public Opinion by consent against ——————————— Limited for the full amount claimed."

It was frontier justice with a vengeance but it was based on the most honest intentions and proved most effective in a period when the affairs of many people were in a topsy-turvy state.

The Court was particularly good at winning jobs back for men who had been cavalierly sacked, and at recovering deposits for folk who had been talked into deals they couldn't afford by silver-tongued salesmen. Maybe it was blackmail of a sort but it was on the side of the angels.

Nothing moved *Smith's* more quickly than a mother's tears. The paper took the attitude that there couldn't be too much wrong with a man if his mum still loved him, and it was ever ready to give space to a mother's tearstained plea for justice, posthumous or otherwise, for her son.

From this policy came some startlingly successful campaigns. Perhaps the most dramatic in its time was the case of the late Dr Claude Tozer. Just before Christmas 1920, this young doctor, a former member of the New South Wales 1st XI, was found dead in the home of a young married woman.

The matter was a prime scandal. The young woman in question was charged with murder but was found not guilty on the grounds of insanity. Her lawyer told the Court that Dr Tozer had been his client's "lover, her seducer, her betrayer." The lady went to prison and the public was convinced that the late Dr Tozer, sportsman or not, had been a first-class cad.

One person in all the world seemed to feel that justice had not been done. This was Dr Tozer's mother who "Took it to *Smith's*." She insisted that her late son's name had been blackened unfairly. He had been a good boy, she claimed. Her evidence? She could offer no evidence. Just a mother's instinct. But that was quite good enough for *Smith's* which prominently published her claims. It seemed ludicrous to expect that the situation could be changed by such publicity. And yet, strange to relate, the story did clear Dr Claude Tozer's name.

From prison the woman in whose home he had died wrote a letter to *Smith's*, completely exonerating him. "Never did he take advantage of me. All the things he was accused of were absolutely untrue. No one could have been more chivalrous than he. . . ."

Smith's was indeed the hope of the hopeless and the helpless. In this field it was unique as a newspaper, naïve and magnificent.

It was to *Smith's* that the amazing Beatrice Miles went in 1927 with her woes. In later years she was to become Sydney's best known and loved eccentric with her renditions of Shakespeare in the streets and her commandeering of free rides in public and private vehicles throughout the city.

"Madhouse Mystery of Beautiful Sydney Girl," cried *Smith's*, and recited how, though declared sane by five doctors, Beatrice, twenty-four, "a beautiful, vivacious Sydney girl of education and refinement" had been condemned to a mental institution. Following study at Sydney University, Bea had broken down and been placed in hospital. She had escaped and was in the office of the Registrar-General getting married when a relative rushed in and stopped the wedding.

Escaping again she had gone to Brisbane and submitted herself for examination to three doctors who, according to *Smith's* had judged her (1) Abnormal but not insane, (2) Peculiar but not insane, and (3) Certainly not insane.

Despite these judgements Bea had been placed once more in an institution. Escaping yet again she had gone from Sydney to Melbourne where she had been placed in a Victorian institution.

Smith's reckoned Bea had not been getting a fair go and

befriended her, providing her with cash and comforts. In return Bea roamed *Smith's* Sydney offices reciting long orations from Shakespeare and challenging one and all to match her in this antic. When she found listeners hard to pin down she would recline on the floor in front of the Editorial Floor lift door. While people were staring in amazement at her from the interior of the lift she would take the opportunity of playing the part of a prostrate Portia or Henry V or King Lear. She asked a fee of one shilling for a long piece, sixpence for a short bit, and three-pence for a snippet. All donations were placed in a kid's leather schoolbag she wore like a sporran. No one ever told Bea to clear out over the decades she visited the office. When the paper espoused a cause it did so with a loyalty that was seldom short of inspiring but was often quite exhausting. That Bea collected 295 convictions for disrupting traffic and life in Sydney did not worry *Smith's* a bit. If anybody ever got a fair go from *Smith's,* Beatrice Miles did.

When, in May 1927, the cook at Central Police Station, Sydney, decided that the world should know his true identity he naturally went to *Smith's*. In consequence of his visit *Smith's* printed an exciting banner, "Police Cook Claims He is King's Son." The cook was Guisseppe di Savoia who claimed that his mother, "a member of a distinguished Italian family," had called him to her death-bed and told him he was the son of King Humbert of Italy. That made him the half-brother of King Victor Emmanuel, of course!

Guisseppe told *Smith's* that he had been only thirteen when he had got the message of his identity from his Mama. He had been given certain important documents which would have certainly established his true identity had they not been destroyed by fire.

He had gone from Italy to England and then to Australia where from 1901 to 1908 he had been head waiter at Federal Parliament House, Melbourne. In 1921 he had gone to Italy to reveal himself to his half-brother, King Victor Emmanuel. Alas, the King would not allow Guisseppe to be revealed to him, and the poor fellow had been obliged to return to Australia and take up the lowly function of police cook in Sydney.

Smith's revealed all these details to the world. Nothing happened, but Guisseppe could not but say that however cool the Italian Royal family had been towards him, *Smith's* had been his friend.

You did not have to be a completely lovable character to get a bit of space in *Smith's* to state your case. You didn't even have to be the possible half-brother of a king. Just so long as your belly-ache came from your heart *Smith's* would print it.

Stoker W. Molineaux, Royal Australian Navy, got the front page in January 1929 on which to air his allegations that he had been victim of an unfair Naval trial, had been refused the right of appeal, and had been deprived of £40 deferred pay.

The Stoker came to *Smith's* fresh from doing three months "hard" in Long Bay Gaol. He had been found guilty of the dread charge of "inciting to sedition" while serving on the H.M.A.S. *Brisbane*. And what had he done? Just stuck some poetry on the ship's notice board that's all. In his opinion the craft has been "a blood ship" and he felt a certain officer needed a bit of guidance. And so he had written a poem addressed to this officer thus:

Oh Mr ——————— think you well
Before you sweat the men below
And make their life a hell.
I advise you to take it slow.
Britannia rules the Seven Seas
And Britons won't be slaves.
Be tolerant of your working hands
And save a lot of strife.
Drive us you will not.
So raise the heavy hand a bit
Before things get too hot.

This verse with a message had been regarded by the officers of the ship as a threat to mutiny.

Stoker Molineaux at least had the pleasure of getting his side of the story over to the Australian public thanks to *Smith's*. And perhaps that was a good thing too.

A case like that was a one shot. But now and then *Smith's* got on to an issue which it decided to champion officially. It would then set out to fight doggedly and desperately for what it considered to be justice. Campaigns fought in this way won *Smith's* countless friends.

The paper fought for little folk and for famous citizens. And it had many fine victories. The case of John Emmans represented a classic fight for a little man. Emmans, an English migrant, had been employed as a gardener at the Sydney Botanic Gardens, a State Government institution. He had been sent to lop some high trees in the grounds of a private home. While doing that job he had fallen and broken his back. Emmans' injuries had caused

him to become paralysed. He was unable to support his wife and
two young sons. The Government refused any compensation because the accident had occurred while he was working at a
private home.

This was the situation when *Smith's* came across the case in
April 1930. Immediately the paper went into the attack claiming
that the gardener had been ordered to go to the private home
and had not gone through any wish of his own.

The Government ignored the attack. For week after week
Smith's hammered at the issue. It hit the Gardens wherever
it could. A statue of the Venus de Milo disappeared from the
Gardens and turned up in the grounds of a Blue Mountains pub.

Smith's demanded an investigation of the Gardens to probe
that matter and others.

It got opposition leader John Thomas Lang to raise the
Emmans case in the State House. It turned fierce pressure on the
Premier Thomas Bavin.

From April to November, *Smith's* kept up the fire. The Government suddenly broke and granted Emmans £600, quite an
impressive sum in those Depression days. *Smith's* was proud of
that victory.

The paper also fought bitterly to get proper rewards for great
Australian airmen like Bert Hinkler and Charles Kingsford
Smith. It seems odd from this distance that such fights should
be necessary. They were necessary. They were not won. Hinkler
died poor enough when his plane crashed on Mount Proto-
mango in Italy in 1933. Kingsford Smith was a poor man
when he was lost in 1935.

In December 1931 *Smith's* demanded to know: "What was
Kingsford Smith doing last Saturday and Sunday? He was taking
casual passengers for brief joy rides at 10/- a trip. Australia's
greatest pilot is broke and Australia stands idly by and lets him
carry his cross. His plight is Australia's shame. Air Commodore
Kingsford Smith has flown more miles than any man or bird...."

To the day it died *Smith's* grieved that it had never been able
to force Australia to do more for Kingsford Smith than give him
a barren knighthood.

Passionately it believed that Australia should reward finan-
cially without stint any of her sons who won her fame. In 1929
it found Olympic champion sculler Bobby Pearce out of work.
"The Champion Sculler of the Earth, Bobby Pearce, an Australian, has been walking the streets of Sydney in search of a job
ever since he returned to Australia wearing the Olympic laurel

wreath on his brow. For three months he has tramped into almost every store and shop in Sydney only to be met with the sickening response of 'nothing doing'." After that blast rent the air Bobby Pearce was not unemployed for long.

That was a minor victory of the Depression days. A major victory that *Smith's* always ranked high among its battle honours was scored during World War II when the paper espoused the cause of Evelyn Owen, the man who had invented the famous Owen submachine-gun.

Owen had worked on the gun from the time he had left school in 1931, until 1936 when he had taken it to Victoria Barracks, Melbourne, only to find the authorities not interested.

In May 1940, when the A.I.F. was about to go the Middle East, Mr V. A. Wardell, Manager of Lysaght's Port Kembla Works, forced the Australian military authorities to take another look at the weapon. It was then realized that an Owen gun which could be quickly manufactured at home for about £10 was every bit as good a weapon as the complicated Thompson submachine-gun which cost us £60 each to import from America — when we could get them.

Australia began mass production of the Owen gun and the inventor was given a royalty of 5/- per gun.

Smith's discovered in 1944 that while royalties due to Owen were £11,250, the Government was taking £8,750 of this in tax, and the inventor who had entered into certain commitments was in danger of bankruptcy.

The paper's rage was white hot and it launched an initial attack on the Federal Government's meanness on August 1944. The campaign ran for months, with the Government gradually giving ground, until it finally allowed Owen to retain between £9,000 and £10,000 of his £11,250 royalties, and not a miserable £2,500 as originally intended. Evelyn Owen wrote to *Smith's* to say "Thank you." Never did the paper wear a medal more proudly.

In spite of its tough exterior, *Smith's* had a great sympathy for nuts, particularly those of a religious variety, and was prepared to transmit to the public any messages they might feel were important to mankind.

Over many years it recorded the progress of an Adelaide man who first considered himself to be the reincarnation of the old King David. On later reflection he decided he was really Paul of Tarsus. And finally he renamed himself "Julian Christ" and, taking a *Smith's* reporter to a pub for a beer, outlined his plans

CAESAR: *"Ha! Ha! Ha! Why has the Christian raised his hands?"*
ATTENDANT: *"Ho! Ho! Ho! He's appealing against the light."*

for the future. He did not intend to work any miracles but he did not intend to die.

Strange, sad nonsense, but it was part of the Australian scene, and *Smith's* gave it space along with the doings of such as Daddy Edwards, the sage of Moonee Ponds, Melbourne. Daddy was convinced the second flood was coming. He grew a beard and began building an ark with tarred paper in his backyard. Day and night he never removed his old army greatcoat because "it might start raining any time." From time to time he issued official statements. Only *Smith's* bothered to print them. It printed them with a smile, never sarcasm or ridicule. And that was one very nice thing about *Smith's*.

Cruelty to any helpless creature, human or otherwise, stirred *Smith's* to uninhibited rage. One of its editors saw a man beating a horse. He found out the man's name and published it with the bitter snarl, "You were born a million years out of your time, you brutal ape!"

Dogs had a special place in *Smith's* heart, probably because

Claude McKay liked them, although he liked to pretend they were a confounded nuisance. All stops were pulled out in August 1935, in defence of the natural rights of "The Cocker of Kooyonga."

There was, it seemed, an aged cocker spaniel named Nigger who, for nine years, had formally attended very important golf matches played at the famous Kooyonga Golf Course in Adelaide. Nigger, the pet of one of the club's founders, Mr H. L. Rymill, had suddenly been ordered to keep away from the course by the Match and Greens Committee.

Smith's investigated and found that Nigger, who had seen the course built as a pup, had never chased a ball in his life, or done a mischief on tee, fairway, or green. He had never barked while a stroke was being played. Indeed the only evidence against him was that he was a dog and not a human.

The paper invited the world to judge the rights and wrongs of the affair. It gave as its own judgement, "Getting OGPUED in Russia is bad. Getting DOGPUED at Kooyonga is worse!" The nicely blended mixture of fact and fun presented by *Smith's* let laughter into the tension at Kooyonga, and Nigger was permitted to continue enjoying the spectator privileges that had so long been his.

Almost the instant it was born, *Smith's* discovered or rediscovered the white-collar worker. And it was righteously indignant at what it saw. By June 1919, it was loudly calling attention to "The Genteel Poverty Of the Poor Bank Clerk." It claimed that the bank officer's salary ill-compared with an artisan's wage, and that his life was regulated by official tyranny which insisted on determining when he might marry, where he might go for entertainment, and so on.

The paper found one big bank with four directors aged a total of 328 years. It cheekily demanded to know how such ancients could know the needs of young men.

From bank officers, *Smith's* moved on to insurance officers, law clerks, and school teachers, shouting loudly and even rudely for a new deal for all of them.

It found out what masters were paid at Sydney's exclusive Great Public Schools and, in 1926, published the details. The headmaster of the Sydney Grammar School received £30 a week, *Smith's* declared, but some of his teachers got only £4. One teacher's wife was forced to run a poultry farm, and other masters took boys as boarders to keep the wolf at bay. There was, insisted *Smith's,* a master at Newington College getting only £175 a year.

All these details may not have been completely accurate, but the white-collar workers of Australia became conscious that, at last, someone with a voice that could be heard, cared a damn about them. They rallied to *Smith's* and, being educated citizens, even if underpaid, were able to pass on to their neighbours in clear terms their admiration for the paper. This form of propaganda was the best kind and contributed greatly to *Smith's* circulation growth.

The paper had great faith in the Australian working man — in all working men. It admired them far more than it did the employer group and it was forever damning the boss who was "mean in spirit, mean in actions, and mean in his rates of pay."

It even found sympathy — rare for a newspaper in those days — for the coal-miners who marched against the police lines in the tragic affair at Rothbury, New South Wales, in 1929, when a man was killed by a police bullet. *Smith's* did not blame the miners but their militant leader, the notorious Jock Garden, who had "urged the men to excesses while he hid himself."

Never did *Smith's* write more bitterly of any man than it did of Garden over that affair: "In the catalogue of cowards there is a depth to which the basest cur will not descend. Even in cowardice there are decencies. Even in the cur there is a code. *Smith's* awards the four feathers of cowardice to Jock Garden. He sent men out to die at Rothbury while he hid in the Trades Hall. Cringe up, Jock Garden, and crawl into your garden of Gethsemane!"

In the same issue of the paper there was a joke block depicting two miners talking:

First miner : "They tell me Jock Garden was the first to be hit in the clash with the police last night."

Second miner: "Yes, they sneaked up on us from behind!"

CHAPTER EIGHTEEN

Don't Forget the Women, By Cripes!

Kindly Cop: Can you describe your home, old man?
Drunk: Ish a bootiful cottage with a terrible woman inside it.
— *Smith's Weekly*, 1922

Smith's Weekly was purely a man's paper and could interpret the Australian male's thinking at any one time with an accuracy that was seldom short of spectacular. Nevertheless, even on its birthdate in 1919 it knew that woman not only existed but had come to stay and, though apparently meek, would eventually inherit the earth — as has now come to pass.

Much against its natural grain *Smith's* sought to salute the female sex because it realized that any living mechanism that failed to do so was doomed. *Smith's* trying to handle women was like a blacksmith trying to shoe a canary. It just didn't understand what it was dealing with. But no man can say that the paper didn't try, in its own fashion, to give the girls a go throughout its lifetime, even from the very first edition, dated 1 March 1919.

Smith's was ready to bust its gut to be something different from any other paper from the moment of its birth. And it was determined to be different in every department. This, anyhow, is one explanation of the first edition story it published under the heading, "Woman — Her Interest and Her Home."

The good housewife was invited to make herself a quite unique mirror for her dressing table with her own pretty hands. First she had to take "the uninjured jaw of a young but well-grown shark," taking assurance from *Smith's* that "the quadrupled rows or horned, glittering teeth could be fashioned into a charming mirror."

The lady was instructed to scrape the jawbones free of flesh and then deposit them on an ant heap to finish the cleaning. What then? Why, place the jawbones on the sand of a wave-washed beach to whiten, of course.

211

"That's her—fourth feather from the left!"

The lovely lady should then steam the connecting cartilage linking top and bottom jaws to soften it and open the jaws out "absolutely straight." The bones and teeth could be enamelled in a colour to suit the good woman's personal taste.

"Then," cried *Smith's,* "a bevelled glass mirror is inserted to exactly fit the jaw, which is mounted on a swing frame, either white or black." And that, bless us, was the paper's idea of capturing the interest of the 1919 vintage female.

Smith's never did get over this initial clumsiness in seeking to court the ladies and, for most of its years, the inclusion of a women's section in such a purely male paper left many readers with the impression that *Smith's* expected ladies to share the well-equipped "Gent's" in emergency.

In January 1924 *Smith's* had a shot at dazzling Australian females with a big name woman writer — Mrs T. H. Kelly, the No. 1 society leader and party thrower of Sydney.

Mrs Kelly, as everyone knew, had been a J. C. Williamson comedy star before her marriage and, as *Smith's* stressed, was very cultured and travelled. Her parties were celebrated. When she gave an evening with, say, a pre-French Revolution motif, the lucky guests were required to arrive in dress of the period, in suitable carriages, and so on.

Mrs Kelly wrote for *Smith's* purple pieces on such vital issues as "Why Ocean Honeymoons Fail." She at least dodged the obvious and did not declare that ocean honeymoons often went crook because either one or the other, or both of the newly-weds were likely to spend more time perking over the rail than reclining between the nuptial sheeting.

Here's Mrs T. H. Kelly's opening gambit on the subject (*Smith's* 12 Jan 1924): "At sea, young people of refined upbringing are forced to become intimately acquainted. I have seen how disastrous this method of starting life is. A young wife often can't understand why her new husband wants to go to the smoke room with the boys, and becomes petulant. . . ."

We modern observers now realize that young married folk are faced with the problem of becoming intimately acquainted wherever they may spend their honeymoon — on land, sea, or in the air. Statistically we can prove that a considerable mass of young moderns don't worry much about being married before they go flat out getting acquainted. And there is reason for believing that with anti-seasick pills being so efficient. . . .

Smith's tried all sorts of odd angles to intrigue Les Girls in the first ten years of its life, and even hopefully gave considerable space to a new religion based on bees and seaweed which was claimed by its founder, a Mr A. W. Hayes of Thornleigh, New South Wales, to be "for women only."

Mr Hayes' belief was that women would eventually rule the world by copying the rules and regulations laid down by bees. Little did he know that women would do just that without the aid of bees and seaweed.

In March 1930 *Smith's* hit on the one women's feature it ever nutted out that was a genuine weekly winner. This was the celebrated Catty Communications, a series of paragraphs written weekly by an anonymous female called "Kitten" to one "Alfreda" and containing items of the sauciest scandal.

The Governor of New South Wales, Sir Dudley de Chair, collected a broadside in the very first take of the feature: "Let us hope, Alfreda, for Sir Dudley de Chair's sake, that the Dominions' Office doesn't search his luggage when he arrives in London 'cos representatives of His Majesty are prohibited from accepting presents. His Ex. has found it impossible to carry out the regulation. . . ."

Sir Dudley got off lightly, for "Kitten" proved to be merciless as she developed her claws with practice. People in the social whirl could pick "Kitten's" targets even if she didn't actually name them: ". . . and that boy with the blond curls who lives at Darling Point is being so kind and attentive to you-know-who while her fiancé is far away overseas."

Society ladies in every State, with a taste for blood, eagerly fed

MAGISTRATE: *"I'm not interested in what your wife said to you."*
PRISONER: *"Neither was I; that's just how the trouble started."*

"Kitten" with saucy bits about their rivals and enemies, and these very genuine Catty Communications were one of the paper's most popular features for many a year. A girl in high society who dared to borrow a frock or boy friend from a friend was sure to get a mention.

Smith's tried from time to time to beat the drum to win sympathy for women living in the bush. It pointed passionately at the heat, the flies, and the hours the good women of the inland had to endure, and constantly called for three rousing cheers for the gallant creatures. Response: nil.

The best woman's story, as far as public reaction was concerned, was printed in June 1947. It was picked up by a fluke.

A journalist was sent to interview a Sydney woman company executive on some dreary subject concerning her organization. The woman spoke long and learnedly while the journalist shorthanded the gabble automatically into his notebook. The newspaperman suddenly realized the stream of words had halted. He looked up at the woman who had a far-away look in her eye. "Who cares a damn about all this money-making nonsense!" she said, "Why don't you write a story about loneliness?"

In a passionate tirade the woman director then declared that

214

she would give all her wealth and station in return for a husband, a simple home, and some children. She claimed that she had been robbed by the war of finding a mate, just as thousands of other Australian women had been robbed.

The idea was tossed up at an editorial conference and Claude McKay grabbed it eagerly. Loneliness, he claimed, was a perfect seller. He remembered back in his public relations days with J. C. Williamson's when, to promote public interest in a new and very pretty actress from overseas, he had handed out an alleged statement from her which tearfully claimed she was lonely, lonely, lonely in Australia because no man would invite her out.

The response to that heartbroken cry had been overwhelming, declared Claude. Johnnies had packed the theatre, the lane behind the theatre, and the street in front for night after night, seeking a chance to invite the lonely lovely out.

Claude declared the most appropriate poster would be:

THE

TRAGEDY

OF

LONELY

WOMEN

It didn't look a world beater then and it still doesn't, but the moment it went on the billboards in June 1947, the edition began to outsell any that had been printed since World War II.

The sales were exciting, but the wave of letters to the editor which followed was the real shocker. Those letters came in by the thousand from women, and their main theme was, "Thank God someone knows our problem!"

What do you do with thousands of letters like that? While *Smith's* was worrying out that problem a new flood started. Men by the hundred began writing in asking, "What about us?"

Smith's then front-paged the melancholy fact:

MEN

ARE

LONELY

TOO

The sales were disappointing, as they invariably are when you try to repeat a smash hit with a variation of the original theme.

It seemed reasonable to put the lonely female letter-writers in touch with the lonely male letter-writers and thus create friendship, romances, and marriages. But what if one of the lonely gents turned out to be a Jack the Ripper in search of easy prey?

Smith's got suddenly scared at the fuss it had created and

"The lady expressed herself in this fashion, sir!"

advised all the lonely men and women to get in touch with churches and social agencies to find an answer to their lonely nights. It was a dull ending to a patch of magic.

From time to time *Smith's* felt it might be able to solve the obvious weakness of its women's section by employing crack women writers. But the bright women writers like Alice Jackson, Helen Seegar, and Isla Brook, when recruited, promptly declared that they would sick up if they had to write social pap, and set about outwriting the best male journalists on any subject anyone cared to name.

It wasn't until 23 September 1950, a few weeks before its death, that *Smith's* found the type of social function it could report in the distinctive and colourful way in which it treated other matters of public interest.

Smith's sent a man along to report on the fiftieth birthday party staged by Mrs Tilly Devine of Sydney. The story he turned in must surely be one of the all-time classics of social reporting:

Wearing £10,000 worth of diamonds the other night — including a diamond pendant presented that day by her husband — Matilda Parsons (nee Tilly Devine), known to some characters as the Queen of Sydney's Underworld, opened the

IRATE HUSBAND: *"If I catch you out with any other man again, I'll get even with you by taking you out myself."*
WIFE: *"No, Hubert; no, never that."*

celebrations of her fiftieth birthday party with a neat speech, "There'll be singin' and dancin' all night. There'll be plenty to drink, and plenty to eat later. Don't any of youse put on a blue or make a rort out of my home. If anyone wants to be a galah they had better fly away now while they've got a feather to fly with."

The party was held at Tilly's suburban address (not to be confused with her city establishments in Palmer Street, Surry Hills, Sydney) at the corner of Torrington and Malabar Roads, Marouba, a quiet and fashionable locality which has never quite recovered from the shock of Tilly's preference for the district.

Tilly spent £500 on her own party, but it is estimated she got most of it back in presents ranging from furs, crystal, and jewellery to orchids, perfume, and monogrammed lingerie. For refreshments there were cases of Scotch, assorted wines, and Sydney and interstate beer.

Supper preparation, supervision, and table arrangements were by husband Eric Parsons who went to bed early after claiming to be the best cook in Australia. Main supper items were two sucking-pigs, four turkeys, two geese, forty chickens and ducklings, twenty lobsters, two bags of oysters, and two crates of North Coast prawns.

Tilly's principal bedroom was transformed into a cloak-room with an ex-boxer as cloak-room attendant to see that "nothing was sent off."

Tilly's expensive overfurnished bedroom was decorated with big pictures of nudes, interspersed with holy pictures. This strange combination she said was recommended by her interior decorator so as to mix "beauty with goodness."

Lefty (Tools) Carpenter, alias Archibald St Clair, in a supper table speech said: "It gets my goat when I see the news-papers giving the coppers the big wrap-up. All they do for Tilly is to go her scone hot. How can anyone compare a good girl like Tilly with a mob of droobs and flat-feet?"

(Hear, hear!)

Tilly compensated for the early and unavoidable indisposition of Mr Eric Parsons, who had sadly misjudged his alcoholic capacity, by remaining the life of the party until the last guests left at dawn on Sunday morning.

After the massed singing of "Happy birthday, dear Tilly" the hostess smilingly carved the first sucking-pig with the gay remark: "Fair dinkum, I wish this 'ere sucking-pig was Bumper Farrell."

(Note: Bumper was a famous footballer who became even more famous as a hardworking member of the Sydney Vice Squad.)

"Now you can all get stuck into the sucking-pigs and the other scran," she said.

Tools Carpenter said: "Cripes, it's a good thing you've got your teeth in, Till."

Asked for the guest list, Tilly told *Smith's* "We don't give out names at my parties. I only put them on to please me friends and Eric's relations. I make the parties extra grouse so as to nark old Kate Leigh (a rival Queen). Her parties are always drac.

"The names of the people don't matter. Just put in the paper that there were jockeys and barmaids, horse-owners, dog-men, tip-slingers, trainers, gay-girls, me bank manager, me interior decorator, and some of me lawyers. Say this; say everyone was at Tilly's suburban menagerie except coppers, top-offs, phiz-gigs, and other mugs."

Noticeable among the gatherings were the large number of handsome and expensively dressed young women who said they had taken the night off for the party.

During the evening some of the guests chatted over the ancient history of the Maroubra home. They recalled how Tilly's first husband, Big Jim Devine, had shot a gent named Gunman Gaffney stone dead on 18 July 1929 (a long time ago, they said with a sigh) as Gunman was climbing over the back fence. It was a case of self defence, see?

In front of the house was Tilly's big new car parked on the very spot where Big Jim shot dead the taxi driver Frederick Harold Moffitt on 16 June 1931. Big Jim was shooting at some friends and one of the bullets went astray and killed Moffitt. It was a case of accidental death.

Sid Devine, Jim's younger brother was a guest. He was wearing an English imported hat that he had bought only that morning. He wore it all night so that it would not be "tea-leafed."

Tilly kept all glasses continually charged with the invitation "Go on boys and girls, there's lashings for everyone."

She got annoyed with her chauffeur. He refused to have double and triple-headed Scotches. "What's wrong with the John Haig?" she asked acidly.

The musical programme was contributed by guests. Linda, a beauteous barmaid sang "Your Eyes Have Told Me All" which displeased Mr Happy Harry Snell, a gentleman who had only arrived in Sydney that morning after a long absence in a certain place in Victoria. One of Happy Harry's eyes was framed in hues of light blue, jet black, and pale purple.

Tilly's singing was so generously appreciated that, for a long time, it was difficult for anyone else to take the floor. She sang "I'll be your sweetheart if you will be mine," followed by "If I had my life to live over I'd do the same things again. I'd still want to roam."

And at dawn, when the fiftieth birthday party was over, and the last of the guests were struggling into their cars, Tilly, still irrepressible, sang (and danced) "Knees Up, Mother Brown" on the front lawn.

That was the end. And the people of this Maroubra neigh-bourhood gave a tired sigh of relief.

How sad that a paper capable of reporting important social affairs as cleverly as that should have died less than two months after publishing the story.

And how sad too that *Smith's* never did get round to under-standing women. For the main part, when dealing with Les Girls, *Smith's* hurried through what it had to say, then scuttled back to the bucks, in whose company it was completely comfortable.

On such occasions as it tarried with the females it tended to collect a thump behind the ear, particularly when it tried to be facetious.

In 1934 it sought to chide, in a chivvying sort of way, one Miss Eve Alwyn, an interpretative dancer, for the way she danced in a Sydney performance. Boldly *Smith's* came out with the headlines: "Australian Dancer Leaves Nothing To Imagina-

DOOLAN: *"An' did Pat die peaceful, Mrs Maguire?"*
THE WIDOW: *"Sure he did. The brick fell on his hid an' kilt him before he cud find out the man who dhropped it on him."*

tion. . . . Nudity On The Stage. . . . Even Brassière Was Dis-carded."

The story alleged that Miss Alwyn had danced on the stage of the Criterion Theatre "naked from the waist up." She con-tributed three dance items to the evening's entertainment — "The Storm," "Dawn," and "The Departure of the Soul from the Body."

"It is not fair for a man who takes his young daughter and his wife's mother to a show," said *Smith's* with heavy humour, "to have to undergo the embarrassment which suffuses his whole body like a pink mantle when these semi-nude women are placed on the stage without warning. Managements should be compelled to advertise they are showing nude women."

Smith's was particularly hard on the dancer's performance in her last item — "She could have got her soul free with more clothes on."

In its next edition, *Smith's* was way down on its knees moving with lightning speed to dodge a writ from Miss Eve Alwyn. "Imputations Gladly Withdrawn," it fairly shouted.

Smith's claimed to have ascertained that owing to a slip on the part of Miss Alwyn's dresser "her draperies" had not been properly fastened on the night the observations were made "and they became partially detatched in the course of the rapid evolutions inherent in the dance."

It fully understood how such an accident could come about, particularly as a change of costume from the dance "Dawn" to the dance "Body and Soul" took place in an interval of six bars of music. . . .

Smith's must have been one of the few papers in the world which insisted there was nothing serious in the friendship between King Edward VIII and an American woman named Mrs Simpson. The paper was sure the girl the King was going to marry was Princess Alexandrina, twenty-two, of Denmark, (*Smith's* 21 March 1936).

Arrangements were well in hand for the marriage, insisted *Smith's*. The young couple had been betrothed for some time before the death of King George V. In fact, a formal announcement was to have been made on the day King George V died!

After stating all these curious details, *Smith's* made numerous attempts to verify them and could only conclude that everyone in the know in England and Denmark had been sworn to secrecy. It complained constantly at the lack of official confirmation and was still chipping away at the subject when the Mrs Simpson affair exploded to prove yet again that *Smith's* was not lucky with the ladies.

CHAPTER NINETEEN

Why Isn't There a Doctor in the House?

Sydney Surgeon Cuts Off Man's Coccyx By Mistake!
— *Smith's Weekly* poster

The things and people *Smith's* liked most were subjected to an endless joshing by the paper. Often a sign that any section of the community had earned *Smith's* displeasure was not so much that it got a tart mention, but that there were no more jokes printed about it.

From the beginning *Smith's* maintained a determinedly straight face where doctors were concerned. It seemed to feel that medical practitioners, as a class, were more interested in their own convenience than in that of the sick, and it took a grim pleasure in seeking to demonstrate this proposition to Australia at large.

From time to time *Smith's* would get one of its bright young men to assume the role of a poor soul suddenly struck by an illness which needed instant attention from a kindly doctor. The reporter would then totter along Macquarie Street, where the specialists of Sydney were concentrated, pressing buttons and calling for succour.

On one wonderful run a reporter was unable to raise seventeen doctors in a row because they were either out, too busy, or maybe sick in bed themselves. *Smith's* made the welkin ring that time. What, indeed, had become of the respect for the Hippocratic oath, by cripes?

And while *Smith's* did not generally like doctors, it is only proper to say that most doctors weren't too keen on *Smith's*. However, there was a group of enlightened medicos who saw that *Smith's*, with all its sabre-rattling, was only trying, in its own enthusiastic way, to keep medical standards high. These doctors had a genuine respect for the paper and its staff, and many of them called regularly at the Assembly pub beside *Smith's* to chat with the journalists and artists.

Among the pro-*Smith's* medicos was one Doctor Ley, a merry soul from Macquarie Street. On dropping into the Assembly one afternoon he sighted Percy Ford, *Smith's* celebrated one-legged lift man, and cried, "Hullo, Percy, how are you?"

Percy hung in his crutches, glowered, and growled back "I won't bloody well tell you, Dr Ley."

The doctor was concerned and feared that he may have offended in some way. He demanded an explanation and Percy declared, "Your question was cunningly put and if I answered it you would probably charge me 10/6!"

That was one anecdote that did *Smith's* no harm in Macquarie Street.

The paper was ruthless in exposing any cases of quackery or medical malpractice it came across, and was prepared to take enormous risks when it felt it was on the trail of a doctor who was using his station against the interests of the public.

In this matter *Smith's* had its finest hour in 1922, when it exposed an unscrupulous T.B. specialist in a most dramatic fashion. News came to *Smith's* Investigation Department that this particular doctor was diagnosing T.B. in patients who did not have the disease, and then treating them needlessly, but expensively over long periods.

To test this dreadful allegation four *Smith's* reporters and another man presented themselves at the specialist's surgery for examination. All were told that they had the disease. The men immediately went to a Government clinic. The first three tested there received clean bills of health. *Smith's* did not wait for the results of tests on the other two but recited the facts to that point under the heading "Sydney Doctor's Ghastly Trade!" It was claimed that numerous people had been duped.

In this story *Smith's* did not print the doctor's name, and said that it would suspend publication of it for another fortnight to give the specialist time to take down his plate. This threat failed to work and *Smith's* grimly printed, "That Doctor's Name Is ————————— " (After the passing of forty-three years it is proper that the name be not remembered.) The doctor vanished from Sydney.

While reserving the right to be eternally critical of medical men, *Smith's* still had a curious faith in their ultimate ability to find the answers to such scourges as T.B. and cancer. It displayed what seemed to be a determination to be in the picture at the moment of victory.

In 1923 Dr Spahlinger of Switzerland was a controversial

figure throughout the world because of his claim that he had devised a serum which would definitely cure tuberculosis. Some quite sound authorities were inclined to think he had discovered something important. The majority of experts were critical.

Smith's, which was genuinely concerned at the grim fact that one death in fourteen in Australia was due to T.B., made a dramatic move seeking to cut through all the controversy. It sent its London man to Switzerland to invite Dr Spahlinger to Australia to demonstrate his serum, and guaranteed that if any cures were effected it would immediately pay the doctor £5,000 from its own purse and raise further funds from the public.

The paper, and its readers, imagined the offer would be most attractive to a pure scientist. This was not good judgement. Dr Spahlinger said he would come to Australia for £105,000 cash.

He never did get to Australia.

Smith's, however, kept its columns wide open to any person with scientific qualifications who wished to bring to public attention any ideas he might have about a cure for any serious disease.

In 1926, the paper asked the question, "Has New South Wales Man Discovered Cancer Secret?" It presented the theories of an agricultural scientist, Robert Kaleski, who claimed that "in dead soils he had tracked down one of the prime secrets of life — a toxin which could cause cancer in plants or animals — a clear limpid fluid. He had also found a way of neutralizing it and had reached the point where he was ready to make large-scale experiments on human beings."

Apparently the Kaleski dead soil toxin, limpid fluid that it was, didn't make the grade, for within twelve months, *Smith's* was championing a completely different approach to the cancer problem thought out by a doctor from Wellington, New South Wales.

Smith's asked excitedly, "Can a diet of Minced Sheep's Tonsils, Eaten Raw, Indefinitely Check the Progress of Inoperable Cancer?"

A Mr J. Mylecharane, "a businessman who should have been dead" had assured *Smith's* that on following the doctor's advice he had eaten two minced sheep's tonsils a day over a period and cured a cancer he had upon his face.

Silly? Who could be sure? *Smith's* at least gave it an airing. It also gave space to a chemist who felt he had the antidote to T.B. in mutton bird oil.

In 1936, it printed with a thinly disguised thrill that Dr W.

Withers Ewbank of Melbourne claimed that ninety per cent of all heart diseases were curable, and that it was not necessary to operate on appendicitis or gastric and duodenal ulcers. According to *Smith's*, the good doctor was backing a serum devised by an American scientist, one Dr Rosenow who, "taking streptococcus germs from the teeth of a man suffering from a duodenal ulcer, made a culture which he injected into a dog. Within forty-eight hours the dog had developed a duodenal ulcer." In similar experiments dogs were given appendicitis.

Smith's was so enamoured of any type of medical scientific dreaming that it had a bad habit of over-accentuating. It could even get excited over the menace of the common tick which regularly bit most people along the Sydney seaboard. Thus in October 1926, under the eye-catching headline, "Sydney Scientist's Startling Discovery," it announced that "A tick temporarily lodged in the human body may set up a permanent defect in the brain. Sydney medical men have now proved the ordinary scrub tick of the New South Wales coastal area to be one of the greatest menaces to health and life."

Time has proved that, of all the menaces to health and life on the New South Wales coastal area, the bush tick is one of the least important.

A psychologist would probably have had a rare old time analysing the factors which encouraged *Smith's* to show the enthusiasm it did over monkey gland operations in Australia in the 1930s. It made great play of the fact that a doctor, H. Leighton Jones of Dora Creek, New South Wales, was performing the celebrated operation of the Russian, Dr Serge Voronoff, on local gentlemen who felt that age was defeating them.

Smith's sought out a number of Dr Leighton Jones's patients and took their case histories from them in exciting detail. One man of sixty-six, *Smith's* reported with glee, looked in his early fifties and had just opened a new timber mill in which he insisted on working every day from seven in the morning until dark. Who could have believed that even at fifty-six this vital fellow had been "a nervous wreck and a tired, dispirited old man?"

Cheerfully the fellow declared that the effects of the operation were just starting to wear off, and he was jolly well going to take steps to have another one.

Smith's found another man of sixty-six who had been "old and broken" at fifty-seven at which point he had monkey glands grafted on. "Within a few weeks," the old man orated, "I found I had young ideas. I've had two more operations since then and I'll be having more before I'm finished."

Another patient, old in years but young in ideas, claimed he had received all the benefits mentioned by the gentleman already quoted, and, in addition, his failing eyesight had improved no end.

While *Smith's* was prepared to spread medical messages of hope and good cheer across its pages, it never abandoned for one moment, its self-adopted right to beat doctors about the head, often in brutal fashion.

Here, taken from an issue in 1926, is an example of *Smith's* at its terrifying best in doctor belting.

An old man was dying in Launceston hospital. Beside his bed, as the grim reaper hovered nearer, sat his sobbing wife. The grim reaper did his work! The bereaved woman, performing her last act of love towards her dear departed, closed his eyes. An undertaker boxed the remains. They had to be buried but, meanwhile, what more natural than that the widow should desire to gaze once more on the features of her life's mate?

One look of loving tenderness was followed by the sound of a body falling across a coffin. The woman had seen, not the normal face of her dead husband, but that of a man mutilated about the head.

It appears that unless a relative of a person who dies in the Public Hospital of Launceston notifies the hospital within twelve hours, any Tom, Dick, or Harry, licensed as a medical practitioner, can push his scalpel into the body and slit, hack, and tear the remains to his heart's content in an exploration for the cause of death.

Pretty grim hitting below the belt that lot.

The only known laugh *Smith's* sought to raise in association with doctors was when it printed a poster:

SYDNEY SURGEON

CUTS OFF

MAN'S COCCYX

BY MISTAKE

In the story, *Smith's* solemnly explained that the coccyx is the human tailbone which, when removed, caused some people to lose their balance. Allegedly a Sydney surgeon had removed such a bone in error, causing its owner to suffer considerable inconvenience.

One way and another it would probably be accurate to say that *Smith's* was not at its best in covering the medical field.

CHAPTER TWENTY

Australia Über Alles

"Every Australian should constantly bear in mind that he is the richest man in the world"
— *Smith's Weekly*, 20 March 1926

When *Smith's* was not singing, "Advance Australia Fair," it was reciting, "I love a sunburnt country," or orating, "Every Australian should constantly bear in mind that he is the richest man in the world." To be Australian born was, to *Smith's*, to be born in the purple. Other people were simply Pommies, Froggies, Bolshies, Yanks, Chows and — duck your heads quick — "that greasy flood of Mediterranean scum that seeks to defile and debase Australia."

Smith's gave no heed to the allegation that Australia had originated as a convict colony. Its vision was incapable of going further back in history than the first Anzac Day, 25 April 1915. But its capacity to see into the future was completely limitless. And as far as its eye could see it saw Australia ever more glorious and victorious.

The paper could never understand why everyone in the world didn't want to live in Australia, and was in a constant sweat that all the coloured races would arrive together when the Federal Government wasn't looking. The "Yellow Peril" was a very real thing to *Smith's*, and the White Australia Policy something to be developed full toot.

As a result of such pressures on its brain, *Smith's* came out with a fantastic proposal on its front page in July 1921.

"SHIFT BRITAIN!"

Smith's idea was that Britain should come out to Australia lock, stock, and barrel, and in quick time Australia would contain "a purely British race that will easily number 100 millions. This is the real meaning of White Australia," the paper predicted excitedly.

Amazing to relate, Britain did not pack up and come to Australia as suggested. *Smith's* was slow to forgive such blind pig-headedness. Fancy anyone refusing a chance to settle in "The Land of Opportunity!"

In the early 1920s, the paper ran a regular feature heralded by a map of Australia across which was blazoned the line, "The Land of Opportunity." Specific cases of migrants making good in jig-time were presented with plenty of impressive black type thus:

> Denis McEwan arrived in New South Wales a few years ago with a few pounds — just enough to get to the country from Sydney. A baker by trade he set up in business with a couple of bags of flour and 17/6 in cash. Today he has the leading bakery business in Murrurundi and is making £15 a week alone selling hot pies to train passengers passing through.

Denis McEwan took the bun for finding his way to a speedy fortune in New South Wales. But what about the four Italians in Queensland?

> Up at Innisfail, in North Queensland, where Bolsheviks howl about the down-trodden worker, four Italians purchased a sugar-cane farm in August 1917. The price was £6,000. All they could scrape up between them was the ten per cent deposit of £600. By hard work they paid off the farm by September 1920. It is now worth £10,000.

It was odd to find a kind word about Italians in *Smith's*. Usually it referred to them as "Dirty Dago Pests" and suspected them of trying to trick dinkum Aussies out of their birthright. The paper fairly had a tantrum in January 1926, when it heard that some Australian broom manufacturers intended to import Italian millet with which to manufacture hard brooms. The headlines cried,

> Dirty Dago Pest
> Ruin Threatens Australian Farmers.

The story ran:

> Australia's safety is threatened by a handful of broom manufacturers who, in order to obtain cheap Italian millet, are prepared to unloose on this land the most dreadful insect pest to agriculture known in the world — the European corn borer!

An anonymous expert was quoted as saying that the introduction of the European corn borer would ruin Australian agriculture. Whether or not that millet was imported into Australia was not mentioned in later issues of the paper. But it is a happy fact that the corn borer never did get into Australia in sufficient number to ruin our agriculture.

Although Italians were *Smith's* No. 1 target, it wasn't too keen on Greeks either; it tended to pin on them the "Dirty Dago" badge, rarely giving them the benefit of any doubt.

The paper was resentful that some Greek merchants in Australia sought to disguise the fact that they were Greeks. It had a regular Roman holiday on the occasion when a certain Greek merchant was fined for having a dirty shop. The Greek had had the name "Michael O'Flaherty" painted over his dirty door. Following the prosecution, according to an indignant *Smith's*, he took down that honourable Irish name and replaced it with "Patrick Ryan."

In the mid-1920s in Sydney, Greeks interested themselves in the confectionery trade and *Smith's* kept a grim eye on "Sydney's Dirty Dago Confectioners," saying things about them that were anything but sweet. Interestingly, *Smith's* never seemed to find a locally born lolly seller worthy of mention, good or ill, in its columns.

In 1926 *Smith's* expressed great fear, in headlines of appropriate size, that Australia was in grave danger of being "dragged down to the level of a South American Dago republic." There was, *Smith's* declared, a conspiracy among foreign wool buyers to rob Australia of her most priceless asset by the dreadful process of lot-splitting. The foreign friends planned to buy our fine wool cheaply.

"Our monopoly must vanish," *Smith's* insisted. "Our graziers might as well grow bad wool as good wool."

It was a very genuine pride of country and race that caused *Smith's* to sound off so violently and, alas, so inaccurately, so often. Were the paper still alive it would have been a leading champion of the New Australian and would have double-damned anyone who dared use the dreadful word "Dago."

The Australian male was the most heroic of creatures according to *Smith's* which kept its columns wide open to stories proving this happy fact.

For instance, it called for applause for Mr Harry Fielding, a "sturdily built suntanned young man of Queensland who fought a fierce duel with a crocodile in a pool in the Calvert River where it flows into the Gulf of Carpentaria."

It had been a rare old battle, the croc opening the hostilities by knocking Mr Fielding out of the saddle, grasping him by the waist, and dragging him underwater. Later the croc shifted its grip to one of the young man's legs. Things looked grim for Mr Fielding. But trust a sturdily built, suntanned young man of Queensland to find an answer to such a situation. Mr Harry Fielding "poked an index finger into each of the croc's eyes until he was freed." He then hunted down his terrified horse and rode to a blackfellow camp for assistance.

Smith's wanted all other young Australians to develop the same courage and ingenuity as Mr Fielding had displayed. It also wanted everyone to learn from the commercial success of Sydney brothers, Bruce and Ron Anderson who, after World War II, demonstrated that Australia was ever a land of opportunity to those with the wit to exploit it.

These young men, *Smith's* declared with pride, had been discharged from the Second A.I.F. after honourable service with the 2/17 Aust. Lt. A.A. with nothing but their deferred pay and a complex of skin complaints — a pretty thin foundation upon which to build a fortune.

They took no leave but busied themselves hunting for something worth having a go at. As they poked around they heard that Army Disposals was looking for someone willing and able to clean and block old army hats for sale to farmers and bush-whackers.

No established organizations wanted the job because there were some technical tricks to it. For instance, how would you get rid of the press-stud at the side of the hat which held up the brim in traditional fashion?

The Anderson brothers didn't know anything about cleaning, trimming, and blocking hats, but as hundreds of thousands of Digger hats were involved they decided to have a go. In a junk yard they dug up an abandoned hat blocking machine and reconstructed it without benefit of any mechanical knowledge. By experimenting they taught themselves how to trim and block hats. They made a simple but effective gadget to remove those confounded press-studs. As factory space was impossible to obtain, the brothers settled for a room which had been used in the manufacture of peanut butter and scrubbed until smell and grease had gone.

They couldn't afford dry-cleaning machinery. In any case none was available. So they got a price from an existing company to dry-clean hats *en masse*.

Then they went to Army disposals which was in a state of embarrassment with warehouses full of greasy old hats. A deal was made and the Anderson brothers got cracking, working a sixteen-hour day, seven days a week.

As they prospered they installed a small dry-cleaning unit to clean some of the hats and, more important, learnt the techniques of cleaning. Shrewdly they began accepting garments for cleaning from the public, and by the time the supply of old hats had dried up they were no longer cleaners and blockers of hats, but among the biggest dry-cleaning businesses in Australia.

This was a typical *Smith's* "Go Thou And Do Likewise" story. While it was full of thunderous applause, it was also strictly accurate and in no way exaggerated.

To *Smith's* such a story was front-page stuff and demonstrated many of the important basic facts of life — any man can grow rich by working hard, Australia is the perfect land of opportunity, you don't need to be born with a silver spoon in your mouth to succeed.

When the mere whisper of such a tale came into the office, there was no rest for the reporting staff until it had been tracked down. Consequently there was unusual excitement at a *Smith's* editorial conference in 1949, when a reporter announced that a detective had told him one of the most spectacular figures in Sydney's underworld had become a highly successful businessman by the purest of methods.

The man in question had been shot eleven times in various parts of the body and grazed another five times. He had been given up for dead on a number of occasions. His life story had never given any indication of business acumen.

A hardened reporter went out to an inner suburb fully expecting to discover that the report was a phoney. But it wasn't.

In 1942, in spite of a shortage of materials because of the war, and with a capital of only £40, the much wounded man had decided to make something of his life and had set up a small factory to launder extra-dirty overalls for railway men. He became interested in soaps and began studying their chemistry. Then he began experimenting and discovered a "cold process" of manufacturing soft soap which became the key to his rapid success in business.

Soon the man was making several types of soaps and disinfectants. He installed power pumps and agitating tanks. And all this he did with one hand, the other being crippled with bullets. Both legs were partially paralysed also. It was one of his prides that he did not need to employ outside labour during the war years when manpower was scarce.

The businessman the *Smith's* reporter interviewed in 1949 was quite a different character from the one of whom these words had been written in 1936: "He dropped to his knees, two bullets in his back. The gunman stood in front of him to finish him off. Four times the gunman fired at his victim's head from a distance of two feet. Each time the wounded man twisted his head as he saw the trigger-finger tighten. His right ear, his left eyebrow, and his top lip were nicked. A bullet passed through his hat. . . ."

Smith's gave its front page to this success story and declared:

> There are object lessons and high inspiration in this story for many kinds of people — for cripples disheartened by their physical handicaps; for men who have failed in life and lack the courage to start afresh; and for those who have lost faith in the power of the individual man to make a career for himself starting from scratch.

YOUNG AUSTRALIA: *"If I've ever got to wrestle this chap, 70 days' training will not be too much."*

And, best of all, the setting of the story was in Australia, Land of Opportunity, Second to None!

Smith's was supersensitive about Australia's security and there were many critics who sneered that the paper was always seeing bogies behind every bush.

These critics had to eat their hats — and *Smith's* made sure they did — before World War II ended. As early as 1919, *Smith's* was worried about Japan, even though that country had been our most honourable ally between 1914-18. In its edition of 24 May 1919, just two months after its birth, *Smith's* devised what was to become one of its most telling weapons — the Candid Communication — to warn of danger from Asia.

The Candid Communication was an open letter carrying plenty of sting. The first ever was addressed to "The Rt Hon. W. M. Hughes, London." The Prime Minister was then overseas for the Peace Conference which ended World War I. *Smith's* told him, "While you have been fighting with such vigour at the Peace Conference for a White Australia, Japanese and Chinese have been entering this country in unprecedented numbers."

From then on *Smith's* never took its eye off Japan and read menace into every overture that country made to Australia.

In the mid-1930s it sent one of its staff, Major Paul Goldenstedt, on a tour of northern Australia in search of answers to many questions, including, "Are crews of Japanese sampans naval ratings?" (The discipline of such crews was so strict that the answer appeared to be "yes.")

By the end of 1937, *Smith's* was convinced that Australia was in danger from Japan and sounded a call to arms. It said:

The ruthless advance of aggressive nationalism on the Asiatic mainland has served one useful purpose to Australia in giving timely warning of the character and intentions of these people. The Japanese have revealed a ruthlessness and primitive barbarity which, allied to their command over modern scientific techniques, form a dangerous threat to more liberal and civilized people. . . .

In the light of history this was first-class insight. At the time it was expressed there were many who sneered at it. And there were many who jeered in 1933, when *Smith's* began warning Australia to beware of Adolf Hitler.

While *Smith's* was never very pro-Jewish in sentiment, it became very irritated with the way in which Hitler was treating Jews in Germany in the early 1930s. To put Hitler in his place, *Smith's* printed a full page broadsheet on "The Jews' Place in the National Life of Australia."

The lesson to be learnt was that "in contradistinction to the plight of the Jews in Germany, where they have been assassinated and assaulted by Hitler's Nazis, the Jew in Australia lives in harmony with his fellow citizens." *Smith's* then paraded for Hitler's irritation the important Jewish figures in Australia's public life, leading with Sir Isaac Isaacs, the Governor-General; George Judah Cohen, the Sydney Banker; Colonel Harold Cohen, the Melbourne brewer, and judges and political notabilities.

To this time, *Smith's* had been fond of turning its comic artists loose on Jewish gags, many of which were cruel though perhaps funny enough to Gentiles. The angle of the Jewish businessman burning down the premises to collect insurance often seemed little short of an obsession with the paper.

However, from the moment *Smith's* developed a hate of Hitler and his works it took up the cause of Jewry and never jeered at it again. On the other hand it fired continual barrages of fiery rockets at Hitler who, *Smith's* felt, was threatening Australia.

On 4 August 1934, it printed a big swastika on top of one of its pages and ran the banner: "The Mark of the Beast. By This Sign Shall Ye Know Him!"

Smith's declared Hitler to be the "Mad Dog of Europe, defiler of everything it touches." It warned that the rape of Belgium in 1914 by Germany, and the war that followed were as nothing compared to what Hitler was planning.

In 1933 and 1934 there were few voices in the world speaking out so clearly as that of *Smith's Weekly* — a quite remarkable performance for a weekly paper some 12,000 miles away from the target area on which the comment was being based. Perhaps the secret lay in *Smith's* abnormal love for Australia which enabled it to sense threats quickly.

Curiously, the paper, though a hundred and one per centum Australian, was not very enamoured of sport. It acknowledged the turf and boxing regularly over the years, but only pecked at the rest of the sporting spectrum.

Nevertheless *Smith's* could never quite understand how any Australian star could be defeated by an importation. And its blood pressure reached popping point over the cricket bodyline business in 1933.

Smith's at first treated the tour of Jardine's Englishmen with a nice dash of humour, poking fun at the fact that the visitors were allowed to talk to the press and give advertising endorsements while the Australian Board of Control kept the local lads stricty muzzled.

After Australia's opening bat, Jack Fingleton, had been well bruised by bumpers, *Smith's* cheerfully came out with a cartoon on 7 January 1933:

Ambulance man: Where do you feel it most?

Fingleton: I can make no statement without the Board's sanction.

In the same issue *Smith's* leaned heavily upon the English skipper and his association with a certain advertisement.

At this moment the most distinguished cricketer in the game is Mr D. R. Jardine, amateur captain of England. Beyond his cricket prowess he must be complimented on the gallant amateur spirit in which he advertises Enos Fruit Salts. . . .

Smith's held that Australian players should learn a lesson from Mr Jardine. Instead of seeking prominence by scoring centuries they should score 1 and 0 (Jardine's recent scores) and "come into public notice by proclaiming the value of a dose of fruit salts."

Two weeks later, *Smith's* wasn't being humorous any more; it was claiming that "England had sent a basher gang for the Ashes," and Mr Jardine was using "frightfulness." It added, "If

Douglas Jardine, English Cricket Captain.

cricket is to become a game of foul play through deliberate body bowling, *Smith's* would rather see an Australian XI refuse to take the field and surrender the Test series."

The paper then recited a list of Australian casualties.

SYDNEY TEST:
Fingleton — eight body blows.
McCabe — four body blows.
Ponsford — bruised arm, hand, thigh.
Kippax — knocked on ribs, shoulder, leg, arm.
Richardson — hurt hand. Bruises hip and thigh.

MELBOURNE TEST:
Fingleton — three body bruises.
Woodfull — blows to heart, hip, thigh, chest.
O'Brien — hip bruises.
ADELAIDE TEST:
Woodfull — blow over heart.
Ponsford — seven bruises.
Oldfield — concussion.
Richardson — thigh bruises.

This simple recitation of Australian injuries up to, and not including, Australia's second dig in the Third Test had a profound effect in Australia, and brought into the sharpest focus the danger inherent in bodyline. As ever, *Smith's* had been game enough to take the lead and deliver first stern judgements that others were to echo later with tardy courage.

Smith's may not always have been discreet but, by cripes, it was always brave.

It's just a shame that *Smith's* didn't have a few pounds more to spare in 1936, because it could well have immortalized itself along with the poet Henry Lawson.

The paper found that Henry Lawson's old home "Eurunderee," four miles outside Mudgee, was up for sale and demanded that the Federal Government buy it as an historic edifice. The paper argued that if the Government could spend £20,000 on new homes for the new Governor-General, Lord Gowrie, and £500 on a portrait of the then Prime Minister, Joseph Lyons, it could purchase Henry Lawson's old home for the nation. The home had been built of sawn timber in 1876 and, according to *Smith's,* would be an ideal place in which a returned soldier on a pension could live as a caretaker.

But the Federal Government would not buy. Nor would the New South Wales Government. And *Smith's* either didn't think of buying, or didn't have the spare cash. Price: £330. A pity!

CHAPTER TWENTY-ONE

Exposure of Evils Real and Alleged

(With which are incorporated matters of public hatred, ridicule, and contempt!)

"Writs for Libel? Fight 'em all!"
— Sir James Joynton Smith, 1919

"Libel actions are the price a newspaper must pay for saying what it thinks!"
— Sir James Joynton Smith, 1927

"Libel actions are best avoided. They are of little benefit to anyone."
— Claude McKay (sadly) in writing *Smith's* post mortem, 1961

Soon after its birth in 1919, *Smith's* assigned to itself the function of The Public Guardian and immediately set out to prove itself worthy of bearing the title. It went peeping into the dark corners of Australian politics, commerce, sports, and life in general, waving an ink-stained waddy in eager anticipation of finding wicked heads to crack.

Thus began a campaign of courageous newspaper crusading in the public interest which will probably never be matched for fearlessness and expensiveness. In its first seven years of existence *Smith's* received writs totalling £400,000 and in those years it paid legal costs of almost £50,000.

Because it was constantly in court battling against the claims of people who alleged they had been held up to public hatred, ridicule, and contempt and had their characters lowered in the estimation of right-thinking people, *Smith's* retained the services of many brilliant libel lawyers. In the early 1920s, the paper was continually tapping on the door of a bright young chap named Bert Evatt. Indeed, *Smith's* constant briefs helped speed young Evatt on the path to legal glory. The crusading did that much good at least.

When the paper first set out on the trail of wickedness it did not take long to find something in the public interest it considered worth exposing in big black type.

A man came to the office immediately after World War I claiming that he had been sacked by a German boss. What! A Hun sack an Australian! (This was 1919 psychology, remember!)

The details made quite a dramatic story and attracted wide attention. But they had a basic weakness in them. The boss had sacked the man all right. But although the boss had a Teutonic-sounding name he wasn't German at all, as was made very clear in the libel suit that followed. Verdict for the plaintiff. Thus *Smith's* was knocked down in the very first round of its crusade. But it was quickly up and fighting harder than ever, laughing at its bloody nose.

Haunted!

In February 1920 it sighted the very sort of target Claude McKay had been dreaming of — a rack-renting landlord.

Smith's found that a waterside worker with four children was to be thrown from his home by the landlord on what the paper considered to be a mean technicality. It provided a barrister to defend the worker in Court and not only printed the harsh things that lawyer said under privilege — that the landlord had hundreds of houses and was everywhere dismissing tenants and doubling rentals — but added its own observations such as, ". . . is a public menace whose actions are worse than any Russian Bolshevik's."

Smith's had a special hate for Bolshies at that time and was giving the landlord the full treatment in dubbing him "worse than any revolutionary Russian."

In came a writ for £10,000 which *Smith's* fought with magnificent gusto and the legal brilliance of Dr Bert Evatt. The paper was overjoyed when a verdict of one farthing damages was given against it, regarding such a verdict as first class publicity.

Unions and tenants who lived in the man's houses all wanted to send round the hat to reward *Smith's* but with fine dignity, Claude McKay insisted on his paper's right to be The Public Guardian at its own risk and expense.

The case had been heard by one Mr Justice Pring, and *Smith's* sought to reward him for his conduct of affairs by giving him its "Man of the Week" feature spot. George Finey did a brilliant caricature of His Honour and beneath this was

Dignity and Impudence.

printed an excerpt from *The Merchant of Venice*:

It doth appear you are a worthy Judge.
You know the law; your exposition
Has been most sound. . . .

Sir Joynton Smith celebrated by devoting the leader, "Why I Publish *Smith's Weekly*" to his thoughts on libel: "A newspaper is known by the writs it receives. Writs broadly come in two categories: (1) Pioneer work in public service, or (2) typographical or reportorial errors. So far this paper has been immune from those in the latter category. This paper began with convictions and cash — the latter to back the former. . . ."

And then, to round off the celebrations, *Smith's* took another whack at the landlord, who, a good fighter himself, shot in a second £10,000 writ. Battle was joined once more in Court, and this time *Smith's* had a complete victory, not even being obliged to spar up a farthing.

This case did much to convince *Smith's* that the publishing of truth in the public interest was a divine mission. The pursuit of this policy was to cost the paper large sums of money.

In the interests of Australia's good name in Asia, *Smith's* published a story concerning the activities of an Australian trader. A writ for £20,000 arrived promptly. *Smith's* sent a man throughout Asia collecting evidence — a trip which alone cost £16,000. *Smith's* got the verdict with costs. But the plaintiff had no money and the paper had to pay the bill. "Mark it off to public service," said Claude McKay who was never calmer than when fate was being harsh.

Many who worked close to Claude swore that he loved trouble, and he was at his best when everyone else was holding his head shouting that "things were crook in Tallarook."

It is quite certain that Claude loved libel cases. He didn't laugh when the paper dropped verdicts, but he entered into the defence of libel cases with the enthusiasm of a small boy playing trains. Besides a quite brilliant grasp of libel law, Claude had an instinct for tactics that prevented many a case against *Smith's* going to Court.

Claude was at his tactical best soon after World War II, when he worked *Smith's* out from under £30,000 worth of writs. Had the case gone to Court the paper would never have stood a chance.

A special writer in *Smith's* had charged one of the biggest advertising agencies in Australia with "buying off left-wing newspapers by giving them large advertisements." The allegation could not be supported by one tittle of evidence. Garfield Barwick, K.C., when consulted could offer *Smith's* no comfort. Claude alone refused to abandon hope of getting out of the mess. He accepted the fact that the law was against him. The aim should therefore be to stop the case getting into Court, he decided.

How?

Three days before the case was to be heard, Claude's busy brain tossed up an idea which would have brought tears of admiration to the eyes of a star-stunting American lawyer. Claude got a list — and it was a very long one — of every client large or small the advertising agency had. He then arranged for the paper's solicitor to obtain from a Judge in Chambers, subpoenas on all those clients demanding particulars of where all their advertising had been placed in the previous twelve months. Immediately these subpoenas were served, angry recipients began ringing Claude complaining that their office routines would be completely ruined if they had to carry out the order. Countless manhours would be wasted.

Claude expressed the keenest sympathy but said the matter was out of his control. Only the advertising agency could do anything about it — by withdrawing their case from Court.

The night before the hearing was to have taken place the advertising agency caved in under pressure from clients and offered to settle, each side paying its own costs. When *Smith's* lawyers joyfully passed this information on to Claude they were startled by his reaction, "We'll only settle if they pay our costs."

Claude had the opposition checkmated and knew it. On the morning of the hearing the agency agreed to pay all costs. At the time it was popularly estimated that Claude McKay had saved the paper between £40,000 and £50,000 in damages and costs with a touch of tactical genius.

One unhappy case for *Smith's* was that of "Wizard" Smith, the Australian racing driver who collected £10,000 in damages in 1932.

With much excited publicity "Wizard" Smith and party went from Sydney to New Zealand in December 1931, with a special car with which it was hoped the world's land speed record would be broken. The Wizard, in a parting statement, said he would go 300 m.p.h. "as sure as the sun rises."

Eagerly Australia awaited results. It got a daily stream of reasons why the attack on the record had to be postponed, postponed, and postponed. To many it seemed that most of the reasons were thin excuses, and a sense of irritation developed in Australia. The track and weather were never right.

Smith's ever quick to sense public temper in Australia, printed a very clever piece of satire on the subject written by Kenneth Slessor who claimed to have got hold of "Wizard" Smith's "Special Diary." Slessor offered these alleged extracts:

Monday: As soon as I woke up this morning I knew that conditions were crook. "Look at that!" I said to the Governor-General of New Zealand (Lord Bledisloe), "Bright sunlight!" He nodded his head gloomily. "Wiz," he said, "You're the unluckiest cow in N.Z."

Someone else stuck his head inside the tent. "There's another worm been making casts on the track," he hollered.

We rushed out, me strapping on a gun as we went, but it was too late. The worm had gone. Turned I guess. Anyhow the track was all ploughed up and mucked about by worms.

Wednesday: Woken up by voice screaming "Ware seagulls!" Rushed outside and found a large, adult seagull polishing his beak on radiator cap. There were also distinct marks of scratching on the track. I sat down bitterly and buried my face in my hands. . . .

This satire, published in February 1932, caused much amusement, and if "Wizard" Smith didn't like it he made no sign.

Three months later *Smith's* made a less subtle criticism of "Wizard" Smith's failure to get speedy results in New Zealand. It published a front page story with the headline, "Yellow Flag For 'Wizard' Smith."

The story alleged that on returning to Sydney from New Zealand after months of fiasco which had humiliated Australia throughout the world, Norman "Wizard" Smith was formally handed a big yellow flag by racing drivers. *Smith's* added some punches of its own. And to publicize the fact that the story was in the paper it put out a curious poster on which some words were written large and others small. Viewed from a distance the poster was a cruel attack on the driver:

WIZARD SMITH
handed

YELLOW
flag

It was a pretty rough old piece of journalism, and when the Court found against the paper there was no evidence of a public move to take round the hat to help meet the bill. However, this sort of attack was rare for *Smith's,* which normally reserved its critical fire for those who were acting against the public interest.

Its exposures, without fear or favour, of wrong-doing were celebrated particularly in the first decade of its existence. Snide business agents were *Smith's* pet hate. These creatures sought to exploit first the Diggers returning from World War I with their gratuities and, later, the victims of the Depression who could be talked into investing their last few pounds in the hope of making a regular income.

Smith's had a team of investigators who specialized in responding to such ads as, "Energetic man with £65 can secure interest in city firm. Salary £5 a week and a quarter share of profits divided quarterly."

Just as it never pays to punch a policeman, so it never paid a snide business agent to play rough with a *Smith's* investigator. At minimum the agent could be assured of an enthusiastic exposure in print, and he would probably get a thump behind the ear as well.

One business agent who was foolish enough to kick a *Smith's* man collected:

COMMERCIAL PARIAH'S OUTRAGEOUS EFFRONTERY.
CHICANERY IN THE HIGHEST — OR LOWEST.

The story ran:

The public will now learn that a prospective buyer of a business has paid the firm of —— £150 and cannot get it back.

Regularly *Smith's* printed a black-list of business agents, surely one of the most courageous acts in Australian newspaper history. Many of them issued writs but not one of them ever scored a win.

Next to the business agents, *Smith's* hated the go-getters and it exposed every new lurk they devised. In the Depression years *Smith's* had one or two mean tricks to spike each week.

Snide photographers would ring up women on charity committees and say they wanted photographs of them for "The Press." Would the ladies please make an appointment? Pictures would be taken and submitted to the ladies who would be invited to sign any they considered okay for publication. Later a rubber stamp would be applied above the signature making the picture a signed order form. Women who refused to pay — two copies for six guineas — would be threatened with being dragged through the Court.

Smith's pounded these photographers — giving their names and addresses — until they were out of business. In the relatively unsophisticated Australia of the 1920s and 1930s this was public service of major importance.

As the great Depression deepened, go-getters switched fast from one trick to another in pursuit of the ever-dwindling store of cash in the hands of the public. And *Smith's* constantly breathed over their shoulders.

The stocking racket lasted only a fortnight before *Smith's* broke it. Good silk stockings went right out of the buying range of office girls who still had jobs. Go-getters aimed at exploiting the hunger of such girls for good stockings and invaded the offices. They would demonstrate a sample stocking, subjecting it to many violent tests to prove its qualities, and then offer pairs at an attractively low price. Girls would spend their last shillings only to find that what they received was far inferior to the demonstration sample.

Smith's busted the large-scale charity racket being worked by professional showmen during the two world wars. A group of showmen would offer to conduct a fête or carnival in the name of a charity and give the profits to the charity. The gimmick was that the charity people didn't have to lift a finger — just lie back and collect the profits.

The paper found that a carnival held in the name of a Boy Scouts' Group in Sydney had returned the showman £822.9.8 and the Scouts £16.0.1

A New South Wales country show staged a celebration which included a carnival. The showman got £1,242.0.2. and the charity £11.9.0.

Due to *Smith's* exposures there are now laws to stop practices such as these.

One racket *Smith's* couldn't bust, although it tried long and hard, was car minding — an industry which grew up in the Depression and has been with us ever since. In 1931, when *Smith's* was investigating the self-appointed white-coated car minders in one part of Sydney, it came across a most interesting secondary racket inside the general racket of car minding. The minders got to know just how long certain car owners would leave their vehicles parked each day without coming back to look at them. They used some of these cars to run a cut rate "taxi" service.

A *Smith's* reporter hired a number of these "taxis" and decided that the time was ripe to print the story when he was driven round for half a day in a car owned by Charles Ulm, the famous aviator. The Ulm car, he was assured, was available almost any day.

Spiritualists and astrologers were natural targets for the paper which regarded them as the epitome of humbug. John O'Donnell, twenty-stone head of *Smith's* Investigation Department for many years, specialized in messing up seances and then ridiculing them in print. He attended a spiritualistic seance staged by "The Mentodial School of Philosophy" in Sydney in February 1927. He noted with a newspaper man's interest the presence of a former Commonwealth Solicitor-General, an M.L.C., and other important citizens who, he felt, should not have been supporting such nonsense.

The lady medium went into a trance while a gramophone played the "Barcarolle" and "Silver Threads Among The Gold."

The music faded, the lights went low, and the medium began to speak in a strange foreign language which O'Donnell took down in shorthand:

Shulamacow, iskamulla,
Kong Sing.
Nam Ping, Sikamulla,
Kong Sing.

The medium cried "Are you there?" O'Donnell kicked the table and everyone, including the medium, became very excited. The table then began to jump until O'Donnell leaned against it. He, a mere twenty stone mortal, proved stronger than the spirit forces, for no matter how the medium exhorted them to push the table around they were unable to oblige. In consequence the seance broke up in disorder and *Smith's* got yet another story.

Except for a short period when it ran weekly astrology features, just before World War II, the paper waged a constant war against astrologers and had its happiest moment when it published exclusively the results of probably the only scientific test ever made on astrological prediction in Australia.

The Australian Society for the Advancement of Science, encouraged by *Smith's*, set up an experiment in 1940 to test the accuracy of astrological prediction.

Some twenty-nine men and women were chosen at random and asked to answer "yes" or "no" to a long series of simple questions such as "Will Winston Churchill die this year?" "Will more than one inch of rain fall in Melbourne in November?"

An astrologer who was popularly considered to be the "best" in Australia was also invited to answer the questions. The answers were sealed in envelopes and locked away for a year until the actual answers were known. The guessing competition was won by a housewife with eighty per cent correct answers. A chemist was second. The astrologer was in the last five.

Smith's was always ready to expose bureaucratic acts which were not proper, and on occasion some amazing cases were brought to its attention.

On Christmas Eve 1924 an English woman migrant delivered a still-born child in Adelaide. It was permissible in those days for such a body to be taken to the Government Cemetery on West Terrace. The father, Charles Hoskins, who had only 6½d in his pocket, took the body to the cemetery but the man in charge there refused to take delivery unless a fee of 15/- was paid. "The scale of charges is there to be obeyed," insisted the officer.

The father then had to wander the streets bearing the tragic parcel.

Smith's had much to say about that Christmas Eve in Adelaide, often referred to as "The City of Churches."

Canberra, the Federal Capital, was originally established as a dry city, and it irritated *Smith's* that officialdom should insist that no liquor was being drunk there. To spike such hypocrisy, *Smith's* set up a secret census on the increase in the empty bottle population of Canberra over a three months' period in 1927. The increase was 864,000 bottles. (*Smith's* did its checking through bottle yards.)

This was good healthy criticism, and *Smith's* was the only paper that cared or dared, at the time, to point a scornful finger at the new capital. It probably should be pointed out however, that *Smith's* had no love for the Federal capital in Canberra's infancy and insisted that it was attempting to govern Australia through "a screen of gum leaves and goannas."

Most newspapers were slow to take a smack at any of the armed services during World War II. But *Smith's* went looking for opportunities to criticize the services — particularly the Australian mainland end of them — in the solemn belief that a little bloodletting was good for the body as a whole. And *Smith's* demonstrated that its watchdog services were worth while by printing every now and then an exposure story which knocked some brass hats for a loop.

In December 1940 it produced a beauty. With France defeated and the cause of freedom very much "in the balance," *Smith's* discovered that the Royal Australian Navy had called for tenders to supply the Victualling Yard at Pyrmont, Sydney, with silver labels for liquor decanters, and silver trays for the serving of drinks. The required quality of the silver was so rare and expensive that Australian merchants could not supply it out of stock.

Smith's pointed out tartly that the list of items required included "1,200 dessert forks coated with thirty pennyweights of silver per dozen forks." Someone in the Royal Australian Navy "has gone stark, staring mad," complained *Smith's*. The comment may not have been very original but it certainly was apt.

One of the most fortunate "exposures" Smith's ever made concerned William Dobell, the artist. Following the excitement and much publicized lawsuit which followed Dobell's winning of the 1943 Archibald Prize with his portrait of Joshua Smith, Dobell ceased to be a news topic.

In July 1948 two young artists who occupied a garret on the top floor of *Smith's* Sydney Office — Douglas Albion and Tymall Downing — decided they would find out why the great artist had not been showing any new works. They journeyed to Wangi Wangi on the shore of Lake Macquarie, north of Sydney, and found Dobell sitting on a veranda, bare feet on a rail, looking into space.

The young men introduced themselves and began asking questions. They returned to Sydney with a startling story. Dobell had abandoned painting! He was living on about £2 a week! He just wanted to be left alone. The storm of criticism that had been stirred up by his prize-winning Joshua Smith portrait had created in him a nervous and spiritual malady.

The young visitors saw a huge pile of unopened letters on a desk in Dobell's home. Dobell said he could not open letters least they contained more abuse. There had been so many horrible criticisms hurled at him he could not face any more.

Albion and Downing told their tale to *Smith's* which gave its front page to "The Tragedy of William Dobell." The paper damned those whose abuse had driven the artist into hiding. It declared Dobell to be of world importance and mourned the fact he had ceased painting.

Two weeks later Dobell had his feet off the rail of his waterside home and was back in front of his easel. At the same time he made this statement:

I have not painted anything for two years and believed I was finished and forgotten. A fortnight ago I called at the butcher's shop in Wangi Wangi to collect meat for my sister who was housekeeping for me and the butcher asked me if I had seen the big story *Smith's* had printed about me. He showed me a copy. Suddenly I felt confidence coming back. I was still remembered. Some people wanted me to paint more.

Inside a year Dobell had made a dramatic comeback, winning the Archibald Prize with his now famous portrait of Margaret Olley, and the Wynne Prize for Landscape with his equally famous "Storm approaching Wangi." Dobell's creative genius had been rekindled, and the credit was due to *Smith's Weekly*.

Smith's was ever ready to fight for genius ignored, with particular accent on scientific genius. Every now and then the paper would boil over with rage at the relatively low salaries Australia paid its scientists in comparison with overseas countries.

It was *Smith's* which let Australia know in 1949 that Dr Adrien Albert at Sydney University was getting £14 a week. Dr Albert had been the first man in Australia to synthesize acriflavine dyes during the war and to make "monacrin," the only antiseptic which could be applied direct to the brain. At the same time *Smith's* declared that R. McCulloch, Rhodes Scholar and the man who licked the dreaded scrub typhus in the islands, was getting "less than £12 a week" with the New South Wales Department of Agriculture.

Smith's constantly claimed that a plumber could earn more than most scientists if he cared to work a spot of overtime. Government authorities constantly snarled that *Smith's* was irresponsible — until in a post-World War II edition of *The New South Wales Government Gazette,* advertisements appeared seeking the services of a botanist and a plumber. The plumber was offered £2 a week more than the botanist.

Many a young Australian scientist of today who never saw a copy of *Smith's* can thank the paper's ghost for a considerable proportion of the respect in which he is held.

For thirty-two years *Smith's* fought the good fight as it saw it, in the public's interest. It particularly sought to protect the people from those who would prey upon it, defraud it, and mislead it. The result?

Claude McKay, who did most of the fighting, provides the sorry answer in his classic autobiography "This Is The Life."

"Anyone thinking of founding a journal to clean up the business underworld would be wise to pause before doing so. In the first place, today nobody appears to mind in the least who preys on whom; secondly, it seems that the more crooked the method, the closer the contact of the operator with his legal advisers. These latter make it next to impossible for a newspaper to defend successfully actions for libel — a state of affairs that will persist until the laws are amended to allow no loopholes to the fraudulent."

These are the sad words from one well qualified to utter them. Claude McKay, the crusading editor, finally discovered that he had been a Don Quixote.

CHAPTER TWENTY-TWO

Smith's on the Subject of Sex

"Populate or Perish!" — Prime Minister Billy Hughes.
"Do as Billy says!" — *Smith's Weekly*

From its beginning in 1919, *Smith's* sensed it had a pioneer job to perform in opening up for public discussion the sleezily shrouded subject of sex. Lots of courage was needed to fiddle around in this field three decades ago, for a large section of the public mind then considered that even a mild sex article was plain pornography designed to inflame unbridled passion.

Smith's waded in with its usual courage. It quickly became clear that the paper had no basic objection to sex *per se* — provided it was exclusively the good old homey type blessed by wedding rings and performed without too much shouting in the sanctity of the formally constituted home.

But for "sex whacko" and "sex by jingo" performed for fun or experiment in the unmarried state, *Smith's* could never find whips and scorpions big enough.

In its time *Smith's* introduced to a vast audience the problems of teenage immorality, the development of *de facto* unions as a substitute for marriage, the danger of the falling birth rate, the growth of perversion and, perhaps most important of all, the large contribution failure to obtain sexual satisfaction in marriage made to the divorce rate.

It's all everyday and even boring sociological phenomena now, and it is no longer possible to understand why an army of critics cocked their eyebrows at *Smith's* as it shouted lustily for more and happier marriages and (in duet formation with Billy Hughes) "Populate or Perish."

To compensate for urging married people into sexual activity, *Smith's* railed fretfully against *de facto* unions, illegitimacy, and the fact that the motor car could be used as a mobile bedroom by illicit lovers.

In its second edition 8 March 1919 it declared war on divorce, and to married women sent out the warning headline: "Beware the Male Idler and the Motor-Car!"

Some very proper advice was given to the ladies of the day. Who could miss the lesson in such ringing assertions as these:

> The woman who wrings out clothes has no time for adultery. Idleness is the breath of adultery and work kills it.
>
> The woman who eats forbidden fruit may be relied upon to make her women friends eat it too.

The mass use of washing machines and vacuum cleaners might well have sent *Smith's* crazy had it been alive today.

In spite of its dislike for sexual hanky-panky, *Smith's* still insisted that even the most wicked, unfaithful woman had certain rights. In an era when such a female could expect a clip on the ear from everyone, from her grandma to the shocked judge who pronounced divorce against her, *Smith's* came out with a defence of the right of "a mother to share the guardianship of her children even when that mother is a convicted adultress!"

Not content with putting forward that startling proposition, *Smith's* produced a poem "with apologies to Robbie Burns":

> Is there a woman strays aside
> And hangs her head for a' that?
> She yet may have a mither's pride
> And mither's heart for a' that.
> For a' that and a' that.
> A man may tempt her errin' steps,
> Her soul's her ain for a' that.

The modern "mither" who gets herself a divorce when caught in adultery can probably thank *Smith's* considerably for the fact that, unless she is a complete no-hoper, she is now popularly regarded as being worthy of remaining in contact with her children.

The modern cynic canna but wonder how R. Burns Esq, allegedly as loose a lad wi' the lassies as ever was, would have reacted to the use to which *Smith's* put his muse.

Smith's constantly concerned itself with the problem of why more and more marriages broke up. It investigated a multitude of possibilities all of which skirted the matter of sex.

Just after World War II, a *Smith's* reporter seeking yet again to explain the divorce rate, called on Father Thomas, head of the Catholic Welfare Bureau in Sydney. He maintained that "The primary cause of seventy per cent of marriage failures is the inability of the couple to achieve sexual satisfaction. If the marital act is made to mean the very apex of mutual affection, satisfying completely both the mental and physical desires of the partners, then the marriage will be completely happy."

The priest claimed that if sexual satisfaction was achieved, a couple could be completely happy in a tent. If there was no satisfaction there could be little lasting happiness even in a castle.

This bold statement staggered the reporter who sought confirmation of it. He went to St Andrews, the Anglican Cathedral in Sydney, and consulted the man in charge of the Family Welfare Bureau there, Dean Babbage. He agreed with Father Thomas: "Some eighty per cent of marriages which crash fail because of physical maladjustment."

Other experts supported the point, and *Smith's* gave the front page to "Churches Denounce Sex Ignorance." Publication of that story opened windows to many thousands of married couples in Australia.

Smith's was concerned with the falling birth rate in Australia and constantly campaigned to check it — with precious little success — but it did uncover a lot of interesting reasons for the situation.

The public was interested to learn that sterility in marriage in Australia was widespread — a surprising fact in a nation which imagined itself to be admirably virile. But the main cause in the collapse of the birth rate between 1911, when one in every five married women capable of bearing a child was confined, and 1948, when only one in ten was confined, was found to be economic.

"Lack of security" from want and war was a major reason put forward by women. Lack of domestic help discouraged many women from having big families. And there was a popular cry, "Why should I spend my life tending child after child and growing drab while everyone else is looking pretty at cocktail parties?"

Smith's was putting its finger on a new approach to life by which Australian women were determined to grab a bigger share of the delights of the affluent society around them. Sternly the paper pointed the way back to national duty for good married women. But no amount of newspaper sermonizing could halt the trend. As *Smith's* had to admit sourly, the vogue was for cocktails before kids.

While *Smith's* wanted babies and lots of them, it insisted they must not be illegitimate. It campaigned for proper sex education among young people and it constantly held up lessons from life to show how good girls could be tricked.

There was, for instance, the case of Jill (pictured in a mask) aged twenty. "She eloped with Prince Charming and lived through a week of marvellous happiness. Then she received a hideous revelation — she was a youthful criminal's paramour, destined for a house of shame, the intended victim of a vile white slaver in Queensland (1929)."

After reading some *Smith's* warnings many a young miss pre-World War II vintage must have been scared of accepting an invitation, even to the flicks.

White slaving in Australia has always been a rare thing, but immediately after World War II, *Smith's* really did come across what amounted to white slaving at King's Cross.

A young ambulance officer dropped into the office and spilled the story. Tenement owners at the Cross had found a simple but foolproof way of running brothels without any risk of being caught by the Vice Squad. Instead of employing girls to act as prostitutes, these people rented rooms at abnormal rentals. Rooms in the city area were desperately hard to get, and it was not difficult to induce homeless young women, whose moral standards were not high, to make enough money to pay big rents by "entertaining a few boy friends."

Smith's busted that racket by getting the Fair Rents authorities on to it. Oddly no one rang up or wrote in to say "thanks" but some anonymous folk — probably unhappy tenement landlords — rang to express opinions of *Smith's*. None were suitable for publication.

Racial purity was another drum that *Smith's* liked to bang. The paper was convinced that genius bred genius, and moron bred moron. It would have been happy if the Australian population had consisted entirely of professors of both sexes.

One sure sign of lack of intelligence was marrying when very young, as far as *Smith's* was concerned. In 1926 it pointed sternly to a Brisbane family as "Australia's Most Degenerate Family."

Two only out of its eleven members had made good. The reason for such a poor record was, *Smith's* claimed, "a strain of degeneracy and mental weakness traceable throughout the off-spring of youthful parents." The girl-mothers involved had all had weak intellects and had passed these on to their offspring.

Some fifty-three years previously, a couple from England had presented Australia with seven daughters and four sons. *Smith's* recited accusingly "Two of the sons made good, the rest were epileptics! The women lived lives of notorious debauchery. The men were loafers and thieves. Four of the women married three times — first to British men and then to Chinamen and Afghans. The nine bad persons had sixty decendants in Queensland."

The story ended with the tart observation, "Early marriages are for men to dodge criminal prosecution."

Australian men of intellect were counselled from time to time by *Smith's* to protect their family trees by choosing wives with bright brains and plain faces rather than bird brains and pretty faces.

In 1949, *Smith's* made the horrid discovery that, in spite of its endeavours to maintain national mental standards, the average intelligence level in Australia had fallen two per cent over the past thirty years and was still falling.

The blame lay at the door of the country's male intelligentsia, some of whom selfishly preferred to come home to a decorative if dumb blonde who could be squeezed, rather than to a plain, high-class conversationalist who could match them on most any subject they cared to toss into the debating ring.

Smith's could never bring itself to believe that nudists were sunworshippers pure and simple. It took many a suspicious peep at them but was never able to prove anything. So it had to content itself with simply poking fun at the practitioners.

It poked around in nudist magazines for targets to pot shot at, and on one occasion, was cleverly fascinated by a series of pictures portraying a day in the life of a long-haired blonde named Mavis and a muscular lad named Ted. Ted and Mavis were presented as "revelling in the wonderful things of life."

"Wonderful things," according to *Smith's* "included Ted holding Mavis to his bosom while pointing out items of interest; Mavis wiping Ted's back with a towel while he tried to climb a stump; Mavis standing on Ted's knees and roaring with laughter; Mavis pretending to be Venus on a rock, with Ted admiring; Mavis very nude in the fork of a tree; and the happy couple standing hip-high in barely adequate feather grass, Ted looking very sonky."

These pix were available at two guineas each per enlargement, *Smith's* grumbled. *Smith's* tried to get reporters into nudist camps but strangers were not welcome. It was very frustrating as the paper was sure that, people being people. . . .

A dream-type nudist exposure dropped right into *Smith's* lap in 1950. A reporter was chatting with the Rev. George Van Eerde, the celebrated slum parson and superintendent of the South Sydney Methodist Mission, when the minister said, "I've just come across a nude dancing outfit in my area!" A number of men and women had visited the Rev. Van Eerde seeking his aid.

They complained that the Child Welfare Department was threatening to take their children from them. Why? Van Eerde thought they replied, "Because of the new dance." It wasn't until he got them to describe the dance that he realized they had said "nude" dance.

Investigating, the minister found that a shrewd operator had set up a twice-weekly nude dancer under the guise of a nudist cult. Entrance fee was 25/- plus 7/6 for supper. A few husbands and wives had attended together, but most of the customers were men who went alone and were introduced to young females.

During his investigations the Rev. Van Eerde came across four unmarried girls who were pregnant following participation in the dances which had been simply orgies. One married woman complained to him that her husband had been attending the dance twice a week, spending £3.5.0 on the entertainment and cutting down on her housekeeping. Triumphantly *Smith's* printed the exposure. Its worst fears that all nudists were not nice had been happily realized!

Coloured folk always worried *Smith's*. The yellow hordes of the Orient haunted its dreams. Black people it could not abide at all. And if there was one thing that was likely to send *Smith's* right off its wick it was coloured men in sexual association with white women — the ultimate horror!

Soon after World War II ended, *Smith's* found that "Sydney as a terminal port of U.S.A. liners is becoming a moral sink. For Australia's good name the waterfront must be ridded of revolting scenes which white women and negro crews enact."

It was sadly true that whenever an American ship came into Sydney Harbour, a number of local girls rushed to the wharf to vie for the attentions of negro members of the crew. "And when American ships sail," reported *Smith's*, "decent people turn their faces in dismay from the revolting sight of local girls hysterically mauling black men and begging them with tearful voices to stay. According to white Americans, in no other Pacific port do white women behave in such a depraved and abandoned fashion."

This may sound bigoted but there was much merit in the story. Sydney Police were disturbed at the racket local white girls were making out of "clipping" visiting negro sailors. These girls, said the police, were specializing in negroes.

At the time the story was published there were people who claimed it was fabricated. It wasn't. Senior police officers had supplied the basic information. They were anxious to have the wharf spectacles stopped. *Smith's* story did that at least.

Many Australians did not take kindly to the flood of "New Australian" men brought to Australia in the immediate post-World War II years. The daily press seemed to be full of reports of fights and stabbings among these people. *Smith's* had the wit to look for a reason and, to its credit, abandoned its long-standing policy of being critical of the alien to plead for understanding of the newcomers.

The violence stemmed mainly from "emotional tangles," *Smith's* found. After being brought out to Australia, husbands and wives were being separated. The women, for instance, might remain in migrant hostels while their husbands went to jobs in the Outback. From this forced separation jealousies were generated, marriages jeopardized, and nerves became raw.

Smith's reported:

Husbands are sent away from migrant camps to directed occupations while wives remain in camp waiting for jobs or until their husbands can find accommodation for them. Married women without children are then moved from married quarters in with the single girls where they are exposed to the attentions of the single men in the camp. Loneliness breaks down barriers, and when a wife steps even a little out of line there seem to be gossip-mongers eager to write to an absent husband. . . .

Smith's found in migrant camps wives whose husbands had completed two years of directed labour in Australia (the price of entry) and were free to work anywhere they cared. But these men could not find homes for their wives.

A migrant showed the paper a letter he had received from his wife in Europe.

Letters are not enough to save me from loneliness. There was no one here to care for me or the child. I met "————" who was kind to me. He was lonely too. Now I cannot go to Australia. . . .

There were some sociologists who considered that it was *Smith's* disclosures of these facts that caused Old Australians to begin to feel some sympathy for the newcomers.

If *Smith's* were still printing today it probably would have accepted the fact that *de facto* wives are a legal reality. In its last few years before closing down in October 1950, it was deeply concerned that the Federal Government was placing irregular associations between men and women on the same plane as normal marriage.

The point had been reached, *Smith's* considered, where the unmarried wife was better off than many legal wives. She enjoyed the latter's privileges but was not bound by the same responsibilities.

Smith's blamed the Federal Labor Government for "socializing matrimony" in 1942 when it passed legislation recognizing *de facto* wives, making them eligible for pensions, repatriation, compensation as wife of an injured worker, widow's pension, and so on.

When *Smith's* finally closed it was still making a last ditch stand to preserve the dignity of formal marriage. "Our nation is founded on the family, and if that collapses we go down in disaster."

Dear old *Smith's*. It was considered such a tough, old unconventional scrapper in its time. By modern measures it was a cautious old conservative. Australia could still do with a roaring voice to warn it that easy-come easy-go marriages are no good to the national interest.

CHAPTER TWENTY-THREE

"That's All—And So Goodbye!"

"But we lived well and it was a good life while it lasted. That's
all — and so goodbye!"
— Claude McKay, *Smith's Weekly*, 28 October 1950

Smith's was a paper that you played by ear, not according to
rules. You needed a rare wit to understand its intricate mechanism, and a good nerve to laugh at the financial nose-dives it
occasionally took.

When, after the post-war boom, the paper began to show
signs of being trapped by rising costs, Mr W. J. (Gunboat)
Smith, the most powerful shareholder, became restless and began
to demand results of a type that Claude McKay, Edgar Holt
(the editor), and the rest of the team could not produce on call.

A tension spread through the paper's staff and this came to
crisis-point when Claude McKay resigned. To the old hands on
the paper, Claude leaving *Smith's* was like the monkeys leaving
Gibralter — a symbol of the end.

In the few weeks up to 28 October 1950, the last print date,
you could feel the paper dying under you. There were a thousand
rumours. Then came word that W. J. Smith had sold out his
shares and others had followed him. This was it!

Claude McKay got Sir Keith Murdoch of *The Herald*
(Melbourne) interested in taking over and reviving *Smith's*. But
just a little too late. The shares had just been sold when he
showed his hand.

The last edition of *Smith's Weekly* — Volume XXXII, Number 35 — was a sorry looking thing of twenty-four tabloid pages.
The page one lead was on the headlined theme "Inside Story of
The Great Political Crisis of 1950. Labor Party Eats Dirt."
There was a story about "Dirty Dodgers Fleece Customs of Fortunes." (They were smuggling watches.) The once thrilling
feature, Unofficial History of the A.I.F., was down to a mean
single tabloid sheet. J. F. Archibald, that old soler and heeler of

paragraphs, would never have even used the thin paragraph that led the Strange But True column, "Nep's bar about the noisy minah recalls that in the early days it was known as the 'lag bird.' Its squawking guided soldiers to escaped convicts."

In that last edition there was no sign of the great sparkling spirit that had long inhabited the paper, except for one little panel.

Claude had reappeared to say goodbye!

THIS IS GOODBYE TO YOU AND TO *SMITH'S*.

This issue of *Smith's* is the last. Bad news is best told baldly, and that's how we write the hail and farewell to a national journal that has had a vivid and living part in Australia's newspaper history since March 1919.

The tasks of journalism did not beat *Smith's*. Mounting costs did. The controlling interest in National Press Pty Ltd was recently purchased by new interests. These interests decided to dispose of *Smith's Weekly* and other assets.

And so this is goodbye. It's goodbye to many Australians. To the tens of thousands of readers in city and bush in every State.

To newsagents whose friendly co-operation has made the nationwide distribution of *Smith's Weekly* possible.

To the advertisers.

It's goodbye to a loyal and devoted staff. Artists with grand reputations and talents. Journalists who relished the freedom to speak their minds.

The death of a newspaper is a melancholy event. But we lived well and it was a good life while it lasted.

That's all — and so goodbye!